Andrew Simms is ~~~~~~~~ is ~~~~~~~~~~~~~~~~~~ economics foundation), an a~~~~~~~~~~~~~~~~~~~~~~~ o tank. For ~~~~~~ ~~~~~ ~~ ~~~~~~ ~~~ ~~~~~~~~~~~~~ ~~~~~~~~~~~ ~~~~~~~~~

~~ of *Ecological Debt: The*
the Wealth of Nations. His other pub~
numerous reports on climate change, globalizati~
tion, international development issues, debt, corpora~ ~unt-
ability, GM food and tackling hunger. He lives in London with
his wife, daughter and bicycle.

TESCOPOLY

How one shop came out on top and why it matters

Andrew Simms

CONSTABLE • LONDON

Constable & Robinson Ltd
3 The Lanchesters
162 Fulham Palace Road
London W6 9ER
www.constablerobinson.com

First published in the UK by Constable,
an imprint of Constable & Robinson Ltd, 2007

A copy of the British Library Cataloguing in
Publication Data is available from the British Library

ISBN: 978-1-84529-511-0

Printed and bound in the EU

9 10 8

To my daughter, Scarlett Iona Snow,
in hope of a world as alive, surprising
and beautiful as you are.

Contents

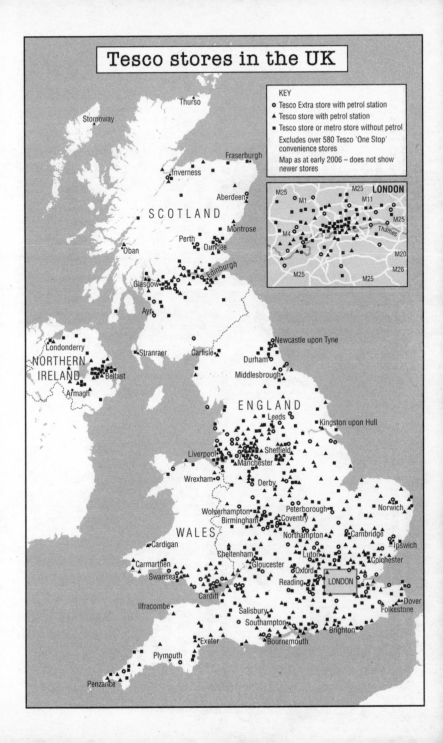

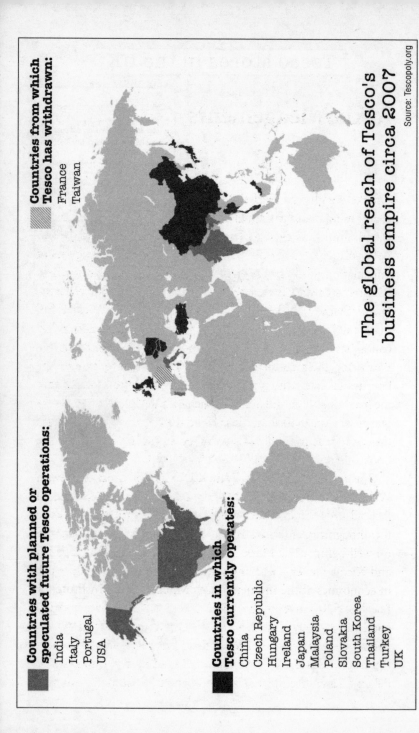

Countries with planned or speculated future Tesco operations:
India
Italy
Portugal
USA

Countries in which Tesco currently operates:
China
Czech Republic
Hungary
Ireland
Japan
Malaysia
Poland
Slovakia
South Korea
Thailand
Turkey
UK

Countries from which Tesco has withdrawn:
France
Taiwan

The global reach of Tesco's business empire circa 2007

Source: Tescopoly.org

Acknowledgements

Thanks are due to Rachel Maybank and Scarlett for happily abandoning me in my room to get on with writing; to June and David Simms, as ever; to David Boyle, Nick Robins and Ruth Potts for being good and interested friends and drawing lots of information to my attention and to Ruth in particular, for help with research on Chapter Nine. Thanks also to Judith Whately, Jacqui Mackay and Josh Gilbert who, along with Vicki Hird, made the Tescopoly website happen; to Vicki again, and to her colleagues Robin Webster and Sandra Bell at Friends of the Earth, for their consistent and excellent work to expose the liberties taken by the big retailers. Alain de Botton kindly gave me his thoughts, as did Stan Thekaekara and Colin Tudge. Becky Hardie at Constable & Robinson said the right things at the right time, and was probably as astonished as I was that I wrote the book in time.

Guy Rubin, John Taylor, Petra Kjell, Corrina Cordon, Stewart Wallis, Elna Kotze, Lindsay Mackie, Dan Keech, Liz Cox (and, in fact, all my friends at nef) are the kind of colleagues you hope for: thoughtful, enthusiastic and committed. The team working on well-being – Nic Marks, Sam Thompson, Saamah Abdallah and Nicola Steuer – is doing some of the most important work in economics at the moment. Stacy Mitchell at the Institute for Local Self-Reliance in the US is taking on bigger adversaries; good luck. Molly Conisbee, Julian Oram and Jessica Bridges-Palmer were at nef when a lot of this really started and still share the vision. Pat Conaty, Larry Elliott, Rosie Boycott, Ann Pettifor, Felicity Lawrence, Jack Clarke, Joanna Blythman, Jonathan

Prynn, Alison Hogg, Mark Brozel, James Marriott, David Woodward, Rina Hossain, Peter Maybank, Maureen Maybank, Sue Carter, Tom Pilston, John Broad and Deborah Doane all helped in different ways.

A guitarist I heard busking in the London Underground called Carlos Herrera sold me a CD that I have listened to dozens of times while writing; thank you, you play beautifully. Everyone at the Marsh Farm project in Luton, and Ben Patten, Graeme Fisher, Amy Higgs, George, Monika and all who sail in Trinity Stores, Balham, are among the thousands making available the myriad alternatives to the supermarkets. To everyone else who helped, you know who you are; thank you.

Alexander the Great, King of Macedonia, once ruled much of the world known to ancient Western civilization. He rolled over resisting tribes and cities from the Danube to Greece, and was welcomed as the ruler of Egypt. After spilling lots of blood in the city of Thebes, the humbled Greeks invited him to lead their war against Persia. When Alexander accepted, a crowd of notables, politicians and philosophers came to ingratiate themselves and offer congratulations; but the well-known philosopher Diogenes was not among them. He was a thinker in the Greek Cynic tradition – the word is not meant here in its modern sense of 'pessimistic and bitter', but describes one whose ethics told him to live in accordance with nature and to exhort reason, self-sufficiency and freedom. Curious, Alexander sought out Diogenes and found him sunbathing. Approaching with utmost courtesy and politeness, the king asked him if there was any favour he could grant him. 'Yes,' replied the philosopher, 'you can get out of my light.'

Every Little Helps

Here are two apples
in one I smell the meadow
the second, nothing

It can take a North American to tell you about the ground beneath your feet. Every Christmas, British families gather to take part in a cultural tradition – not the token visit to church, the family argument or the orgy of materialism, but a ritual of anti-corporate awareness-raising. This is the true history of the iconic game of Monopoly as Francis Moore Lappé, author of the classic 1971 book *Diet for a Small Planet*, pointed out in a casual conversation. Each Christmas holiday, having forced reluctant parents and siblings into playing the game, I would sit smugly grasping my wad of fake banknotes behind rows of streets lined with houses and hotels. Either that, or I would bewail my fall into poverty and landless destitution. I took it to be what the game's modern-day manufacturers see it as: a celebration of brutal, winner-take-all markets. As the rules said, 'The idea of the game is to buy and rent or sell property so profitably that one becomes the wealthiest player and eventually monopolist.'

Unsurprisingly perhaps, growing up in suburban Essex, I didn't come across the fact that the game was actually invented by a Quaker called Elizabeth Magie-Phillips in 1903 to teach the evils of land speculation and the tendency of badly regulated markets to create monopolies. Lizzie Magie's early game had properties called Beggarman's Court, Lonely Lane, Easy Street and, curiously, Slambang Trolly. If you trespassed on Lord Blueblood's estate, you went to prison. Another corner of the board had a Poorhouse. In place of the now-usual stations and utilities, in a nod to the concerns of her time about robber-baron businessmen, there were coal- and oilfields, farmlands and forests. Income for basic goods could be collected on squares marked 'absolute necessity'. Before being swiped by a sharp sales rep during the Great Depression and sold as his own idea to a games manufacturer, the game acquired folk status among Quaker communities. Many developed their own variations of the rules and street names, but all the early players understood the game's true purpose.

The clue was a property name in Magie's design: George Street. Like many of her contemporaries she was a 'single taxer', a follower of the ideas of the colourful, radical economist Henry George. The game was explicitly devised to teach his ideas. George was a former seaman and itinerant printer who developed his theories working as a journalist in nineteenth-century San Francisco. There he witnessed at first hand the fallout from an earlier era of globalization. He wrote about the suffering of bonded immigrant Chinese labour, the land grabbing of the railroads and the injustice of unearned income linked to land speculation and landlordism. His simplistic solution to all these ills was a 'single tax' on land to effect the redistribution of wealth.

If you hunt around the Internet today you will find a game called Anti-Monopoly. Developed and sold by a retired American economics lecturer, and following a long legal dispute with Monopoly's current makers, it seeks to restore something of the game's original purpose and put its history straight.

Similarly, our modern problem of emerging monopolies is a struggle of memory against forgetting. A strong element in the success human civilization is our adaptability. The downside is that we quickly acclimatize to circumstances that are far from ideal. Once something appears to become the natural order, it's difficult for many to imagine how else things could be organized. So it is with the supermarket capture of our days. In a human life, along with shelter, little is more important than how we meet our basic needs for food, drink and a few other essentials (Lizzie Magie's 'absolute necessities'). The way they are controlled carries with it a sort of DNA for society. It determines how we relate to our neighbourhoods, and whether communities thrive or decline. It sets out how towns and cities relate to the countryside. To an extent, it determines how we think about ourselves, either as passive consumers or active citizens.

At the very least, it matters that the gene pool stays rich and diverse. We all know what happens when you start to breed from one that is too restricted. This is the problem to which this book is addressed, namely: What happens when you grow an economy from ever-shrinking combinations of retail genes?

To be clear from the outset, this is unapologetically a case against the current and growing domination of the supermarkets. The major players all have multimillion-pound advertising budgets for self-promotion in newspapers and on billboards, radio and television. Together they have thousands of stores in which, unedited and unquestioned, they can also put forth their side of the story. This is the other side; at least, it is one alternative version of events. It is also an invitation to think differently about how we shape things to meet our daily needs.

For the sake of clarity, let's deal briefly with a few of the most common arguments supermarkets make in self-justification. Then, balancing the case made in the rest of the book with your own life experience, the reader can decide for him- or herself. Many other issues to do with choice, value and jobs, for example, are treated in more detail in the following chapters.

Supermarkets argue that proof of their popularity is in the number of customers who shop at their stores. On one level, this is an empirically ridiculous argument. People need food, and if most other grocery shops have been put out of business there is little choice left but to shop at a supermarket. This argument is like a motorway making a similar claim according to the number of cars driving on it. In itself, this doesn't tell you whether it is a good or bad thing, merely that the road is used. It ignores whether there might be a better way to get around, or what the impact of the motorway is.

Actually, most surveys reflect the fact that the majority of people want a good balance of both: they want a healthy range of local shops as well as the ability to visit a supermarket. The massive loss of independent, local shops is the result of several dynamics. Partly, it's an unintended consequence of changing shopping patterns. Nowhere is it written on the sliding super-market doors that by crossing the threshold your vibrant, distinctive, local economy will begin to wither. It's also the result of numerous anti-competitive practices by the super-markets, plus a range of rules, subsidies and decisions about infrastructure that work in their favour.

Moreover, the amount of 'positive feedback' is unrecognized by most policymakers and economists (here, 'positive' doesn't imply 'good', just that one thing feeds off another); this means that beyond a certain point of dominance, the market fails and supermarket dominance becomes self-reinforcing whether the job the companies are doing is good, bad or awful. History is littered with examples of winners who were not the best in their fields, from the 'Qwerty' keyboard designed to actually slow down typing to the triumph of the VHS video format over the superior Betamax; from the privatized UK telephone directory enquiry services in which one provider, 118 118, became the market leader despite being one of the most expensive and only eighth in a league table of accuracy,[1] to broadband providers of which, again, the largest are not the best.

The reason this occurs is that real people almost never behave like the 'rational actors' of conventional theory, which states that the wider economy can be understood from the behaviour of lone individuals and is, unfortunately, the basis for how our economy is managed. One less orthodox economist put it down to experiments with ants (though he did allow for the fact that people can be a little more complicated).[2] Research was done in which ants were given the choice of different food sources at equal distances from their nest. There was no reason for any individual source to be more advantageous than any other. On this basis, assuming normal probability and rational behaviour, each source would be chosen by a roughly equal number of ants. In reality, nothing like that happened. Instead of a 50–50 split one source would end up getting nearly all the visitors for a time before the ants' collective choice flipped.

What appeared to be happening was that a few random acts and choices early on in the experiment set up a self-reinforcing process that led to a dominant outcome: the ants copied each other. After a while, a new dynamic was created, the balance shifted and the pendulum swung back again.

Under experimental conditions, however, there were no structural changes in the availability of the food sources. A pile of rice winning ant popularity at one moment could later become the loser. The difference with a real, human market-place should be clear. A range of often arcane decisions at national and local levels on everything from road-building, to store sizes and pricing policy, coupled with a playing field that is anything but level, set in motion a self-reinforcing dynamic of supermarket dominance. Size brings with it the opportunity to dominate markets, set terms and conditions, advertise on national television and gain direct, influential access to deci-sion-makers. There's also the power to control the supply chain, and certain unearned benefits such as access to cheap money to build even more stores. Because of this, in the human marketplace, the pendulum doesn't swing back. You get a monopoly, or Tescopoly.

The other basic claim made by supermarkets, and a major reason they have been let off by regulators, is that they provide cheap food – especially important to people living in real and relative poverty. But here too, things are less straightforward than they seem. Fresh fruit and vegetables, for example, are typically cheaper at no-nonsense street markets. These in turn tend to be good training grounds for enterprise, better at providing information about what they sell, flexible about prices and operating more in harmony with other local shops.

Yet planning decisions can work against them in favour of supermarkets, as happened at Queen's Market in the East End of London, as we shall see later. Some research shows that when supermarket branches open in areas where other food shops are lacking, the consumption of fruit and vegetables goes up. But this is as useful an observation as pointing out that thirsty people will drink water if you locate a tap where none stood previously. It also leaves unaddressed the forces that created the food desert in the first place. (Step forward, the rise of out-of-town shopping centres driven by the supermarkets.) Even here, the truth can be very different from the hype. In late 2006 the National Consumer Council assessed supermarket performance on providing the nation with healthy food. It found that, in particular, 'Low-income consumers are being short-changed on health. Many economy range foods contain more salt, fat and sugar than their standard equivalents.' The survey also revealed that there were fewer low-price promotions on healthy products in supermarket outlets most likely to be used by low-income shoppers.[3] That said, household spending on food and drink has fallen steadily over more than two decades. In 1982 we spent

21 pence in the pound on food and non-alcoholic drinks; by 2005 that had fallen to 16 pence.[4]

But much of this book argues that there is no such thing as cheap food. It usually means that someone or something else, like the environment, is paying the price. Investigative writers like Felicity Lawrence and Joanna Blythman, in their respective books *Not on the Label: What Really Goes into the Food on Your Plate* and *Shopped: The Shocking Power of British Supermarkets*, have detailed the impact of supermarket methods on food quality. However, it doesn't stop there. When you add up the supermarkets' impact on local distinctiveness, local businesses, jobs and the social glue that holds communities together, I believe they contribute to a *culture of poverty*. By way of response to such criticism, supermarkets use the 'clawback of trade' argument, which suggests that town centre stores (already something of a distraction: the central thrust of Tesco's business model is building more edge- and out-of-town hypermarkets) attract customers to other local shops. In specific circumstances this might be true, such as when local shops don't compete with the supermarkets' range of products and when the road layout encourages it. But supermarket ranges are so large these days that few opportunities are left for others, and town layouts can just as easily cut small shops off. Any benefits are, regardless, minuscule when measured against the devastation wrought on independent local shops by the overall impact of the chain stores.

Here, then, is a summary of key arguments in this book. It's an attempt, at times quite personal, to redress the daily barrage of phoney cheer and self-serving propaganda (sorry, advertising) thrown at us by the major retailers. After all, every little helps.

Shopping in supermarkets gets us down; according to a survey in *The Grocer*, more people seem to experience a range of negative emotions in Tesco than at other major supermarkets. Under pressure from the anti-competitive practices of the supermarkets,[5] small, independent retailers are passing through a 'mass extinction event' at the hands of the supermarkets – and in the process an important part of the social glue that holds communities together is being dissolved.

Over time, a buildup of changes, each one apparently relatively innocuous, has turned the country into a 'free-fire zone' for the supermarkets. The result is businesses that feel they have the right to do what they want, when, where and how they want to do it. Changes to shopping hours, planning rules, how goods are priced, regulations on special sectors like pharmacy and attitudes toward monopoly have all conspired to create the corporate equivalent of overgrown teenagers who think the world revolves around them. Now, regardless of the impacts on others, senior supermarket executives expect to be able to sell anything at any price, anywhere, at any time, and from stores of any size.

The big, centralized logistical operations of the super-markets are driving the homogenization of business, shopping, eating, farming, food, the landscape, the environment and our daily lives. In the process, Britain is being sucked into a vortex of US-style, chain store-led, clone retailing, both in towns and in faceless, soulless 'big-box' out-of-town shopping parks. They are spreading like 'invasive species' spread in nature, lacking checks and balances and killing off diversity and 'native' (in other words, local) species. Tesco is the largest driving force – if not the only guilty party – behind the spread of clone towns in Britain. The store's already monopolistic control of the British grocery market is set to get even more suffocating, with huge further growth already planned and underway. Ironically, Tesco seems to cling on to an image of itself as an upstart and a maverick outsider. It may be a genuine delusion or a trick, like the politician who uses outsider-status as a veil behind which to hide real power.

Whenever supermarkets may boast about creating employment, they hide the fact that someone else is paying the cost, through jobs lost as a result of smaller shops going bust or suppliers broken by the supermarkets' unreasonable demands. So-called low prices also drive low pay, long hours and the casualization of the workforce all along the supply chain. Coupled with their impact on town centres and other retailers, the supermarkets are, in effect, pushing a social and economic culture of poverty.

In wealthy Britain, farmers and suppliers live in fear of the power of Tesco. Now Tesco is moving into less-developed Central and Eastern Europe, and into developing countries in Asia. Across Asia there are hundreds of millions of small-scale farmers who have even fewer defences against Tesco's ability to control the market. The store is symptomatic of a wider problem in the global economy. In every sector, a shrinking number of ever-bigger corporations are wresting and centralizing control of the market. Similar if varied stories could be written about the French Carrefour, the Dutch Ahold, the German Metro and the US stores Kroger, Home Depot and Wal-Mart.

The supermarkets' global business model, increasingly built on sourcing from poor countries around the world as they diversify into selling things other than food, and dependent on energy-intensive production and distribution, is set to walk into the 'perfect storm' of climate change and permanently high and rising oil prices.

In terms of the original purpose of the corporation, which was to encourage people to invest in projects of public interest, the legal form of the corporation has become a living corpse – a walking zombie. Hope that voluntary 'corporate responsibility' would answer public mistrust of multinationals died along with it. It is time to re-invent the corporation so that it works to the benefit of the whole of society. A 'corporate reformation' is overdue. Investigations by official regulators into Britain's biggest retailers will show whether or not these officials have become an arm of the industry they are supposed to regulate, or whether they are prepared to meet the challenge of steadily growing monopolies.

On the brighter side, in Britain and the US national rebellions are growing, made up of hundreds of community campaigns set to challenge the supermarket steamrollers. Well over 100 individual campaigns in Britain are focused on Tesco alone. The first signs of a turning tide are beginning to emerge. At the time of writing, the latest consumer research showed customer loyalty to the company to be either stagnant or in decline. Popularity was lowest among younger shoppers, boding badly for Tesco in the future.[6]

Ever since the 1960s, that decade has been the scapegoat of choice among a certain class of commentator alluding to any example of social breakdown. To understand what really destroys community cohesion, however, I think we've been looking in the wrong place. Communities are held together by thousands of threads that directly connect people in social, cultural and economic interactions; but real, face-to-face human relationships that occur in the neighbourhood are being designed out in countless, seemingly insignificant ways. They're going because an economic system that is meant to be our servant has instead become our master, and it sees people too often as costly and inefficient. The cash machine replaces the bank clerk; automated voice-activation stands in for someone at the end of a phone. Unlike local shops, the supermarkets buy in services and goods with logistics that are remote, centralized and automatic. Even at the till – the last post of human interaction – they're switching to auto-checkout.

Over time, with less and less direct human contact through a vibrant, distinctive and locally rooted network of shops, cafes and services, we become strangers to the people we live around. Then it spirals. We feel less connected to and therefore less inclined to invest time and energy into the community. We retreat into virtual electronic worlds where fewer social and emotional skills are needed than the full spectrum of senses we require for real life.

It almost certainly wasn't intended to end up like this, but when you turn around and wonder why the idea of community seems to be turning into an item for display in a museum, a large part of the blame must lie at the foot of unmanaged market forces. In the crime caper of 'who killed community' and wore away social cohesion, it isn't a lost decade that should be blamed but an economic system that cannot distinguish between financial price and human cost. The market did it. It's also possible that the battle to correct this enormous imbalance and to protect the things that matter to us will look different from older struggles. Rather than a clash of left and right, political certainties are breaking down into a fight between big and small.

In some ways the supermarkets take away our choices about where and how to shop, by foreclosing on the possibility of local variety and by only stocking products that fit their fast-turnover model or come from suppliers prepared to accept their terms. In other ways they give us choice paralysis, or choice fatigue. We get lost in aisles of endless jars, tins and ready meals – food remotely mass-produced and stripped of cultural context. All of this is for sale in big, impersonal, self-interested supermarkets that have no concept of limits. In response, we understandably seek more authenticity, a sense of place, connection and human scale. Then there are the problems of climate change, global shortages of water to drink and with which to grow crops, rising drought, threats to agriculture and the need for low-carbon, productive food systems that are controlled by the people most in need. Against these sorts of challenges, supermarkets are looking increasingly out of place in the modern world.

My father ran a small business and voted Conservative. He thought the party was a friend to entrepreneurs like him. His rude awakening came in the early 1980s; the national political embrace, it turned out, was a group hug for the rich and big businesses only.

Shortly after the Labour Party took office, it appeared things might be different. Refreshingly, an enthusiastic new adminis-tration looked ready to confront the abuse of corporate power. In 1999 the Chancellor, Gordon Brown, endorsed a campaign to end 'rip-off Britain'. Speaking at the Party's annual conference he promised, 'In the new Britain of enterprise open to all, we will expose and end anti-competitive practices.' In March 2001, in a meeting with a group of farmers, Prime Minister Tony Blair criticized the supermarkets' dominance.

Terry Leahy might have become Chief Executive of Tesco the same year that Blair came to office but, publicly at least, the retailer and the government seemed to be heading in different directions. Then it all went quiet – silent, that is, apart from the soft, brushing sound of a revolving door steadily turning.

Behind the scenes, people were on the move. Tesco hired one of Blair's closest advisers, a strategist called Philip Gould, to shake up its approach to public affairs. His reshuffle also brought the prime minister's former private secretary David North to Tesco to handle government relations, joining Lucy Neville-Rolfe, who had already brought inside knowledge of government to Tesco from the Cabinet Office in 1997.

When the Labour government was still quite young, Tesco generously helped it out. The government inherited the great plastic folly of London's Millennium Dome and was desperately short of friends and funds. Then Tesco pledged millions to the Dome. Coincidentally, a proposed tax on shopping centre car parks under discussion in a government paper on transport, which reportedly would have cost the supermarket heavily, was quietly dropped from legislation.

An old (and not very good) joke about American politics had it that the Republicans were the party of big business and the family, whereas the Democrats were just the party of big business. Not far into the long day of Blair's government, the morning dew of many progressive ambitions quickly evaporated. The same bad joke could almost be made today in Britain, substituting Conservative and Labour for Republican and Democrat. Neither, though, can claim to stand for family and community if they continue to put the interests of global corporations first. The year after Blair said that the supermarkets had the country's rural livelihoods in an 'armlock', Leahy was knighted for his services to British business and became Sir Terry Leahy.

But It's Not All Their Fault

Belatedly, I should mention an important caveat. I appear to be loading a lot of criticism on to Tesco. But at one level, the company is merely doing what the system, or lack of one, allows it to do, and what City investors expect of it. Its dominance, with all its attendant problems, is merely a logical consequence of a badly designed and failing marketplace. Misplaced priorities mix with confusion about what appropriate economic goals should be.

At a deeper level, Tesco and the other big supermarkets thrive because governments have yet to understand our greatest challenge: how we can meet all our basic needs, including the pursuit of happiness and well-being, while living within the world's environmental limits. The enterprising management of Tesco couldn't solve this problem, even if it wanted to. Fundamentally rethinking the legal form of the corporation is not a technocratic issue. It is not even a call for newfangled innovations. It is a call to remember the thinking that heralded the birth of the modern industrial age. Back then, a Scottish academic whose name has been too frequently taken in vain understood that what we needed a 'moral economy' to guide the building of a new age. His name was Adam Smith and, surprising as it might seem to people who associate his work with the brutal rise of 'free market' economics, he was one of history's fiercest critics of corporations. If he were alive today, I like to think that after a hard day campaigning against the new corporatism manifested by companies like Tesco, he would sit down in the evening to a nice game of Anti-Monopoly to witness, once again, how people pay when markets fail.

CHAPTER ONE

Identity Theft

'There is nothing in front but a flat wilderness of standardization either by Bolshevism or Big Business.'
G. K. Chesterton, *The Outline Of Sanity*, 1927[1]

Quiet Death of the Soul:
Six Months of Your Life in a Supermarket

A part of me is dying. I'm standing in the chilled-food aisle of a Tesco supermarket. I think I can feel my soul wither. But this is my neighbourhood; I should feel comfortable and at home.

On the site of the former South London Hospital for Women, this store was built in 2006 against local opposition and after a long planning dispute. The council and a government planning inspector rejected the supermarket, but Labour Minister Stephen Byers overruled them. Even abandoned, the building had retained a fading pride. Large, distinctive lettering on the façade spelled out its name, keeping alive local history and a sense of place. Anyone passing in the street would see a quiet monument to caring and social purpose. Those traces disappeared, sandblasted away when the building was eventually remodelled into the store. The only memories salvaged of the building's former public service are chiselled into two old discoloured foundation stones. The exterior was further disfigured by an ornamental staircase that would have seemed more at home announcing the *nouveau*-Essex mansion of a London gangster.

For more than a year after opening, Tesco operated on the site, without planning permission. The building had been listed, situated in a conservation area and described as a Wren-style landmark. Conditions were set with the original permission to protect its character. But virtually all that remained after the visit from Tesco's demolition crew was the building's brick front. Residents and councillors were 'shocked'. The store had to reapply for retrospective permission. Had the council known of Tesco's track record ignoring planning rules, it might have watched developments more closely.[2]

Three things confront you as you step through the glass entrance doors. To the right is a Krispy Kreme doughnut display. Exclamation marks almost equal the doughnuts in number: 'See us soon!' 'Any time!' 'Store locations!' 'Pick up our doughnuts!'

To the left of the entrance there is a whole wall of cigarettes for sale. Straight ahead is a CCTV monitoring station. A bored employee in uniform stands watching aisles of produce. Clearly the store is vulnerable to attack at any moment. By manipulating a joystick, the guard has the ability to track individual customers around the store. His presence near the front door establishes a tone of distrust. As you move further inside, the unease builds into evidence of mild corporate paranoia.

There are cameras everywhere. Notices on each aisle remind customers, each apparently a potential shoplifter, that the supermarket is part of a 'civil recovery scheme'. It takes time to translate the euphemism. One avenue of shelves is heavy with wine and spirits. Each bottleneck is ringed with a security tag. Together they look like a prison party allowed out only on condition that they remain in chains; a chain gang within a chain store.

Tesco is proud of its market share and the sheer number of customers it attracts through its doors. But having worked so hard to attract them, it doesn't seem to trust them very much.

This matters in ways that are not immediately obvious. Extensive research into human well-being shows that a lack of trust is one of the most powerful drivers undermining individual happiness and a sense of community – what academics like to call social capital.[3] Whether or not people are fundamentally trustworthy is an endless source of grumbling by moral guardians. But perhaps the time has come to ask if supermarkets are really people-worthy.[4]

Interestingly, and this is bad news for supermarkets, the same body of research also shows that rising levels of consumption do nothing to increase our sense of life satisfaction, and that the culture of 'shop till you drop' also ends up making us more listless and depressed.[5]

The sullen atmosphere in the store is underlined by its downbeat staff members, who seem to slump from place to place. They are strangely nothing like the perky perma-grins seen in television adverts. Almost cruelly, they have to wear contradictory, bright red bibs spelling out promises of customer support.

It would be hard to design an environment more capable of inducing alienation or, for that matter, family arguments. On cue, I've stepped into the store with my wife and our two-year-old daughter. Within seconds of entering, we have a mild disagreement about how to juggle a child with a tricycle in tow, and my intention to gather information. This is, after all, a research trip. I have no intention of buying anything despite the full-spectrum, 360-degree assault by carefully refined marketing tactics. For a moment I worry, reacting as I have to the surroundings, that I have become overly sensitive. But I grew up in the suburban sprawl of Chelmsford, Essex. I am accustomed to spiritual wastelands.

Moreover, it seems, I am not alone in sensing that a quietly corrosive nothingness, imported through a culture of unquestioning consumerism, is beginning to hollow me out from within as I wander through the land of the major multiple retailer. Big supermarkets make us feel bored, frustrated, stressed and overwhelmed. The bigger the chain, the worse they make us feel. Tesco, in particular, makes us feel more bored and stressed than any other major supermarket, and equally as frustrated and overwhelmed as the next worst.

Here are some numbers. According to *The Grocer* magazine (required reading for supermarket-watchers and the retail trade), 56 per cent of Tesco customers were 'bored' by the shop, 53 per cent were 'stressed', 52 per cent 'frustrated' and 51 per cent 'overwhelmed'. That means over half of Tesco shoppers were unhappy in their stores in one of four variously unpleasant ways.

Of the big food retailers, only in Waitrose – tiny in comparison to the 'big four' of Tesco, Asda/Wal-Mart, Sainsbury's and Morrisons – are negative feelings balanced or overcome by more positive sensations, such as being 'pleased', 'organised', 'interested' or 'satisfied'.[6] Tesco customers experiencing these positive feelings were few in proportion: only 24 per cent (pleased), 29 per cent (organised), 15 per cent (interested) and 24 per cent (satisfied).

It would matter less were it not for the fact that, according to current trends, the average British shopper is set to spend six months of his or her life in a supermarket.[7] We choose to spend so much time making ourselves miserable in order to fill our cupboards and fridges with what we need to keep going. If there were no alternatives (and, unfortunately, in many places there increasingly aren't) it would be understandable, but would still be a trigger for change. Yet even where choices exist, we are complicit in a kind of corporate coercion that lessens our quality of life.

The way we shop is forming the backdrop of an ideological death scene. If much of how the country and world are run is based on the assertion that people behave rationally when they make economic decisions, the rest of our lives are nevertheless loaded with contradictions. So, it's always been odd to assume that, where numbers are concerned, we would suddenly become cool and logical. History shows quite the reverse to be true. From tulip mania in seventeenth-century Holland to the stock market crash of 1929 in the US, and the executive crimes and denials of the twenty-first-century energy firm Enron, we have known, where money is concerned, of the power of popular delusion and the madness of crowds.[8]

That a form of misery-making, daily dependence on supermarkets has emerged is by itself important, symptomatic, and something I shall return to later. But walk through the doors of a major supermarket, and you walk into a much wider world of dysfunction. In this other, less than attractive place it is possible to see how the global economy is being engineered in ways that will also make people poorer, foster an environmentally destructive culture of over-consumption and blow a suffocating fog of banality over the communities we live in. Although this book contains more than enough information about the particular phenomenon of Tesco, it is really about looking through the lens of the dominant supermarkets to observe a flawed economic system. To understand what is going wrong and why, it is necessary to look beyond the bland reassurances of wall-to-TV-to-magazine-to-billboard-to-wall supermarket advertising. Then we can start to think about how to do things better.

Just then, at precisely the moment when I have nearly convinced myself that all is lost, something happens to revive my crushed sense of being and makes the forthcoming battle seem almost like fun. My daughter reappears, squealing with delight. She barrels around a corner into the chilled-food aisle, pushed by my partner in an otherwise empty trolley, and rushes headlong towards me. At this point, under the gaze of disapproving security guards and anxiously pivoting CCTV cameras, we leave Tesco and head into the park outside. We were made to

feel a bit like criminals and bought nothing. Out in the sun, our
hands are empty of shopping, but our souls are a little lighter.

Engineers of the Human Day

Before we even start to think about how to level the shopping
playing field in a world rigged in favour of the supermarkets and
against independent and local shops, consider: is it actually
possible to live without them?

The innovative campaign group Anti-Apathy (strapline: *Because waking up is hard to do*), invited ten people to try and live
without supermarkets for one month.[9] Unsurprisingly perhaps,
considering that the 'big four' control over three-quarters of
Britain's grocery market, the results were mixed. The following
personal accounts illustrate a range of responses.

One participant, Meredith Cochrane, struggled: 'I've broken
down and bought small bits and pieces (no big shopping trips
though!).' She spent much of the time without milk and bread in her
house, and resorted to liberating food from her colleagues at work,
going hungry and 'eating out A LOT'. But Meredith also came away
with a profoundly different awareness of what supermarket dominance meant: 'The difficulties I faced have spoken volumes about
what the large supermarkets have done to local accessibility. I've also
found it liberating not going to my fridge every week after a massive
shop and throwing out tonnes of rotting food from "overshop-
ping". I have thrown out a total of one carrot.' After the experiment
Meredith said she thought she would use supermarkets again, but
the experience has changed her approach to shopping. She said she
would use them less, and smaller shops more.

Participant Nadia Raafat, on the other hand, happily settled
into her 'supermarket-free life', without being dogmatic about
it: 'I like spreading my money around,' she said. 'I enjoy going to
the markets. My diet has become healthier as a result – less of the

chemically-subsidised [*sic*] crap and much more fresh and organic produce.' She didn't vow not to use supermarkets again, as she did not feel the need to be that rigid. She said she would take it 'a week at a time' and not feel guilty if she did use one.

Another participant, Lucy Hughes, conveniently spent the first few weeks of the experiment in Bourg-St-Maurice in the French Alps. There she gorged on locally produced vegetables, quiche, cheese and sausages. Things got more difficult when she returned to Essex to visit her mother. Still, she managed to obtain fruit and vegetables from a farm shop, as well as some locally made strawberry jam. Being at home in London was a 'shock', she wrote; however, she 'managed very easily not to go to a supermarket'. Instead, Lucy bought all she needed at her inexpensive local Turkish shop. Her conclusion at the end of the experiment is worth reading:

> The last month has made me realise how much of what I eat is processed and/or imported. I have also realised that I didn't miss going to the supermarket at all. Everything I need, I can get from elsewhere. It is sometimes more expensive (particularly cleaning products and toiletries), however the amount I saved by walking to the shop instead of driving to the supermarket probably balanced [that] out. In fact, I probably saved money, because every time I went shopping I just bought what I needed instead of being wooed by a load of advertising, 'special offers' and cunning shop layouts, and leaving with a load of stuff I didn't need.

Tesco, Tesco, Everywhere

By the time this book is published, Tesco will be Britain's biggest retailer – not just the country's biggest supermarket, known for selling food and groceries, but its biggest for everything that isn't

food as well. Tesco alone takes £1 out of every £8 spent by British shoppers, and its share is rising. The company's chief executive, Terry Leahy, really isn't joking when he says that still leaves the other £7 left to go for.[10] Suddenly, a twisted Orwellian vision of an economy centrally planned, not by the state but by a single, unstoppable commercial enterprise, begins to emerge from the realm of paranoid delusion and creep into the world of distant but credible possibility.

The UK is divided up into 121 postcode areas. In a single year, Tesco rose from being the dominant grocer in sixty-seven of these areas to dominating the market in eighty-one. In an additional twenty-four areas, the store is the number-two retailer. In six areas, Tesco takes over 50 pence of every pound spent on groceries. Communities in these areas have become known as 'Tesco towns'. In Southall and Truro, that figure was 57 pence; in Swansea, 54 pence; in Inverness, 52 pence; in Twickenham and Perth, 51 pence each. Only four areas were silent in 2006 to the ringing of Tesco's cash tills: the Outer Hebrides, Lerwick in the Shetlands, Kirkwall in the Orkneys and the well-preserved northern town of Harrogate.[11]

Having outgrown all the other UK supermarkets, Tesco is also leaving in its wake the UK's previously biggest non-food retailer, ARG, owner of Argos and Homebase. According to the analysts who predicted Tesco's ascent to the shopping throne, such unprecedented dominance by a single retailer will lead to 'casualties from almost every corner of the market'.[12]

' In Orwell's vision, endlessly copied in literature and film by anyone seeking to paint the dark side of highly centralized societies, the state does everything for you. There is little, now, that Tesco does not promise in terms of meeting our daily needs. It is the fulfilment of a decades-old dream held by supermarket chains. In 1970, Harry Cunningham, the founder of the huge US discount store chain K-mart (which would later be eclipsed by Wal-Mart), promised to 'take care of the needs of the typical American family'. But exactly how many corners of our lives would Tesco like to inveigle itself into?

Start with the simple things: Tesco can provide the ingredients for breakfast, lunch and dinner, and any snack or drink you fancy in between. You'll obviously be tempted with a few loss leaders and promotions on popular items (the costs of which will be met by the suppliers, not Tesco).

You can pick up your reading material there, too. But you might find it difficult if you want anything other than a newspaper, one of the top mass-circulation magazines or the latest mass-selling pulp novel or celebrity biography. You'll find it difficult not just because Tesco doesn't sell anything else, but because by taking the market for high-volume, fast-turnover items, it also destroys the economics of smaller, more specialized outlets. Look for one of those and increasingly you will search the town centre in vain.

In retail, there is something called 'the 80/20 rule'. It suggests that retailers make 80 per cent of their sales and nearly all their profits from the best-selling 20 per cent of their products. In other words, a relatively small range of products creates the economic underpinning by which, for example, an independent newsagent is able to stock a much wider range of titles. The supermarket, on the other hand, only sells the smaller range of high-turnover titles. But by taking the market for the bestsellers, it pulls the rug out from under the smaller shops, which used them to underwrite a much wider selection and remain financially viable. Tesco, of course, don't want special-interest publications, untried modern literature or dusty old classics hanging around on the off-chance that someone might buy them. Who but a freak would want to read them anyway? The same market logic is applied to music and film, and with the same consequences. Some say that the Internet age has rendered the 80/20 rule obsolete; others hold that it merely reinforces the power of the leading retailers.

Tesco will also sell you a range of drugs and supplements to fill your medicine cabinet, and feed the fears of the worried-well. And if it gets its way with the government and licensing authorities, it will provide an in-store pharmacy and GP too. Gradually, and literally, the operation will build into a cradle-to-grave service. You can buy the alcohol and junk food with which to ruin your health, and then the drugs and 'healthy options' to pull you back from the brink.

At home, you can have your house decorated, furnished, lit, heated and powered courtesy of Tesco. Listen to your music (top-selling titles only) and watch your films (mostly popcorn hits) on electrical appliances also bought from Tesco. The store will clothe you, provide you with plates and dishes to eat off and also sell you the washing machine and dishwasher you need to clean them. Of course, it will also sell you the cooker for that vital in-between phase from supermarket-prepared TV dinner to plate. If it's summer and you feel like sitting outside, there is a range of garden furniture for sale to keep you off the ground.

With such a significant stake in your home already, it's only natural that Tesco wants to actually own it, too. To make that dream a reality, it also offers loans and mortgages (if you fail to keep up payments your home could be at risk, and all your Tesco products will be in the back of a bailiff's van heading back whence they came). But if you pick yourself up again financially, since moving into property development, it's now possible to buy a new Tesco-built home. Did I mention that you can also do your Tesco shopping with the benefit of a Tesco credit card or loan? But be careful; it's a bit more expensive than the range of finance deals you can get from mainstream banks.

If you want a brief respite from the rigours of living in Tescoland, handily, Tesco can sell you a holiday. It also offers you the chance to buy insurance, not just for your holiday but for your pet, car (it'll also pick you up if you break down), home and life as well. Just as a footnote, you can capture all those holiday memories on camera and get them printed at your local Tesco store, too.

Want to phone a friend from your mobile or home phone, or surf the Internet? Tesco is there for you. Work from home? Tesco can kit out your office with everything you need, from furniture to computers plus software. If that doesn't work out, you can apply for a job at the store and take out a Tesco savings account for somewhere to put your pay.

Then, if life itself doesn't work out, Tesco can provide the paperwork to make a will, get divorced, sue your boss, sue another trader, sue your neighbours, sue anyone. But don't worry, if someone else uses the power of Tesco to sue you, the store can provide you with a paper shredder to get rid of any evidence.

As an afterthought, people with a particularly bad sense of direction can make a special request for Tesco staff to come and find them by using the new radio frequency identity tagging system. This enables a store to follow goods that have radio tags attached wherever they go. The reader must understand, however, that this is not a service advertised by Tesco and would have to be negotiated in individual circumstances – unless, of course, you forget to pay for something, in which case the store will be following you anyway, or using the information on your Tesco Clubcard combined with CCTV footage to arrange a home visit by the other boys in blue – not Tesco managers, but the police. (Note: These are real systems that have already been introduced, and the circumstances described are either technically possible or have already happened; see Chapter Three for one example.)

If you're not feeling claustrophobic yet, it might mean that you have already become institutionalized. Don't feel bad if you didn't see it coming. The past is full of uninintended consequences; I'm sure the Vikings never planned for the sheer, tacky awfulness of the clunky, animated mannequins celebrating their past at the Yorvik, the Viking tourist attraction in the city of York.

Not only does Tesco aspire to become the commercial equivalent of the nanny state, providing every product and service imaginable – something that is unhealthy for many reasons – it also aspires to have a store format for every location. There they are on the petrol forecourt, the high street, and the roundabout at the edge of town. Then, as you drive along the dual carriageway between towns, that huge building over there is not an aircraft hangar or medieval feudal village (but then again . . .), it's one of the new, huge Tesco Extra 'big-box' outlets that will enable the company to double its size. No, that is not a printing error: if retail analysts are correct, the nation's already dominant retailer is set to double in size if its current UK expansion plans are allowed to continue unrestrained. What is going on, and what will it mean if they do?

Invasive Species

Sometimes it's easier to see a trend by comparison or analogy, and nature has a lot to teach economics. Massively expanded global trade and communications also carries many unintended consequences. Different species of plants and animals, for example, are able to mix across geographical boundaries at a scale and speed never before seen. The Chinese Mitten crab (*Eriocheir sinensis*) is now common in Britain after being carried here in the holds and bilge water of huge international freight ships. It wrecks both riverbanks and local habitats, and controlling its expansion might mean having to hunt the crab for food. (It is one of the more curious lessons of globalization for fusion cuisine that in Asia, the gonads of the Mitten crab[13] [which ripen during migration] are a prized delicacy.)

Natural scientists use a whole new term to describe the current epoch of comprehensive, global human interference in ecosystems. Our time, they say, should be called the 'Homogocene' to describe the way distinctiveness and difference are being eroded.[14] A combination of the creep of invasive species and habitats destroyed by development is driving a mass extinction event. The World Conservation Union warns that such 'invasions' are leading to the 'irretrievable loss of native biodiversity'.[15]

Invasive species, scientists tell us, are 'organisms (usually transported by humans) which successfully establish themselves in, and then overcome . . . native ecosystems'.[16] Typical characteristics of an invasive species include the absence of predators, hardiness and a generalist diet. Whatever the reason for their arrival and proliferation, invasive species often cause a 'disruption' of the ecosystem that is 'catastrophic for native species'.

Superweeds are sometimes introduced into an ecosystem by experiments that go wrong, or emerge because they are highly efficient, new predators. Take Japanese knotweed (*Fallopia Japonica*).[17] It was introduced to Britain by enthusiastic, if naive, Victorian gardeners, who considered it an ornamental delight that could also be used as cattle feed. They didn't realize it could grow through tarmac, pavements and brick walls, from just a scrap of root no bigger than a pea; or that, over a century later, its virtually unstoppable spread would be considered such a threat that planting or dumping knotweed in the wild carries a fine and a two-year prison sentence. The government believes it will cost, nationally, over £1.5 billion to control. Knotweed is so hated because it suffocates other plants, squeezing out anything in its path and replacing it with an unproductive, leafy monotony.

Then there is the Nile perch (*Lates niloticus*), branded one of the 'world's worst' invaders by conservationists. It's a freshwater fish that can grow to huge proportions, weighing up to 200 kg and stretching to 2 m long. Again, with good intentions, it was introduced in 1954 to Lake Victoria, which straddles Tanzania, Kenya and Uganda. Since then it has helped push over 200 well-established local fish species to extinction. The Nile perch ate them, and it ate their food. The Nile perch is also a cannibal, and eats its own young. It eats, in fact, pretty much anything it comes across. It breeds all year round, producing up to 16 million eggs per breeding cycle. If you struggle to find something positive to say, you can point out that the fish has been turned into an export crop. But it has also caused social upheaval in lakeside communities and killed off many of the fish that were relied upon for food. Perversely, the fact that Nile perch is traded for export means that it is also often too expensive for many local people to eat.[18]

Bufo marinus, otherwise known as the Cane toad, is another case of good intentions gone badly wrong. It was deliberately introduced in many places around the world as a natural way to control pests that affect cash crops like sugarcane. But like the Nile perch, it eats almost everything it comes across. The toads' original habitat was subtropical forests but, unfortunately for other species, they're happy to set up home in everything ranging from drainpipes to ponds, piles of rubbish around or under houses and building sites. Cane toads are not good neighbours, nor much fun to hang around with. They're noisy, fast-spreading, ready to eat you if you're the right size and have glands on each shoulder that exude venom.[19]

The Invasive Species Specialist Group of the World Conservation Union lists 100 of the world's most invasive species. Tesco is not mentioned . . . yet. But the omission might be an oversight, perhaps explained by the fact that the store is yet to be assigned a Latin name for classification. It might not appear so, but this is actually a serious point. Remember the characteristics of an invasive species: the absence of predators (think of real commercial competition or effective regulators to hold back the supermarkets); hardiness (think of legions of corporate lawyers, financial leverage and endless commercial cost-cutting); and a generalist diet (supermarkets will sell anything to make a profit, and chain stores operate according to a low common denominator).

If you want diversity in the world around you rather than a single kind of plant in your garden, a single variety of fish in your lake and only one type of venomous, croaking toad under your shed, then you have to manage for that outcome. When we garden, we hold back aggressive, opportunistic plants in order to keep space open for a celebration of variety and colour.

There are serious parallels between the way that both ecosystems and local economies function. An ecosystem with little diversity might be less productive, less able to absorb nutrients, more vulnerable to disease, climatic shocks and upheaval and bad at recovery afterwards. A system that is richly diverse and has more species to call upon during hard times to enable adaptation is likely to fare better. Invasive species are not only hard-to-control nuisances. They're also unsightly, cause mass local extinctions and reduce the overall productivity and diversity of ecosystems. This, in turn, undermines the ecosystems' strength, stability and resilience.

In many ways, local economies are like ecosystems. In others, the analogy with nature is less straightforward. Commonly within ecosystems, some sort of bumpy balance struggles to establish itself. For example, the relationship between predators and prey can lead to boom and bust population cycles. If a predator that lacks its own higher predator gets the upper hand, its population increases. But then its own prey is over-consumed, decimating the population, destroying the predator's food supply and allowing the prey to recover. In these kinds of relationships, a kind of balance, if brutal, emerges over time.

In local economies, however, that doesn't happen. Superstores and chain retailers are not examples of either symbiosis or of species that sit in a balanced food chain. They are much more like invasive species, like Japanese knotweed, Nile perch or Cane toads. They are not in balance, nor even a boom–bust cycle with other similar, local species of shop; they are permanently displacing them. Just like invasive species, they are invariably introduced with good or at least benign intentions, by planners, town councils or governments too much in awe of big business.

But then they prove to be hungry, indiscriminate, antisocial and destructive. When no one is paying much attention, the superstores and chain shops grow to dominate and suffocate the economic ecosystem. They pass through planning regulations as easily as knotweed pushes through tarmac, devouring smaller and independent retailers with as much reflection as the Nile perch cleansing Lake Victoria of competition. And, like the Cane toad, they were often introduced to provide a specific service but outgrew their habitats until their cash-till song could be heard on every street corner, forecourt, roundabout and out-of-town centre.

Like it or not (and it is something about which most policy-makers and economists are in deep denial), weakly regulated markets tend towards monopoly.[20] This is the great modern economic irony. Advocates of free markets argue against checks and balances to counter the power of big business, but in doing so ultimately destroy the possibility of markets that could meaningfully be called free, or rather, 'open'. They resist anti-monopoly regulation in the name of providing consumer choice, and in the process they ultimately destroy it.

In some important ways, we are returning to an earlier phase of corporatism. Henry Ford told customers they could have any colour of car, as long as it was black. The scale and seriousness of Tesco's ambition means that, before long we will be able to shop anywhere we like for our groceries, as long as it's Tesco.

This Will Be Out of Date by the Time You Read It

But Tesco is not the only ambitious store with a design on our lives. Invasive economic species don't wait to be counted. Here are snapshots of some of them in action as they spread across Britain so quickly that the following figures are guaranteed to be out of date by the time this book is even printed.

Starbucks first arrived in Britain not very long ago; I remember it. There was a coffee shop near Covent Garden in London that I had been to. One day, in early summer 1998, I walked past and saw that it had changed into a Starbucks, which at the time, seemed exotic. It's hard to believe now, but the corporation only arrived in the UK and in Europe as a whole in May of that year, when it bought sixty-five outlets of the Seattle Coffee Company.

Within three years there were over 200 Starbucks branches.

By mid-2006 – a year in which the company plans to open 2,000 new outlets globally to add to the 12,000-odd it has already – there were over 500 in the UK.[21]

Starbucks promotes a laid-back, US West Coast image, offering its shops as an extension of your own living room. It invites you to 'relax and linger' in its, 'cosy and intimate' outlets, where you can 'huddle on a sofa' if you're looking for 'an intimate [again] place to meet friends'. How much warmth and intimacy can you handle? Some people might be relieved to know that Starbucks' business methods actually – how should I put this? – rather *contrast* with its self-styled fireside warmth. But you might also be surprised that Starbucks refers to its own approach in terms of economic cannibalism. When it opens stores in clusters to squeeze out any competition, the practice is so aggressive that it has sometimes undermined its own outlets.[22]

Beneath a thin top layer of careful marketing, there often lies a much less attractive coat of managerial paint. Three large supermarkets near where I live offered to cash in each other's discount vouchers in order to spoil their respective competitors' promotions. A friendly delicatessen and coffee shop opened in the neighbourhood, triggering a small quality-food renaissance, with a successful Sunday farmers' market and an organic fruit and vegetable store opening within a year. Then came Starbucks. While the coffee chain's new premises were being fitted, the local delicatessen took a lead from the supermarkets and jokingly declared (in its regular email to customers) that Starbucks vouchers would be redeemable at the farmers' market. Almost immediately, a letter arrived from Starbucks.

Given the supermarkets' precedent, it's hard to imagine what rules if any were being broken, but the global coffee corporation threatened legal action. The delicatessen was to 'cease and desist' from making such offers, or Starbucks would get nasty. As though the charge-list against clone stores were not already long enough, legal intimidation now sat where the company's sense of humour should have been. Some people will go to any lengths to protect a bland, hot coffee milkshake.

In 2004 the international development agency Oxfam colla-borated with Starbucks to promote fair trade. That relationship didn't last very long. Coffee makes up nearly half of Ethiopia's income from exports, and 15 million Ethiopians depend on the trade. Speciality coffees like Sidamo and Harar, which earn farmers between 30 and 59 pence, are sold for up to £14/lb in the coffee shops of rich countries. To capture more of the value of the coffee for its own people, the Ethiopian government tried to trademark the names of several types of coffee beans like Sidamo, Harar and Yirgacheffe. Oxfam estimated that this could earn an extra £47 million for Ethiopia, where eight out of ten people live on less than $2 per day. But when the trademark applications were filed with the US Patent and Trademark Office, Starbucks prompted complaints; at least two of the applications were denied. In a single week, more than 60,000 outraged people faxed or called Starbucks to 'express their support for Ethiopian coffee farmers'. Starbucks: 'cosy, intimate, relaxing'.[23]

Blockbuster, the US home entertainment chain, is yet another example of winner-take-all clone retailing. The first Blockbuster store opened in the UK in March 1989 in London's Walworth Road. After that, for millions of people during the 1990s, Blockbuster became synonymous with Friday and Saturday night trips to pick up a film, some ice cream and popcorn, not to mention additional trips to make 'late payments' after forgetting to return the videos on time. In just two decades, the company has established 9,000 stores internationally, with over 700 in the UK – its largest presence outside the US.

The history of McDonald's in the three decades since its arrival in the UK (which has been extensively explored else-where) is one of a dramatic rise to power. The company's extraordinary proliferation in that time shows that, in fact, the paint is really still wet on the chain-store backdrop of our communities.

The first McDonald's outlet in the UK also opened in south London, in October 1974. The company now has around 1,250 fast-food outlets nationwide, though its seemingly unstoppable expansion has been hit by several factors. Long, embarrassing legal cases have been fought, ironically to protect the company's reputation, which instead have put more health and environmental information into the public domain than a burger-munching public might have wanted to know. Films followed about the impact of McDonald's food on people's health. Then a new, invasive fast-food outlet arrived to profit from its ill fortune. Early in 2006, McDonald's actually closed twenty-five UK outlets.[24] Was the tide turning for the imported US chains?

Probably not, because the sandwich chain Subway arrived and, in 2002, announced plans to open 2,000 outlets in the UK and Ireland by 2010. Store #700 opened in July 2006 in Bilston, West Midlands. New outlets began appearing at the rate of fifteen per month, or roughly one every two days. (Subway began life in 1965 – the year I was born – and now has over 25,000 sandwich shops. It makes me feel like such a slacker.)

In Britain and the US, concern grew linking an epidemic of obesity to the massive growth of fast-food outlets and their penchant for 'super-sizing' portions and tempting you with 'guilty pleasures'. The movement rose like a protesting wave of nausea. Subway likes to be seen as a healthier alternative to the burger chains; the last time I passed a local branch, however, its window advertised a special offer to buy one large sandwich overflowing with cheese and layers of cooked meat, and get one free. The other window promoted Subway's own special cookies. The enormous private profits made in the fast-food sector are passing equally overweight costs on to the public health service, as doctors and hospitals must cope with a wide range of problems connected with the effects of overeating.

This epidemic does, however, create a market opportunity for the last of the chain stores in our short survey: The Gap clothes shop. The bigger range of body sizes, coupled with our watching our weight balloon up and down as the result of endless failed diets, mean good news for The Gap, seller of trousers for multiple waistlines. The Gap, like the other global brands, has been a lightning rod for critics of globalization. It is part of that same generation of multiple retailers, having started out in 1969. Now, with over 3,000 stores around the world, iconic advertising and an income of $16 billion in 2005, it has become a major part of 'Brand USA'. Because the retail model for selling clothes is very different from that for fast food, The Gap has fewer outlets; but with over 130 stores in the UK and growing, it is a dominant force.

In case anyone suspects or detects a discomforting under-current of anti-Americanism in this overview, some Americans think it possible that Britons have suffered from the opposite problem. The award-winning American investigative journalist Greg Palast suggests that people in the UK have been seduced by the cultural myth of Americana, and been blinded to its darker realities. Writing at the turn of the millennium, he concluded:

A conspiracy of British travel writers has sold the image of America the Beautiful: Georgia O'Keefe sunsets over New Mexico's plateau, the wide-open vistas of the Grand Canyon. But to get there, you must drive through a numbing, repetitive vortex of Pizza Hut, Wal-Mart, K-Mart, The Gap, Kentucky Fried Chicken, Starbucks and McDonald's. All the separate tastes – New Orleans jambalaya, Harlem ham hocks, New England crab boil – the uniqueness of region and town have been hunted and herded into a few tourist preserves. The oppressive ubiquity of contrived American monoculture has ingested and eliminated any threat of character. The words of McDonald's late chief executive Ray Kroc – 'We cannot trust some people who are non-conformists' – have become our national anthem.[25]

Homogocene: The Death of Diversity

Palpable consumer excitement greeted the initial wave of new American retailers like The Gap and Starbucks, just as it did the early supermarkets. It has been replaced by a listless malaise closely resembling boredom. Why?

At first, the new shops seemed new and compelling and promised variety, like distant relatives from the other side of the world visiting at Christmas. But the global brands just delivered a lasting 'latte-cino' blandness. In the supermarkets, with their ostensibly large range of products, rather than a celebration of genuine cultural diversity we are presented with a boiled-down universal experience. A gap has grown between promise and reality. The image that comes to mind is of science-fiction astronauts, told they will dine in space on sumptuous three-course meals like honeydew melon with fresh figs, blue cheese soufflé with leaf salad and lemon sorbet for dessert; but when the silver lid is lifted, what they actually have is three differently coloured pills on a plate.

Chain stores try hard to fake being authentic and local, and to promise choice. The reason they can't, and never can, is coded into their centralized operational model. Choice isn't just a matter of picking different products from a supermarket shelf. Real diversity, and therefore choice, comes from the character-istics of the whole supply chain. Cultural richness can be embedded in an enormous local variation of what and how things are grown, made, packaged and where they're sold. But it is all lost if there is no variety. The Slow Food Foundation for Biodiversity estimates that Europe has lost three-quarters of its diversity of food products since 1900, while the US lost over nine out of ten (food products) in the same period.[26] The banter of a market stall or the polite interest shown by a small, independent store differs from the dead-eyed checkout stare of a supermarket. A wider range of human relationships and experiences are possible between shop, supplier, staff and local residents if a diversity of business types and values flourish.

Chains, though, are the living embodiment of standardization. Their logistics function like biological cloning. Instead of random, enriching local variation that produces fabulous, endlessly surprising gifts of diversity, they guarantee uniformity. You might be able to buy a ready-made vegetable korma, 'four seasons' pizza or king prawn stir fry at Tesco, but the korma, pizza and stir fry will be identical in every branch.

My own neighbourhood in London is being sucked into this numbing vortex. Within a few hundred yards around where I live, there are Starbucks, McDonald's, KFC, Subway and Blockbusters. Bringing the phenomenon even closer to home in terms of nationality, there are ten Tesco stores of various sizes within approximately 3 miles of where I live.

The hoped-for tales of adventure from other cultures turned out instead to be banal small talk and formulaic conversation. Unfortunately, our festive visitors obeyed the rule of the old Chinese saying that after three days both fish and guests begin to stink. As with most unwanted guests, now that we realize how tiresome they are, they refuse to leave.

Worse than that, due to the increasing concentration of ownership in everything from coffee shops to clothing stores, the big brands made it harder for smaller and more diverse outlets to get a foothold in the marketplace. By driving up rents, suffocating town centres with their shopfronts, wielding massive marketing budgets and controlling global supply chains, the clone store companies ensure that small and independent stores frequently cannot compete. Banality then takes root.

Identikit commercial culture also has a darker side. The death of diversity can undermine democracy, attack our sense of place and belonging and therefore our well-being, too. It can hand power to unaccountable corporate elites, and ultimately it can pull apart the rich weave of natural systems upon which our livelihoods and the economy depend.

'The diversity of the phenomena of nature is so great,' wrote the sixteenth-century German astronomer and mathematician Johannes Kepler, 'and the treasures hidden in the heavens so rich, precisely in order that the human mind shall never be lacking in fresh nourishment.' Now the slide into corporate sameness, greased by the logistical demands of economic globalization, is removing nourishment for the human mind as surely as the burger and fried-chicken chains took it from our food.

For centuries, scientists and poet-philosophers have understood the importance of ecological diversity. A diverse habitat helps produce equilibrium and is better able to recover from external shocks. Most importantly, it allows ecosystems to be resilient to change. As the biologist and author Barbara Kingsolver wrote:

> At the root of everything, Darwin said, is that wonder of wonders, genetic diversity. You're unlike your sister, a litter of pups is its own small Rainbow Coalition, and every grain of wheat in a field holds inside its germ a slightly separate destiny . . . Genetic diversity, in domestic populations as well as wild ones, is nature's sole insurance policy.[27]

The multiple award-winning science writer Colin Tudge, author of *The Variety of Life* and *So Shall we Reap*, agrees. He applies this logic to the most obvious crossover between natural and economic systems – how we farm to meet our need for food (a subject to which we shall return in the final chapter). 'The way to insure against variability and real world conditions is with diversity,' he says. 'High yield, high input (mono-cropping) is for showbiz, but for safe, long-term, sustained output, go organic.'[28]

There is also a parallel between genetic diversity in the natural world and retail diversity on our high streets. Where loss of genetic diversity threatens the survival of species and makes natural ecosystems vulnerable to collapse, clone towns imperil local livelihoods and communities by decreasing the resilience of high streets to economic downturns, and by diminishing consumer choice. At its most extreme, if a town is almost entirely dependent on a single employer and that business closes, the local economy will collapse – the equivalent of an ecosystem crashing.

Exactly this happened to the town of Consett in County Durham. Massive unemployment followed the closure of its famous steelworks after losing out to cheaper competition from Asia and the US. A similar fate hit the town of Flint, Michigan in the US when its auto industry closed. Economic globalization now hastens the speed with which firms can either go bust or relocate. Think of towns like Truro, Swansea and Inverness, where Tesco accounts for over half of all grocery shopping.

The late North American urban planner and social activist Jane Jacobs explored the parallels between economic and ecological systems. In *The Nature of Economies*, she argued that the degree of diversity in either natural or economic systems determines whether or not benefits actually 'stick' where they are needed.

In the case of an ecosystem, that could mean after sunshine and rainfall. In the case of a local economy, it might mean when money gets spent in a shop. 'The practical link between economic development and economic expansion is economic diversity,' she wrote. But, as a handful of brands capture ever more market share, diversity is being lost both in the US and, through its exported business models, in the UK. Where Wal-Mart leads in suffocating markets, Tesco follows.

Trends like these don't just attack small businesses; they also threaten choice and diversity. Tesco is reportedly following in Wal-Mart's footsteps in the influence it exerts over magazine publishing. In the US, Wal-Mart actively censors by not stocking publications if it disapproves of their content, particularly their covers. In the British media, senior publishing industry sources reacted strongly to allegations that Tesco was set to copy that practice.[29] One commentator said that the supermarkets' increasing control of newspaper and magazine sales 'gnaws at the ankles of democracy' because it also threatens to collapse the unique distribution system that guarantees magazines for sale at the same price anywhere in the country, however small the shop (see Chapter Four).[30]

The loss of diversity is even built into the very fabric of the supermarket buildings. Jonathan Glancey, the *Guardian's* architecture correspondent, has complained that 'Tesco branches are breeding like shrink-wrapped rabbits. Where once we had a church in every village, town and city, now we have Tesco with its Extras, Metros and Expresses.'[31] But whereas churches display considerable architectural diversity, the conservation organization English Heritage has been dismayed by the impact on high street commercial buildings of supermarkets that impose standardized layouts to fit their strict business models. Walls and windows are ripped out to accommodate identical shelving and signage.

High street homogenization is just one manifestation of the march of cultural uniformity. My generation grew up in the

1970s and 1980s buffeted by a rising wave of narrow, sharply self-interested versions of market economics. In case we should flirt with more radical, progressive ideas, the cautionary spectre of dreary, state-run, centrally planned Eastern European econo-mies was forced down our throats. The clear implication was that if you criticized the new consensus, you must be longing for East Berlin behind the wall, or to queue for bread outside an empty store in a Moscow suburb. Only very slowly did I wake up to realize that the prospect of monotonous state socialism used to keep me in line when I was young has merely been replaced by the reality of dreary market economies, centrally planned by corporations.

Anxieties about social 'homogenization' are not new, and can be unpleasantly elitist. T. S. Eliot and Ezra Pound complained that mass culture corrupts the impulses of the Enlightenment. Permeating the writing of H. G. Wells, Aldous Huxley and George Orwell is the threat of some form of totalitarianism triumphing over a population whose senses have been dulled by one drug or another. So is there anything different about contemporary fears? I believe it's a question of scale and range. The power, concentration and international reach of big busi-ness at this moment in history makes resistance to dominant market systems so challenging that even the most dystopian critic of the last century would despair.

In 2001, the British Booksellers' Association reported that against the power of the big chains, more than one independent bookshop in ten had folded in Britain during the previous five years alone. In the US, the American Booksellers' Association grew so alarmed at the retail chains that in 1998 it filed a lawsuit against Barnes & Noble and Borders. Clark Kepler, one of the plaintiffs and the owner of Kepler's Books & Magazines in Menlo Park, California, stated:

This fight is about preserving what America is able to read. A network of healthy, independent bookstores spurs publishers to produce a diversity of literature and to take risks with authors who are of less commercial but greater critical appeal.'[32]

Kepler's shut down in 2005, but was then saved by a local campaign. It had been at the heart of its community, and local people couldn't imagine their home without it.

These tensions reach across global media. Since a controversial merger approved in July 2004, just four companies now own around 80 per cent of the global music market: Universal, EMI, Warner Music and the newly merged Sony BMG. Universal and Sony BMG are now the two biggest music companies in the world, with about 25 per cent market share each. But even that does not represent their true grip. Sony BMG is owned by media giant Bertelsmann, Universal by fellow behemoth Vivendi. Warner cut 1,000 employees and was preparing to sack half of the 170 acts on its rosters. In March 2004, EMI was reported to be cutting 1,500 jobs and dropping one-fifth of its recording artists. Niche and underperforming artists were reported to be on the way out. EMI said, 'We believe that by concentrating our efforts on a tightened roster of artists we will increase our revenue-generating potential while reducing our costs.'

In his book *The Long Tail*, Chris Anderson says that the Internet has revived the independent sector and changed the dynamics of winner-take-all retailing. Yet the dominance of online stores like Amazon.com and Apple's i-Tunes may concentrate the market still further. Rather than overturning the 80/20 rule of retailing, one report mentioned that 10 per cent of the product range on i-Tunes accounted for 90 per cent of total sales.[33]

Then there's the question of how music gets public airtime. 'I don't think anybody anticipated that the pace would be so fast and so dramatic,' said William Kennard, Chairman of the Federal Communications Commission, the body responsible for deregulating TV and radio ownership in the US in 1996. 'The fundamental economic structure of the radio industry is changing from one of independently owned operators to something akin to a chain store.' On this scale and with these economics, it is more profitable for a music company to sell 10 million copies of one album than to sell 1 million copies each of ten albums. So companies constantly vie to sign a 'sure thing' pop act that will be marketed massively.

Still further, there's the lack of diversity of opinion that makes it on to the airwaves. Five corporations control 90 per cent of the news in the US. Mark Cooper, research director of the Consumer Federation of America said, 'News departments get reduced, and culturally diverse and public interest programming comes under pressure. Less popular programming disappears and journalists are evaluated by the corporate-profit-centre logic of these huge organizations.'[34]

Coke's advertising agency requires of magazines that their adverts must only be positioned next to editorial that fits its marketing strategy, which rules out 'hard news, sex-related issues, medicine, health, negative diet information (e.g. bulimia, anorexia, quick weight loss, etc.), food, political issues, environmental issues'.[35] It reserves the right to pull its ads if they end up too close to such undesirable issues.

There is also growing international cross-ownership. Rupert Murdoch's News Corporation, for example, publishes 175 newspapers in six countries and owns about 800 companies around the world that include terrestrial and digital TV channels broadcasting in five continents where the company claims 300 million subscribers, news networks, newspapers, magazines, major book publishers like HarperCollins, film companies, sports teams and record companies. In Silvio Berlusconi's Italy, the former prime minister owned one of Europe's biggest media companies, Mediasat, and controlled 90 per cent of Italian television. An average Italian could spend a Saturday shopping at his local supermarket, relaxing at home, reading a paper, flicking through a few TV channels to watch AC Milan play football – and all these goods and services could have been provided by the same huge company.

The distinguishing characteristic of globalized media is not that it serves as a window on diversity, but rather that it has become a pipeline through which formulaic, cloned programmes like *Pop Idol, Big Brother, The Weakest Link* and any amount of blueprinted reality TV gets pumped into front rooms the world over, regardless of cultural impact or appropriateness.

A hidden victim of the emerging global consumer experience is the diversity of language itself. Only half of the world's 6,000 languages are expected to survive to the end of the current century according to UNESCO, and only 600 are thought to be really safe. There are both practical and aesthetic reasons to be concerned.

Because of the interaction between nature and culture,[36] it's no coincidence that places with the highest biodiversity also tend to have the greatest cultural diversity. As much as the rainforests of Brazil are home to plants containing secret cures to human illness, they have been home to the cultures that held the keys. Since 1900, about one Indian tribe has disappeared from Brazil each year. Ken Hale of the Massachusetts Institute of Technology makes the point that, 'Languages embody the intellectual wealth of the people that speak them. Losing any one of them is like dropping a bomb on the Louvre.'[37]

As Mark Abley describes in *Spoken Here: Travels Among Threatened Languages,* every language also expresses a unique knowledge and interpretation of the world. Their structures can encode different philosophical understandings of our relationships to each other and our position in the greater scheme of things. Abley directly compares the situation of threatened languages to 'locally run stores, confronted by a Wal-Mart invasion'.

In Australian Aboriginal culture, the system of totems that binds together human and animal life is reflected and contained in their languages – like Mati Ke, for example, in which people refer to themselves and others not as atomized individuals but in terms of their relationship to the natural world. The pronoun system of another Aboriginal language, Murrinh-Patha, has four categories instead of simply using singular and plural: singular; dual: paucal (three to fifteen people); and plural (more than fifteen).

Where English has one verb meaning 'to know', French has two – *savoir* and *connaître*, allowing for greater nuance between factual knowledge, understanding and acquaintance. But the French have got nothing on the Inuit, whose language Inuktitut has roughly eight verbs to express different qualities of knowing, not including one that can translate either as 'he/she is nervous' or 'he does not know which way to turn because of the numerous seals he has seen come to the surface'.

However, an award should go to the Boro language spoken in several countries along the north bank of the Himalayan Brahmaputra River. It has verbs such as *anzray* (to keep apart from an enemy or wicked company); *onsra* (to love for the last time); and *asusu* (to feel unknown and uneasy in a new place).

Diversity is under attack even when we look in the mirror. One of the most popular plastic surgery procedures in Japan is for women to have their eyes 'widened' to look 'more Western'. In parts of East Asia, skin whitening creams are among the most popular beauty products, allowing darker-skinned Asian women to also look 'more Western'. In the Philippines, television adverts have even marketed nose pegs that can be inserted in one's nostrils to give a more European-shaped nose.

The reason so much goes unremarked is because the global corpocrats who make decisions about where we can shop, what we can buy and what we can read, watch and listen to are themselves trapped in horribly cloned lifestyles. They meet in identical glass-walled rooms in corporate headquarters and travel in first and business class on international flights. They read the same international newspapers, watch the same global TV channels and stay in identical hotel suites. For global enterprise to be managed, management has to *live* globalization, creating for the managerial technocrat a cloned virtual reality detached from rooted, diverse local existence.

Just Sit There Getting Cloned

I'd watched in Britain as the spread of out-of-town shopping centres killed off the high streets and parades that sat at the hearts of our communities (see Chapter Three). 'Ghost Town Britain' was what I called the phenomenon in a series of reports that we at the new economics foundation (nef) began publishing in 2002. It captured the torpor of too many shopfronts left boarded up or just abandoned, with posters hanging loosely in windows from yellowed Sellotape and dust falling on to sad, useless fittings. But this clearly wasn't the only trend hitting local economies in the UK. In the bigger towns and metropolitan areas where enough money was spent to keep the local economy moving, and in the gaps left by the death of independent retailers, the chain retailers were moving in. The result was that across the country, surviving high streets were starting to look identical.

Sitting at my desk, thinking about the next cup of tea, something struck me in that way that always seems afterwards to have been obvious all along, both to you and to everyone else. At the time, however, it was just that listless dissatisfaction again, an unnamed sense of something not being right. Before I got to the kettle to make the tea, the name came out: 'Clone towns,' I said, probably with a disturbing, thousand-yard stare. If they weren't turning into ghost towns, they were turning into clone towns. That was our next report. The media got excited, fond as it is of new terms. Later, looking through the press cuttings in a kind of linguistic archaeology, it's possible to see the birth of the phrase – from nowhere, there is a sudden, massive spike of the term being used in immediate coincidence with the 'Clone Town Britain' report's publication.

It then quickly crept into common use as though it had been there all along. We launched the first of a series of papers with a special outside broadcast edition of BBC Radio 4's *Today* programme, from the East Anglian market town of Boston. It seemed relevant because the area had a lot of migrant workers toiling in the fields and packhouses to supply the big supermarkets with produce. The other item of interest that day was the ageing footballer Paul Gascoigne's (aka. 'Gazza') arrival at the local football club for one last roll of the sporting dice before retirement. In a way that doesn't happen often, I knew we'd hit a nerve. After the broadcast, which was made in front of a full, live audience including farmers, councillors and a range of local people, everyone wanted to know how the 'cloning' could be stopped. How could the distinctiveness and character of their town be preserved?

That day we launched a simple survey that enabled people in their own towns to measure the balance and range of real, local shops compared to chain retailers. Under a year later we published the results. A scale grouped the surveyed towns into three broad categories: clone towns, border towns and home towns. In a clone town the individuality of high streets is replaced by a monotonous strip of global and national chains, leaving a place that, if you woke up on the street after a very big night out, could be mistaken for dozens of bland town centres across the country, leaving you with a problem finding your way home.

By contrast, a home town has a high street more likely to have retained its character. It would be instantly recognizable and distinctive, both to the people who lived there and to those who visited. A border town would be on the cusp between the two. Results from over 100 towns showed that 42 per cent were clone towns and 26 per cent border towns, vulnerable to creeping homogenization. One-third were home towns.

The survey gave a snapshot of how high streets and parades, once filled with a thriving mix of independent butchers, fish-mongers, newsagents, pubs, bookshops, greengrocers and fa-mily-owned general stores, were rapidly filling up with faceless supermarkets, fast-food chains, mobile-phone shops and global fashion outlets. Not only did the clone towns have fewer, distinctive, locally owned shops, they also had a poorer range of shop and service types.

I wanted to stand in the middle of a high street somewhere, perhaps my home town of Chelmsford, or Reading, whose centre was surveyed by the local evening paper and found to have the score of an almost perfect clone. Both, unfortunately, were eliminated from the nef study on a technicality – they were too large to have a single measurable centre. But I wanted to stand somewhere and shout, 'Call 999, someone has stolen the nation's identity!'

CHAPTER TWO

Welcome to the Dead Zone:
The Rise of the Giant Retailers

'Wal-Mart, the largest corporation in the world, provides the template for a global economic order that mirrors the right-wing politics and imperial ambitions of those who now command so many strategic posts in American government and society.'

Nelson Lichtenstein, *Wal-Mart:*
The Face of Twenty-First-Century Capitalism

A little history

L'Angleterre est une nation de boutiquiers. Two hundred years ago, according to the memoirs of Napoleon's secretary, the emperor dismissed England as 'a nation of shopkeepers'.[1] It's a shame he didn't live to see the irony of shops like Wal-Mart and Tesco succeeding in their plans for international domination where he ultimately failed. The rise to retail power of supermarkets began, by general consensus, in the US on the morning of 6 September 1916, when British minds were elsewhere, literally bogged down in the trenches of the First World War.

A store opened at 79 Jefferson Street, Memphis, Tennessee with the peculiar name of Piggly Wiggly. When its owner, Clarence Saunders, was asked why he called it that, he replied enigmatically, 'So people will ask that very question.' One simple innovation led to large and lasting consequences. In Piggly Wiggly stores, instead of having a clerk collect your shopping from the shelves – the way most shops operated – people did it for themselves. But there was more to it. To compete with the established shops and department stores, Piggly Wiggly and its imitators cut costs by reducing staff and lowering the profit margins it was making.

To compensate, it sold more with faster turnover, bequeathing to us (and Tesco) the unbreakable cliché 'pile high, sell cheap'. Piggly Wiggly became a success. Although later overtaken by more aggressive copycats, it still has around 600 stores in the US. The restless creator of Piggly Wiggly went on to create other chain stores, including Clarence Saunders, Sole Owner of My Name Stores and an early automated outlet called the Keedoozle, slang for 'Key Does All'.

From those humble beginnings in Memphis, an approach to business would grow, leading to global retail brands like Wal-Mart, Starbucks and The Gap. Unusual though it might seem to us now, for much of the last century the US was a country deeply suspicious of big business – and, it can be argued, with good reason.

From a low starting point, between 1900 and 1926, chain stores tripled their market share of American shopping. In the following seven years they more than doubled it again to capture a quarter of all retail sales. In just three decades from the beginning of the century one company alone, The Great Atlantic and Pacific Tea Company (A&P) grew from 200 to 15,000 stores.[2]

But it didn't grow without resistance. By the 1920s there were around 300 organizations in the US with over 8 million members who were opposed to the growth of chain stores. Using language that might easily be heard again today, a 1922 letter from an aggrieved small shopkeeper to a local newspaper derides the chain store as 'a cutthroat competitor managed from the outside by a soulless corporation'.[3]

So-called 'antitrust' legislation (anti-monopoly rules in Britain) was common in the US dating back to the late nineteenth century. There were numerous attempts to control the abuses and outright criminality of the robber-baron coal, oil, steel and railway industrialists. A line can be drawn from the Sherman Anti-Trust Act in 1890 to the Clayton Anti-Trust Act of 1914 and the 1936 Robinson-Patman Act, also known as the 'Anti-Chain Store Act'.

Today, reading the deluge of complaints made to Britain's own Competition Commission in 2006 about the behaviour of our biggest supermarkets, it is impossible to escape the sense of being trapped in a corporate *Groundhog Day*. The Clayton Act in the US was designed to stop predatory pricing by banning exclusive sales contracts with suppliers. The Robinson-Patman Act prohibited 'price flexing', the practice of charging different prices for the same goods in different areas.[4] Both are common anti-competitive techniques still used by big supermarkets in modern Britain.

In recognition of their negative impact on independent local stores that support communities, several states introduced 'chain store taxes' explicitly designed to level the playing field in favour of smaller enterprises that, dollar for dollar, employed more people. These taxes were often designed to escalate: the more stores were operated by a chain, the more it had to pay in tax.

Between 1927 and 1941, twenty-two states successfully introduced chain-store tax bills with charges ranging from small amounts (a top rate of $30 in Montana) to large ($750 per store in large chains in Texas [which would, of course, have the largest stores]). Such sums were considerable at the time, especially considering it was the middle of the Depression. During the 1930s, targeted levies affected 60 per cent of the big retail chain stores. The result was that the chain stores' share of the market fell and stayed down throughout the following decade.[5] By the 1940s, however, clever manoeuvres by chain stores to recruit support from unions meant that the political will to restrain them evaporated. A national tax on chain stores was proposed in 1938, but it was defeated after A&P spent $500,000 (a huge sum then) supporting the political opponents of the congressman who backed it. After 1941 no new taxes were introduced, and the existing ones were either repealed or withered away.

K-mart, a corporation with roots reaching back to the 1950s, is a close contemporary of Wal-Mart, and set the tone for the development of 'big-box' stores. K-mart sought out 'standalone sites with huge parking lots to serve car-dependent suburbanites'.[6] This was because it wanted to avoid having any competition immediately adjacent to its stores.[7] As legal experts on competition in the UK point out today, the much-hyped, hotly competitive nature of the big supermarkets is largely fake. Competing supermarkets are virtually never situated adjacent to each other in a way that would allow the shopper to be selective, buying one thing in one shop and something else in another.[8]

Both K-mart's founders and Sam Walton, the founder of Wal-Mart, were inspired by a small discount enterprise called Ann & Hope, set up in an old weaving mill in Rhode Island. Overheads were low, it was entirely self-service, goods were sold cheaply and the turnover was fast.

It was a simple and effective formula that left a deep impression on Walton. In fairness, many of Wal-Mart's very negative impacts on communities, families and workers that are obvious today were clearly not intended. They were the emergent consequences of what appeared to be a very attractive business model. When the first Wal-Mart Discount City opened in 1962, in Rogers, Arkansas, no one imagined it would become a paradoxical corporation that projected 'faith, family and small-town sentimentality' but co-existed 'in strange harmony with a world of transnational commerce, stagnant living standards and a stressful work life' while squeezing 'the last drop of sweated productivity from millions of workers'.[9]

Wal-Mart grew in little over four decades from a one-man general store to a vast, global brand with over 100 million customers per week and more than 4,000 stores worldwide. Approximately every three days a new Wal-Mart store opens somewhere in the world; along with Mexico, Brazil, Argentina, Canada, Puerto Rico, China and Indonesia, the company is now also firmly rooted in Europe.

According to one US study, 'In the 10 years after Wal-Mart moved into Iowa, the state lost over 555 grocery stores, 298 hardware stores, 293 building suppliers, 161 variety stores, and 158 women's clothing stores, 153 shoe stores, 116 drug stores and 111 children's clothing stores. In total some 7,326 businesses went to the wall.'[10]

Stacy Mitchell of the US-based Institute for Local Self-Reliance calculates that the store is so ubiquitous, and its outlets so large (typically 200,000 sq. ft or larger) that you 'could fit every man, woman, and child in the US inside a Wal-Mart store at one time'.[11] The store takes $1 in every $5 spent on food and sells more clothing, furniture, toys, jewellery, music CDs, DVDs, magazines and books than any other retailer. Wal-Mart also accounts for nearly $1 in every $3 spent on everyday items like toothpaste, nappies and shampoo. In 2004, the company made a surplus alone of $18 billion (more than the total national income of Kenya) on sales of $260 billion (larger than the economy of Argentina, Greece, Ireland or Denmark).

Before the ascendance of Wal-Mart, observe Andrew Seth and Geoffrey Randall in *The Grocers: The Rise and Rise of the Supermarket Chains*, the 'diversity of local markets produced a constant flow of new food ideas . . . some quite unique, and simply irreproducible anywhere else'.[12] Reassuringly, some

stones are still to be turned by the US supermarkets. Discriminating food shoppers will still go to specialist stores and, as the
business analysts say, the 'users of meal solutions'[13] (I think this
means people who eat in restaurants) are still beyond their
reach.

During the 1980s, a number of factors conspired to create a
snowball effect of superstore growth. Regulations were removed
that prevented rapid concentration of corporate power in food
retailing. Existing antitrust laws were ignored by authorities.
Financial deregulation made it easier to raise the huge amounts
of capital needed to finance hostile takeovers. A quarter of the
food retail market seized the advantage in the three years from
1985, either refinancing their own businesses or taking part in
buyouts. Very quickly, though, the downside of winner-take-all
economics started to show itself. The takeovers and buyouts
were financed by taking on big, new debts, and the need to
service these led to harsh pay bargaining, job losses, a squeeze on
suppliers and asset stripping.

One consequence was a practice familiar in the UK. Shoppers
at real street markets can easily compare price and quality from
one stall to the next. It's the closest real life gets to the economic
theory in which consumers have 'sovereignty'. But once you're
inside a supermarket, it's more like being captive in a centrally
planned economy. The whole system is designed to keep you
put, so that you do your whole shopping in one stop. The effort
invested in getting there, the time taken and the unimaginable
inconvenience of buying your apples at Tesco, your oranges at
Sainsbury's and your milk at Asda/Wal-Mart keep you compliantly in one place.

The dirty little secret of supermarkets is that, from the point
of view of shoppers as the free agents referred to in the
economic textbooks, the major multiples represent a clear case
of market failure. This is not an accident. In the UK, different

major supermarkets are almost *never* located immediately adjacent to each other, which would make comparison shopping easy.

As things began to change in the US during the 1980s the supermarkets engaged in a 'geography of avoidance'. Like armies not wishing to engage in combat for fear of taking casualties, they instead kept to their own territories, implicitly sharing out the market between them on terms of strictly limited competition. In only six out of fifty-four areas in the US did Safeway, Kroger and American Stores – the three major players – all decide to compete with each other. (Wal-Mart moved into selling groceries only in the late 1980s, but then quickly became the market leader.)[14]

'Category Killers'

In the US, a retail ecosystem that began with enormous diversity and energy has been carved up between the world's biggest retailer, Wal-Mart, and a handful of powerful, so-called 'category killers' that specialize in a particular range of products such as toys, electronics, hardware or, indeed, coffee. They earned their name, according to business analyst Robert Spector, 'because their goal is to dominate the category and kill the competition'.[15] As sketched in Chapter One, the UK already has experience of category killers from the US.

The category killers divide up roughly according to two different approaches. First are what Americans call 'big-box' outfits like Toys "R" Us, that dominate a neighbourhood with one large store. Second are operations like Starbucks, which open small outlets in clusters to suffocate any potential competition. The 'big-box' stores also frequently group together where land is cheap, outside town, forming malls that the retail trade calls, appropriately, 'power centres'. Wal-Mart increasingly does both. Its core business occupies vast, warehouse-type stores but, followed by Tesco and Sainsbury's in the UK, it is experimenting with a store format for every type of location and occasion to ensure its continued corporate growth.

Wal-Mart's killing spree has been particularly effective. It took only fourteen years since entering the market to become the top grocery shop in the US. In the course of a single decade, twenty-nine other chains filed for bankruptcy, with Wal-Mart being a driver in twenty-five of the cases.[16] In 2006, Wal-Mart's US sales, at just under \$98 billion, were over 50 per cent higher than the next-largest US supermarket, Kroger, and nearly three times more than the next company down.[17]

Figure 1: Top Ten US Grocers in 2006

Rank Co. Name	No. of supermarkets (\$ + sales)	Est. annual sales (thousands)	sq.ft selling area (thousands)
Wal-Mart Stores	2,089	\$98,745,400	130,078
Kroger Co.	2,501	58,544,668	103,950
Albertsons. Inc.	1,765	36,287,940	88,904
Safeways, Inc.	1,540	32,732,960	56,082
Ahold USA, Inc.	824	23,848,240	34,603
Publix Super Markets, Inc.	876	18,531,500	33,971
Dalhaize America, Inc.	1,544	16,480,100	45,099
H. E. Butt Grocery Co.	272	10,422,100	13,187
Supervalu, Inc.	619	8,633.040	17,370
Winn-Dixie Stores, Inc.	563	7,091,500	26,104

Note: This is groceries only – excludes Wal-Mart's other sales.
(Source: *Progressive Grocer*, 1 May 2006)

Shopping as Warfare

'Many of the visible differences between the US and European industries are disappearing and a discernibly uniform global model is starting to appear.'

Andrew Seth and Geoffrey Randall, *The Grocers:*
The Rise and Rise of the Supermarket Chains

Separated for decades, British and American shopping lives are beginning to converge in a place called the 'dead zone', a reference in the US to the great suburban sprawl that depends on 'big-box' stores to fill its homes and stomachs. Petrol-hungry 4x4s shuttle its inhabitants between home, work and the store. It doesn't matter which came first, the 'big box' or the suburb. They now need each other, as well as a constant supply of the cheap oil needed to feed the addiction that holds their codependent relationship together. Dead zones may be bigger and more numerous in the US, but the footprint of their soulless, resource-hungry monotony grows ever larger in the UK. As people who can afford to leave big towns and cities seek out suburban space, the zones creep further.

Wal-Mart is the undisputed king of 'big-box' retailing. Tesco founder Jack Cohen reportedly went to the US in 1935 to study how American supermarkets worked. He went when the high point of the previous generation of anti-chain store legislation was waning. The experience was fundamentally to shape his business back in Britain. Today, Tesco's emulation of the US retail market has moved to a whole new level. Fifty senior Tesco executives were sent to the US to 'shop, eat and chill out' with families on the West Coast. Their mission was 'to understand the American way and how best to exploit it'.[18] When job adverts for Tesco's new US venture discretely appeared, it requested some very specific personnel skills taken straight from the Wal-Mart handbook. Senior managers were sought with experience in 'maintaining union-free status' and 'union avoidance activities'. The language indicated, according to the financial press, that Tesco was 'set to follow the non-union example of Wal-Mart'.[19]

But the American way according to Wal-Mart is far from trouble-free. It landed the company in court facing a huge class action suit in response to nearly a decade's worth of abusing the rights of its staff. Employees in Pennsylvania sued and won over claims that during an eight-year period up to 2006, Wal-Mart forced staff to work during rest breaks and outside the hours they were paid for. The court found the company guilty, and a jury awarded damages of $78 million. Under the ruling, nearly 187,000 current and former employees are to receive compensation. A judge was expected to add a further $62 million in damages under obligation by state law, and there was an expected additional bill of around $40 million in legal fees.

The case came to court just as, separately, leaked internal Wal-Mart documents showed that the company was seeking to cut its costs even further by searching for healthier employees during recruitment, in effect weeding out less healthy potential staff and so minimizing its liability for sick pay. It also indicated a practice of hiring a higher proportion of part-time workers, who would have fewer employment rights.[20]

Wal-Mart's antipathy towards and troubled relationships with unions followed it to the UK. In what was described as 'one of the most prolonged stoppages in recent industrial history', the management of Asda/Wal-Mart fell out with its workers over union recognition among its depot staff.[21] The problem came to a head in mid-2006 with workers voting by a ratio of three to one to go on strike. Problems were deep-rooted, covering issues of pay, national bargaining, health and safety.

Wal-Mart has become, according to some, 'the template

economic institution of its age'.[22] For that reason alone, it should be watched. Now Tesco, Britain's biggest retailer, is following Wal-Mart's lead towards so-called 'big-box' shopping and has also begun to compete on Wal-Mart's home turf in the US as well as flirting with some of that company's more reactionary management practices. Now there is real reason for concern; in 1999 Wal-Mart took over Asda, one of the other 'big four' British supermarkets and Tesco's nearest competitor. Combined, Tesco and Asda/Wal-Mart control a mighty half of the UK grocery market (48 per cent, to be precise).[23] The British shopper is being surrounded by people he or she neither knows nor whose intentions can be read. To find out what lies behind the blank corporate gaze of meaningless reassurance, we need to look at the American experience.

Once in a while a single company becomes big enough to affect the fortunes of a nation. In the US, early last century, it was US Steel. By the middle of the century that place was taken by General Motors. Now the mantle has shifted to Wal-Mart. In its kingdom the rest of us – customers, suppliers and workers – have become the new serfs. Missing from the grimness of modern serfdom, however, and to complete the feudal analogy, is even the historical sense of patrician responsibility and the importance of social cohesion. That is because the competitive success of Wal-Mart depends, according to Nelson Lichtenstein, Professor of History at the University of California (Santa Barbara), on the destruction of any vestigial 'New Deal-style social regulation' and its replacement with a 'global system that relentlessly squeezes labor costs from South Carolina to south China, [and] from Indianapolis to Indonesia'.

In the US, countless Wal-Mart suppliers have been reduced to 'quaking supplicants'. But their experience will already be familiar to firms supplying Tesco, which are among the most assiduous students of modern retail feudalism. Images of the thud and clatter of a medieval lord's bonded army also seem oddly appropriate when you read the language chosen by reporters to describe Tesco's international expansion. Anodyne descriptions of gaining points and market share melt away. Emerging from a mist of emollient advertising and stripped of Tesco's chirpy, beloved, family-friendly image is an economic army dressed for battle.

This isn't really about shopping at all, it seems, but war. For all Tesco's commercial machismo, as it prepares to expand yet more internationally the company appears in reality as just another – albeit successful – retail division, fighting on behalf of more demanding generals: investors in the City. Its task, which it willingly takes on, is to re-engineer how the world does business in order to maximize the financial returns to itself and its masters.

Hence the *Sunday Times* reports that Tesco executives were finding 'ammunition' for the 'imminent assault on America' and that 'Tesco carried out similar exercises in China and Japan before invading their markets.'[24] Thus let us name the supermarkets for what they are: occupying armies driven by the City's imperial need for growth and expansion. Even if guns and armour have been replaced by lawyers and multilateral trade agreements, they are the direct descendants of the earliest multinational corporations like the East India Company, which perfectly blended commerce, gunboat diplomacy and warfare.[25]

There are casualties too, in this economic warfare crossing the Atlantic and other oceans and continents. Communities, jobs, cultural diversity, local economic vibrancy, human well-being and quality of life get trodden underfoot: this is the rough equivalent of a military 'scorched earth' policy. The battle's aftermath is a paradox: a culture of poverty growing at the heart of the world's wealthiest nations.

'Tesco has a tendency to stick its fingers in its ears and hum loudly when its impact on small retailers is mentioned.'
Financial Times, 15 March 2006

The Rise of Supermarkets in Britain

Lower Higham in north Kent is unique in character, but its story is typical in outcome.[26] Sitting south of the Thames, the village traditionally grew food for sale in London. In the nineteenth century, its fields were full of hops for beer, but the market collapsed in the 1950s. Then orchards growing apples, pears and cherries were harvested by groups of temporary, travelling workers, which history shows is neither a new nor threatening phenomenon. There were Londoners as well, often poor East Enders, who travelled to the Kent countryside to supplement their modest earnings picking fruit to be sold in Covent Garden.

Two decades ago, there were three shops in Lower Higham. The last one has now gone. There used to be a shop-cum-post office typical of communities like this, run by a couple that had lived in the village for years. According to resident James Marriott, they never made a huge living, but they got by. The last threat to them came in the shape of the supermarkets.

Supermarkets want you to make frequent, repeat trips to their stores. First, in order to persuade us to come in more regularly, they focused on a few of the things we buy in small amounts and often, like the daily pint of milk. (How Britain's dairy industry fell under the cost-cutting control of the supermarkets is a sour tale, something still lamented by Britain's dairy farmers on a daily basis who say they are forced to sell at prices that barely, if at all, cover the cost of production.)

When supermarkets began stocking magazines, it signalled the death knell for Lower Higham's corner shop. There was no longer a special reason for people to patronize it, so the whole shopping trip, papers and all, went to the supermarket. The introduction of Sunday trading also meant that corner shops lost the extra business they got from being open at odd and often antisocial hours.

Lower Higham also used to have a man called Frank who drove around in a reconditioned ambulance. He was a travelling butcher who delivered meat door-to-door, especially to older people. One day, he disappeared; the spot by the village green where he used to park was empty. Some months later, James noticed a new van parked in Frank's old space. It was a Tesco van that had come from Gillingham, 20 miles away.

Bob, a farmer, was one of the few villagers to buy his house from St John's College, Cambridge, which, in some strange feudal hangover, owns most of Higham. But Bob ended up in a caravan, another casualty of upheaval triggered by the growth of supermarkets. He had sold his house because the price of fruit collapsed, in large part due to price pressures from the super-markets. Left in debt, it was cheaper for him to leave his fruit on the trees to rot than to pay people to pick it. Britain has lost three-quarters of its apple orchards in the last thirty years owing to changes in how we grow and sell food.[27]

Bob tried to vary his crops. A supermarket buyer suggested pumpkins. But just as Bob harvested them, the supermarket changed its mind – demand had dropped, and they were no longer wanted. Bob was left with a pile of rotting pumpkins. Such common caprice from supermarkets blithely disregards how long it takes farmers to re-gear their farms to grow different crops.

James says that today the village is like a weakened body. The community networks held together by the shops, post office and the seasonal and sociable gatherings of fruit-pickers are gone. Nor have they magically reappeared in a Tesco car park 20 miles away in Gillingham.

Independent local shops may be on the retreat because of supermarkets, but to remind children of what they once were like, this Tesco own-brand shop toy is available, with guaranteed no-added irony at Tesco Extra hypermarkets. In a nod to social realism, a sign on the back of the box reveals that to survive, even the toy convenience store has to open 24hrs.

Lower Higham itself never saw a supermarket shopfront. What killed the village economy was remote, a ghostly phenomenon that changed the nation's landscape before people were able to connect cause and effect. Its story has been repeated, with different casts of characters, in thousands of other villages and small towns around Britain.

There is something about that slice of the past that is just receding. The great cultural critic Raymond Williams noticed a strikingly consistent phenomenon in literature dating back over 2,000 years. No matter where you were in history, there always seemed to be a golden age that had occurred about fifty years before the present, a time that was beginning to slip from the grasp of living memory. It would typically be painted as a time when doors could be left open, unguarded, where neighbours could be trusted and youths didn't congregate with hooded intimidation or in Fagin-herded gangs; a happy time, a better place.

We still experience the gilding of recent history, but the remembered past in Britain today is a much more ambivalent place. The long, slow recovery from wartime austerity still casts a pall over those who lived through it. It is also synonymous with an approach to food that saw most things either deep-fried or boiled to death. We may have been a nation of shopkeepers, but what happened in the kitchen was another matter.

So when the supermarkets came, did they liberate us or merely exploit our lack of imagination and the fact that we couldn't cook? Tellingly, it is in the countries with great gastronomic traditions based on simple peasant cooking, like Italy and France, where the contemporary backlash against globalization and supermarket culture is happening most forcefully. The French farmer José Bové and Carlo Petrini, the leading light of the Italian 'slow food' movement, are, in many places, now household names.

The question of whether supermarkets have set us free or delivered us into a new kind of captivity, wandering trancelike down soulless aisles of dependence, is important. It must be asked in order to understand their rise to power, and also to grasp the growing disenchantment with them and the character of a new food culture emerging in Britain.

When supermarkets get criticized, often the accusers are in turn disparaged for wanting to return to a golden age that never was. It is a powerful, but self-serving and, I believe, false accusation. The new desire in Britain for good-quality, flavoursome, varied and locally produced food can't be harking after the past because such a past, in most cases, never existed. It is more a reaction to the banality and homogenization of modern life, and a powerful desire to break the resulting spell of alienation. To do that, we seek authentic and meaningful connections to the world around us. Food, because we eat it every day, just happens to be one of the ways that this desire is expressed. Try as they might (and they do), vast, centralized commercial operations like the giant supermarkets and other chain stores simply can't fake authenticity.

G. K. Chesterton's lament in 1927 over standardization's 'flat wilderness' shows that our current, growing concern about clone towns builds on much older worries about the homogenizing effect of commerce on culture. Some aspects of standardization go back further. Once, local variation around Britain even included the time of day. It was only with the growth of the railways and the need for consistent timetabling that the nation's clocks were synchronized. The difference today, compared with Chesterton's equal suspicion of both 'Bolshevism or Big Business', is that bolshevism has evaporated, leaving just big business to do the job.

In fact, chain stores date back in Britain to the mid-nineteenth century. Some of the first chains are still with us, sellers of news sheets like W. H. Smith and J. Menzies that began in the 1850s. Shoe shops also took the step to form early, so-called 'multiples'. But it was the food shops, starting from the 1890s, which led the chain store army.

Some once-large chains like Medova and Maypole Dairies, Home and Colonial and International Tea have disappeared from the surface of modern life. Many of the supermarkets' precursors sold a simple range of goods like tea and dairy products, butter, eggs, condensed milk and margarine. Maypole Dairies opened its first shop in Wolverhampton in 1887 and its thousandth in 1926. Still other names survive, like Lipton, as a brand of tea. But over time companies that were once household names were subsumed in a sequence of mergers and takeovers. These have been a feature of food retailing since the early spread of the first multiples. For a long time, though, the chains had only a small share of the overall market. Only today are we approaching the prospect of an endgame from which true monopoly power emerges.

The key elements for an unstoppable retail chemical reaction were brought together long ago: chain stores with centralized buying and administration, standardization and mass production. At least one name has survived, since first opening as a dairy shop in 1869 in London's Drury Lane: J. Sainsbury, for years Tesco's key competitor.

The chain stores' share of the food market went from around one-eighth in 1900 to one-fifth in 1920. Over the next two decades the number of chain store outlets rose from just under 8,000 to over 13,000.[28]

Between the two world wars a number of other things pushed the standardization of day-to-day life. A national media was becoming more pervasive. Through radio, newspapers and magazines, growing numbers of people across the country and among different social groups began to share a common cultural experience. Inadvertently, the foundations of contemporary celebrity culture were also being laid. Some celebrity gossip magazines only exist today due to their sale and promotion through supermarkets. Together they form a strange, symbiotic relationship, a pact of mutually assured banality. Now the staple paparazzi photograph of celebrities caught shopping at a supermarket, lifting bags into the back of an SUV, is considered to be the ultimate public demonstration of normality.

Although they weren't new, during the inter-war period branded consumer goods advertised and promoted through the new media infiltrated more into people's daily lives. Bird's

Custard Powder became one of the earliest convenience foods; Tate & Lyle's Golden Syrup fed the country's sweet tooth; Marmite divided the nation's palate. The 'multiples' grew alongside these increasingly famous branded goods and profited from a continuing social shift as more people left the countryside to live in towns and cities.

It was the dawn of domestic de-skilling, the beginning of the end of home preparation and the rise of processed food. Now, however, three-quarters of a century later, a meaningful backlash has begun, although it was slow to develop. It is a trend driven partly by an awareness of the richness we have lost and partly by a deep embarrassment at being infantilized by supermarket living. (Families living in the last century would have either been shocked or found it hysterical that the result of the 'progress' around them would mean that adults would come to need special lessons on how to boil an egg from people like television chef Delia Smith.)

This trend could signal a new incarnation of a more independent, self-help culture in retailing born under far harsher circumstances during the Industrial Revolution. In the early nineteenth century, radical magazines like *The Lion* began publishing real-life tales of horror from the factories and workhouses building the wealth of the British Empire. Children were left to fight with pigs for slop in troughs in filthy yards; routinely beaten, abused in every way, their stories eventually found the ears of people like the great capitalist-turned social-reformer (and deeply odd individual) Robert Owen.

From becoming manager of the mills of the New Lanark Twist Company in 1800, Owen went on to campaign for workplace improvement, like a reduction in the working week and the addition of sick pay. Some of his more exotic projects like establishing utopian socialist communities in North America, as well as his theories on the abolition of money and marriage, are largely forgotten. Nevertheless, his reforming zeal transformed not only the mills of New Lanark, but also the whole community. He is remembered as the father of benevolent and cooperative approaches to business, and as a catalyst for the organization of the working classes into unions to improve their conditions. Owen formed the superbly named Grand National Moral Union of the Productive and Useful Classes, and the English labour movement stepped into the light. He was hugely influential, but sometimes it took others to turn his ideas into practical realities. One group, comprising the twenty-eight weavers who became the known as the Rochdale Society of Equitable Pioneers, created the consumer cooperative movement.

In addition to appalling working conditions, many families in the growing towns and cities of northern industrial Britain found it hard to get good, unadulterated food at fair prices. Doctored, overpriced goods were common. In 1844 the Rochdale Pioneers started the first successful retail cooperative society in Toad Lane, Rochdale to tackle the problem. To begin with, they focused just on selling the basic groceries that made up working-class diets. Before long they were operating mills and factories to meet their members' needs. Customers were members of the Society and received a dividend in return for what they spent (a very early and more generous precursor to the loyalty card, the difference being that the societies were run democratically for the benefit of members).

By 1863, the movement – largely based in Lancashire and Yorkshire – grew to 300 cooperatives. In 1872 the Co-operative Wholesale Society (now the Co-operative Group and known as 'the Co-op') was formed. Hundreds of cooperatives across the country had banded together to use their purchasing power to get better deals, but they went further than that. Factories, banking services and insurance operations were started to service the national network and, most importantly, its ordinary members. By 1890 there were 1,400 societies, and by 1950 the cooperative movement supplied and distributed the benefits from nearly one-third of the grocery market.

The movement was always about more than putting food on the table; involvement in a cooperative was about having more control over your own life. It created, unavoidably, a new economic literacy among its members. As historians of the movement point out:

> . . . [It's easy to forget that for those who] participated in the running of their local stores, who attended the cultural and political events of the Cooperative Union, and who voted for the Co-operative Party in national elections, being a consumer was much more than being a wise shopper. It was the first stage in the reform of economy and society and the struggle for the 'cooperative commonwealth'.[29]

Even in the 1950s, cooperative consumer societies had over 10 million members. Although today members still number around 3.6 million, and the combined turnover of the Co-op's food, bank and insurance services is over £7 billion, Tesco has pushed it to one side. The cooperatives lost out partly because their decentralized structures made it harder to coordinate their efforts in the market as a whole (there are still dozens of different societies), and partly because a growing welfare state began to respond to some of the underlying problems that had brought them into existence. Tesco now has almost exactly the share of the food market enjoyed by the Co-op at its peak, and also has the same proportion of active loyalty card users as the Co-op had members in the 1950s. Interestingly, Tesco customers get a much worse deal. In the 1930s, Co-op members could often expect to get 15 pence (3 shillings) for every £1 spent, rather more than the typical single Tesco Clubcard point worth around 1 pence for every £1 spent in Tesco.

History suggests that more cooperative ways of organizing economic life tend to emerge by necessity in times of great hardship and upheaval. Perhaps the most useful outcome of revisiting the history of the cooperative movement is to remind us, as we look dimly into a future that could be shaped by an increasingly frail global environment and economy, that there are fundamentally different and more equitable ways to organize the economy.

Modern supermarkets didn't rise miraculously in isolation, fresh and smiling to improve our day. They grew by putting other shops out of business. The following chapter details several of the legal, dubious and less-than-legal ways that Tesco managed it. But first, let's get a sense of the scale and comprehensiveness with which the fabric of our communities – underpinned by diverse, local economies – has been worn away.

Many changes to our local community landscapes are missed because things happen that are either not noticed or recorded at all, or are not clearly visible from official government statistics. A picture must be pieced together with facts and figures from numerous different sources. Then the deep changes to our local economic lives rapidly become apparent.

In the second half of the last century, the UK lost around 100,000 small shops, according to Professor Tim Lang of City University and his colleagues. The decline of small shops in villages, market towns and district centres still continues. Up, down and across the country their numbers drop by approximately 10 per cent every year. At the beginning of the decade, the Rural Shops Alliance estimated that fewer than 12,000 rural shops were left in Britain. These, however, were closing at a rate of 300 a year, or nearly one per day.[30]

The government's Countryside Agency estimated in 2001 that

seven out of ten rural settlements had been left with no general store or village shop.[31] 'Villages which lose their shops quickly lose their identities,' said Margaret Clark, the agency's director, warning of the socially divisive nature of the trend. 'Those in lower income brackets who do not have cars cannot get to the nearest shopping centre to do their business. They are forced to move into towns. The danger is that villages will become the preserve of the well-off and that threatens the very fabric of rural life.'[32]

A single, dominant force has been behind this tearing up of community life: supermarket growth. As the agency pointed out, while so many villages lack the social and economic glue provided by a local shop, eight out of ten rural households now live within 2.5 miles of supermarket. The phrase 'cause and effect' comes to mind.

At least one of the key regulatory changes that have allowed supermarkets to flourish can be directly attributed to Tesco. Britain once had a set of rules called Resale Price Maintenance (RPM). In effect, it protected small shops by preventing larger stores, with their greater economies of scale, from discounting many goods. The logic was that setting a minimum price level for goods ensured a fair return to both manufacturer and distributor. Official inquiries in 1920 and 1931 supported the policy on the grounds that government should not interfere with the freedom of private citizens to agree contracts. In practice, however, Tesco got around it by offering discounts to customers when they shopped in the form of Green Shield Stamps. Tesco's founder Jack Cohen saw RPM as a restraint on his business, and campaigned vigorously for its repeal. RPM's scope was reduced in the 1950s, and in 1964 Cohen was successful; price maintenance began to be completely removed from a succession of goods. By the late 1970s it remained only on books and pharmaceuticals.

The number of superstores more than doubled between the mid-1980s and mid-1990s, going up from 457 in 1986 to 1,102 in 1997. Their market share of groceries also shot up from 30 per cent in 1987 to 54 per cent in 1996. A decade later, the four largest supermarkets alone now control 75 per cent of the market.[33] In the short duration of their rise to power, the supermarkets have rearranged our landscape, re-engineered our local economies and created a new kind shopping dependency.

St Neots in Cambridgeshire got an out-of-town Tesco store in 1995. When it opened, town centre shops lost business and jobs as a result, and remaining staff ended up working longer hours.

In Fakenham, Norfolk, the opening of an out-of-town food store was followed by a one-third increase in the number of empty shops; a drop in the number of convenience stores; and 'a noticeable deterioration' of the built environment of the town centre. Edge-of-town developments in Fakenham and Warminster, Wiltshire, were accompanied by town centre convenience stores losing a huge share of the market, 64 per cent and 75 per cent respectively. When a Tesco opened on the edge of Cirencester, Wiltshire, town centre food shops lost over one-third of the market and convenience stores lost out too.

Outside Leominster, in Herefordshire, Safeway opened an out-of-town superstore in 1992. Three years later, nearly one-third of convenience stores in the centre were closed, and other food shops lost one-third of their businesses. Within around five years the number of empty shops went up from sixteen to thirty-six. As the out-of-town supermarket was making private profit from the decline of the town centre, £2.2 million of public money was spent in an effort to revive the centre. A few pretty but not very useful antique and craft shops were attracted.[34]

Ample research has shown that after large superstores are built at the edge of towns or at out-of-town sites, local speciality shops and convenience stores lose somewhere between one-fifth and three-quarters of their market share. As a result, staff get laid off or businesses close entirely.[35]

Figure 2: Growth of Out-of-Town Shopping Centres 1976–2000

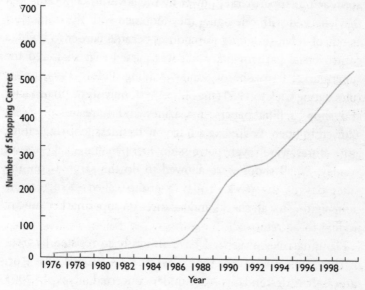

(Source: 'Ghost Town Britain', new economics foundation [nef], 2002)

During the 1980s and early 1990s, it seemed that nothing could stop superstores from pushing up out of the landscape around and outside towns until, in 1993, new Conservative Environment Minister John Gummer introduced curbs via new planning rules. It was a surprising move for many, and perhaps to do with a party beginning to try and escape from the long shadow of its previous leader Margaret Thatcher, a prime minister synonymous with the promotion of unchecked markets. It signalled a modest turning point. By 1997, as the Labour government came to power, the number of people doing the bulk of their shopping at out-of-town stores began to drop. But the new rules were only partially successful. In the five years after they were brought in, still nearly one in six independent food stores and cooperatives were lost.[36]

One reason for the mixed outcome was an inconsistent approach to supermarket power by the government. Reins that they checked with one hand, they loosened with the other. Just as out-of-town shopping warehouses became harder to build, a controversial parliamentary bill was passed that shattered the supermarket-free zone of Sunday trading. Before 1994, under rules dating back to 1950 (the Shops Act), only some pharmacies and shops selling papers, magazines and refreshments were allowed to open. Following a huge big business lobbying effort, large stores were given permission to open for six hours on Sunday. Small shops were allowed to do the same as on any other day of the week. Today a group called Deregulate is campaigning for all checks and balances on supermarket Sunday trading to be removed.

Planning rules in general have always been resisted by free-market ideologues. At the time of writing, Gummer's rules – or, rather, their descendants – are under concerted attack. In 2003 and 2004 they came up for revision. When finally published, the redrafting contained an explicit endorsement for big retail outlets setting up shops at edge-of-town locations. This struck many as a regressive step. Speaking in the House of Lords, Lord Hanningfield commented, 'I think that the guidance is contrary to the discussions we have been having about rejuvenating town centres. This is a licence to build many more out-of-town centres rather than developing the high street.'[37]

Earlier on during the revision process, official comments led retailers to believe that the rules would be strengthened, not weakened. What had happened in the meantime? Research by campaigners revealed a door handle at the Office of the Deputy

Prime Minister made warm by the twisting hands of super-market representatives as they visited officials. Between April and September 2004 the new draft guidelines were discussed twice with representatives from Asda/Wal-Mart, twice with Tesco, with Sainsbury's and with the supermarket trade body, the British Retail Consortium.[38] A study by academics at the University of Stirling mentions the 'belief that considerable lobbying from the industry and pressure from the Treasury contributed to the modification of the policy' and concludes that the supermarkets 'have a considerable impact on the shape of policy'.[39]

Currently, a review under the auspices of the Treasury and, ironically, a new push by the official body charged with regulating supermarkets (the Office of Fair Trading [OFT]) – are both trying to further weaken the planning checks and balances on out-of-town store development.

Town Centres: Vital and Viable or Light Snacks for Supermarkets?

The rules known officially as Planning Policy Statement 6 ('PPS6') are supposed to promote the 'vitality and viability of town centres'. Local authorities are obliged under them to ensure that firstly, enough sites are made available for present and future shopping needs in town centre locations. Only then are edge-of-town and subsequently out-of-centre sites to be considered. The twist, and the reason that these rules are being attacked, is that Tesco (far more than any other supermarket) had successfully amassed a huge amount of land both before and after the rules came into play. Its land bank is now so large that it is thought to present a barrier to competition.

The irony is that one of the only sets of rules available to modestly balance the power of the supermarkets could be ditched because the supermarkets have become more powerful. At this point, the OFT's rationale became even more circular and confused. In May 2006, it once again called on the Competition Commission to investigate the supermarkets for acting against the public interest, pointing out that 'most of the construction of very large out of town retail outlets (frequently selling non-food as well as grocery products) has taken place since the change in rules on out of town developments during the 1990s'.[40]

But instead of calling for the rules to be strengthened, it did the opposite, suggesting that they should be relaxed to allow Tesco's competitors – Sainsbury's, Morrisons and Asda/Wal-Mart – to buy more locations to build new, large stores. This is how the OFT put it:

> The planning system can reasonably be suspected of restricting or distorting competition by raising the cost of, and also limiting the scope for, new local market entry, particularly by way of new large format stores.[41]

According to the OFT, local planning authorities cannot take into consideration whether or not one store already has a monopoly, as we've seen Tesco does in Inverness, for example. A planner could not, they say, 'consider whether there were already four fascias of the same supermarket already [sic] in the area, as long as the new supermarket could meet the retail "need" of the area'.[42]

The situation looked bad several years ago when I started looking at these trends; now it seems worse. In 'Ghost Town Britain' we suggested that when the amount of money circulating locally drops below a certain threshold due to shop closures, a tipping-point could be reached that would lead to the local economy crashing. Some of the more recent figures for the loss of small, independent shops indicate that we could be getting to that stage.

The number of communities to retain local shops has been on a steep downward curve for some time. From 1980 to 2000, the overall number of retail outlets fell from 273,000 businesses to 201,000.[43] The decline was steady in the 1980s and accelerated in the 1990s. While small general stores have closed at a rate of around one per day, specialist stores like butchers, bakers and fishmongers shut at the rate of fifty per week between 1997 and 2002.[44] Following such trends, the Manchester School of Management predicted that there might not be a single independent food store left in the whole country by 2050.[45]

Amidst the confusion of different shop categories and definitions, many rely on figures from the Institute of Grocery Distribution (IGD) to understand what is happening on, or rather to, the shop floor. Its figures show that as predicted, the point may have tipped for independent grocery shops. If anything, it seems that the warnings made in 'Ghost Town Britain' might have been conservative. We warned that if current trends continued, one-third of all essential local outlets including banks, post offices, pubs, food retailers and general non-specialized stores (usually corner shops), all mainstays of the local economy, would be lost between 1990 and 2010. But according to the IGD, in key sectors things were happening much faster. In one category alone – so-called 'unaffiliated independent stores' (shops that are genuinely independent and not part of a bigger buyers' group, or sharing a formula shopfront of any sort) – nearly one-third was lost between just the year 2000 and 2006. Overall the number fell from 35,500 in 2000 to 25,893 in 2006.[46]

The rise of the supermarkets has also seen the infrastructure dismantled on which independent retailers depend. Sidetracked by supermarkets, which prefer to deal directly with a handful of large-scale suppliers, the country's network of wholesale suppliers, abattoirs, dairies and food processors has withered. There has been a self-reinforcing downward spiral. Local shops and local suppliers need each other. As local shops close, suppliers either have to subject themselves to the power play of the supermarkets and accept gruelling terms, or also close. Many, in any case, do not fit into the supermarkets' large, centralized operations.

Britain lost nearly 2,500 food, beverage and tobacco wholesalers in a single decade. The number of food manufacturers also fell. In the two years up to 2003, wholesalers closed at the rate of six per week – nearly one a day.[47] The number of abattoirs dropped from 1,022 in 1985 to just 387 in 2000.

With large amounts of produce being imported and only a small range of British apples for sale in supermarkets, the number of apple orchards in the UK reportedly halved between 1990 and 2002.[48] Over a longer period, the figures are even more dramatic. In 1930 there were 97,886 hectares of traditional orchards in England. By 2004, there were just 16,676 hectares left of traditional and bush orchards combined in England and Wales.[49]

Supermarkets now account for around 80 per cent of milk sales, and their buying power has driven concentration in the UK dairy sector, leading to an unhealthy degree of control over pricing by a few milk processors. In another sector, the growth of supermarket alcohol sales occurred alongside the closure of twenty traditional pubs every month across Britain, according to the Campaign for Real Ale.

Despite government intervention and a commitment to keep post offices open, especially in areas of high deprivation, in both rural and urban areas the branch network continues to shrink. Closure rates in both deprived and non-deprived urban areas are actually very similar. The problem is especially severe in rural areas, where over two-thirds of customers use the local post office as a hub for information and social and general services. In late 2006, the government made clear that around 2,500 more post offices would be allowed to close, almost one-fifth of the total number in the UK. As a result, multiple neighbourhoods will lose their economic keystones. The government argued that without the closures, subsidy to the network would need to rise by £100 million. What it didn't tell the public or media was the scale of wider, cumulative economic losses that could follow. If trends followed typical patterns seen with post offices elsewhere, the cost to local economies could be over £1 billion, more than ten times the raised subsidy. Looking at post offices in isolation, and as a burden, the government failed to see the vital niche they occupy in the neighbourhood business ecosystem.[50]

The same forces of globalization that allowed the rise of the supermarkets also drove deep changes in Britain's banking system. New technology, buyouts and mergers saw Britain lose one-third of its bank branch network in the decade up to 2002. According to the Campaign for Community Banking Services, 800 communities were left with no bank at all, and over 1,000 rural and urban communities with the choice of only a single branch. Community pharmacies are also under threat. Like post offices, they are often some of the last outlets left standing on shopping parades (in this case due to their unique arrangements with the National Health Service [NHS]) after others have been killed off by the supermarkets. A rumbling process of deregulation following another intervention by the OFT could lead to community pharmacies closing at a rate of around one per day.[51]

'The very small "mom and pop" shops are in permanent decline and offer little or no opportunity for the U.S. exporter,' was the curt assessment made in 1999 by the US Department of Agriculture on the state of British retail.[52]

To point out what has gone wrong is not a sentimental plea for the preservation of a fixed idea about Britain's cultural identity. It is not a warning about the decline of 'Olde England', or even an alarm about a world converging towards a single, monolithic notion of a global marketplace in which there are only self-interested individuals leading atomized lives divorced from society. But it *is* a wake-up call to remind us about the real value of what is being lost. When a locally owned shop goes out of business there is a domino effect, just as other plants and animals are affected when a key species is rudely torn from an ecosystem. Window cleaners, carpenters, accountants, solicitors, decorators and plumbers all lose a client. Because supermarkets tend to procure most products and services centrally and not from small-scale local traders and professionals, the business doesn't simply switch; local people lose out.

The dynamic of Ghost Town Britain creates a nation where neighbourhoods become food and enterprise deserts, with poor nutrition and ill health (including diabetes, heart disease and mental health problems). People lose financial literacy because they no longer trade on a daily basis in the community. The poor – unattractive as customers to the high street banks – fall prey to unscrupulous moneylending practices. The unemployed lose informal routes back into work as jobs disappear from the neighbourhood. Local businesses lose valuable local outlets. Communities that lose their neighbourliness as day-to-day contact withers become prone to vandalism and more serious crime. A lack of diversity impoverishes, and the environment and general health suffer as people are forced into car-based shopping.

Farmers' markets, organic vegetable 'box schemes' and car boot sales are evidence of a groundswell of popular resistance to the standardization of how we shop. But these are not yet of a scale to counteract the greater economic forces creating ghost and clone towns.

Several things are to blame: policies that favour supermarkets; the failure to halt the 'downsizing' of banks and post offices and the patchy provision of services to poorer communities; transport systems that encourage car travel; weak planning controls on out-of-town stores; and a lack of support for truly local enterprise. Far from helping, the aggressive move by supermarkets like Tesco and Sainsbury's into new convenience-store formats is likely to further undermine surviving independent, local shops, putting them under even more pressure. Around one-fifth of the convenience grocery market has been captured by petrol station 'forecourt' retailers, operated either by the large supermarkets like Tesco or by major oil companies like Esso, BP, Shell, Texaco and TotalFina Elf.

The Meaning of 'Local'

The meaning of 'local' has changed dramatically in recent years. Previously the images conjured up in the minds of economists and planners by the notion of 'local' were of twitching net curtains, crummy corner shops, small-mindedness and parochial oppressiveness. But now 'local' is becoming to economics what 'organic' has become to the food industry. It means real, authentic, connected. Three decades of rapid supermarket expansion have left a hole where 'local' should be. Nature, of course, abhors a vacuum, even those left by supermarkets. Farmers' markets and local food initiatives have risen to the challenge. But, unfortunately, so have the speech and advertising copywriters who work for some of the world's biggest businesses. If 'local' has a feel-good factor, big business wants a piece of the neighbourhood action, at least rhetorically, to aid in emotional bonding with their customers.

What else could explain the image makeover of the controversial, international, giant bank HSBC? In many ways, HSBC is the very image of finance-driven globalization. It has 7,000 offices in 81 countries, assets of nearly £500 billion and half-yearly profits of over £3.5 billion – much more even than Tesco. Like other multinationals, it has been a lightning rod for criticism by those who oppose orthodox globalization, and was heavily caught up in Argentina's economic troubles. Critics point to the bank's involvement in funding environmentally damaging dam projects, its former role as personal banker to dictators like Nigeria's Sani Abacha and the Philippines' Ferdinand Marcos. More recently, concerns have been raised about its role in the sub-prime lending market, in which poor people often find themselves trapped. The bank is even shadowed by a dedicated freelance newsletter, *The HSBC Watch*. Yet this poster boy for economic globalization clearly thinks something is missing. It chooses to send a quite different message to its potential customers – something much warmer and more human in scale. In search of the feel-good factor, it uses the strapline, 'HSBC – the world's local bank.'

Strange enough, but it gets stranger still. A kind of easygoing informality imbues the idea of being 'local'. But when big business wants to own a piece of something, even a notion that substantially predates it, negotiations can become a little, well, fraught. That's why HSBC, one of the world's biggest banks, found itself in court in the Netherlands, France and Belgium facing Interbrew, another corporation and one of the world's biggest brewers. What was it doing there? It was being sued over who had the legal right to use the phrase 'The World's Local . . .' Interbrew had already described itself as the world's local brewer. All told, an irony wrapped inside a paradox and lightly coated with denial, large marketing budgets and legal fees. Tesco, too, ran into problems over the meaing of 'local' when the Advertising Standards Authority (ASA) ruled that it had misled potential customers in an advert for 'vegetables from your local farms'. The store was in Bangor, but the food actually came from nowhere nearby. The ASA concluded that the advert breached its code on grounds of 'substantiation' and 'truthfulness'.[53] Following the feel-good of all things local, in 2006 Tesco launched a 'community plan'. The next chapter will look at why that, too, is possibly tinged with a little irony.

CHAPTER THREE

Any Shop You Like, As Long As It's Tesco: How One Store Came Out on Top

'We're all things to all men, all women . . . Our market share of UK retailing is 12.5% – that leaves 87.5% to go after.'

Sir Terry Leahy, Chief Executive, Tesco,
interviewed in *Management Today*, 2004[1]

'You can't make this up. It's like meeting a religious leader faithfully reciting a creed.'

Chris Blackhurst from *Management Today*
on interviewing Leahy.

A single anecdote, often retold, is enough to create a reputation. Whether the anecdote is true or the reputation welcome doesn't matter. As Oscar Wilde said in one of his carefully rehearsed but seemingly spontaneous quips, 'Give a man a reputation for early rising and he can stay in bed till noon.'

Here is Tesco's founding myth: A man who became known as 'Slasher' Jack Cohen – a nickname in which he revelled – rose from running market stalls in the East End of London to build the Tesco store chain. (In the banking community that dealt with Tesco in the City of London, Cohen earned for himself the slightly less flattering moniker of 'Old Flap Ears'.)

Back in the early days, Jack managed to procure some cargo (tinned cream from Denmark) from a half-sunken ship. The tins were dispatched to his stalls with instructions attached.

Workers were told to remove the labels, clean the rust off the tins with metal polish and sell them for 2 pence each.[2]

Behaviour like this led supermarkets in general and Tesco in particular to become synonymous with the practice of piling things high and selling them cheaply. As two business journalists have written, 'It was low prices and nothing else that moved business fastest. The product at Tesco was distinctly secondary.'[3]

Today, the public relations departments of the big stores will try to convince you that they are also concerned, for example, about the environment. But the supermarkets' real obsession has changed little in half a century: to extract the highest margin from a price that shoppers can be persuaded is 'low'. This book argues a different proposition: that where prices at the point of sale are genuinely low, this has been made possible only by passing costs on to someone or something else, such as the environment or the wider society. In other words, there is a high hidden cost to 'everyday low prices'; to abuse Tesco's preferred marketing jargon, instead of 'every little helping', somewhere it is actually hurting.

However, judged on limited criteria, Tesco's success has been phenomenal and needs explaining. What did it do to get where it is today?

Having started out in the East End markets, Cohen expanded south of the River Thames to Tooting (where, today, there is a thriving Asian market just around the corner from where I live). He opened his first shops in 1931. Tesco the store was set up in 1932, its name coming from the first two letters of Jack's surname combined with the initials of a business partner, T. E. Stockwell, from whom Cohen bought tea. It wasn't until 1956 that he opened a larger store that was recognizable as a super-market.

Tesco's founder was known for 'tactical thinking that verged on sharp practice'.[4] For years, Tesco was seen as a chain of fairly grotty bargain basements. Even so, by buying lots of other small and mostly unimpressive outlets (culminating in the purchase of a chain called Irwin's in 1960), Tesco became a national retailer. In 1961, pointing to the future of ever larger stores, it opened a flagship superstore – tiny by today's standards – in Leicester. Over the next decade Cohen bought more businesses, including a cafe chain and 300 Victor Value stores. There were now over 800 Tesco outlets in the UK. In the 1970s things didn't appear to be going too well. In the stores, the company's actual prices were higher than its image suggested. Anyone who today leaves a supermarket to visit a street market to buy fruit and vegetables will have a similar experience. The quality of Tesco's products then, 'always known to be poor . . . was actually much worse than any perceptions'.[5]

Cohen was the individualist and entrepreneur of business legend, a barrow-boy capitalist. But his swagger and acumen would have never been enough to create the modern Tesco. That would come when the aggression he bequeathed the company was married to a cold, centralized logistical efficiency. Tesco's growth followed the path for the whole sector, as outlined in the last chapter. Then there was the growth of out-of-town superstores and car-dependent shopping subsidized by the government's road-building programme. Tesco bought more competitors, such as the retailer Hillard, in 1987. Profits doubled over the next three years. The company grew in terms of total floorspace at the rate of 10 per cent a year. Between the mid-1980s and the late 1990s Tesco's share of UK grocery sales grew from around 13 per cent to over 20 per cent. It rose to 25 per cent in 2003, reaching over 31 per cent by 2006.[6] And Tesco already has amassed a bank of land that, if built on, would enable it to increase its market share to 45 per cent.[7]

Jack was eventually sidetracked by modern business methods, but his influence was strong enough to cross the generation gap.

His daughter, Shirley Porter, married her father's ultimate successor, Leslie Porter, and had a high-profile political career with the Conservative Party. It ended ignominiously when she was found guilty of political corruption and gerrymandering in a famous case involving Westminster Council in London. To fight her political battles, Shirley took inspiration from her father: 'I thought of my father, working in markets where they used to blow a whistle and people had to run to get their pitch,' she said. 'It was survival of the fittest. You crumble or stay and fight. Like him, I stayed and fought.' Actually she lost, and was fined £42 million in 2001 for vote-rigging. The House of Lords found her guilty of a 'deliberate, blatant and dishonest misuse of public power'.[8]

Tesco, in its own unique way, has been found guilty of numerous counts of abusing its market power and breaking planning law, but has so far avoided serious legal remedies. At the time of writing the store is again being investigated by regulators for, in effect, manipulating the market – details of which I'll return to. Sooner or later, action will be taken.

From a market stall to Britain's dominant retailer is a big leap. It happened, of course, in stages, and hints have been dropped about how. But the path to dominance is often hidden in details. For that reason, rather than a standard corporate hagiography (dates, chairmen, honours and swashbuckling executives pulling off impossible mergers and winning hostile takeovers – and is it actually possible to buckle a swash in a business suit?), this chapter will look at how Tesco operates. By focusing on a few areas of business, such as how customers are groomed, new sectors entered, finance handled and prices and planning manipulated, you can begin to understand how Tesco came out on top. But first, let's stand back and stare up at its dizzying corporate heights.

Richer than Whole Nations

For the year ending February 2006, Tesco had over £39 billion of revenue (approximately $71 billion), and profit of over £2.2 billion.[9] We'll see below why the revenue figure is particularly interesting, so try to keep it in mind. To put these earnings into perspective, if compared to the income of countries, Tesco would come in fifty-fifth in the World Bank's 2005 ranking of nations, above Bangladesh (the world's eighth-most populated country, with 141 million people) and just below oil-rich Kuwait. Tesco's income was roughly equal to that of Bolivia, Barbados, Bulgaria, Burundi, Bahrain, Bosnia-Herzogovina, Botswana and Bhutan – *combined*.[10] By 2008, Tesco's sales are predicted to hit over £46 billion.[11]

Most of the company's earnings come from the UK, but its overseas expansion is increasing quickly. Tesco is growing faster than its rivals in the UK and steadily occupying ever more of the market. In the five years from 2000 to 2005, the price of its shares rose steadily against the average for UK companies. By the end of 2006, Tesco was set to match the combined share of supermarket grocery shopping held jointly by the next two largest stores Asda/Wal-Mart and Sainsbury's.[12] They added a bewilderingly large two million square feet of additional shop space in the year 2006 alone, thought to represent around half of all the new shop space opened in Britain that year.[13] The City always loves a money-making machine, whatever its business.

Tesco is accused of many things, but a lack of ambition isn't one of them. Having contributed to the downturn of town centres by drawing shoppers to out-of-town complexes, Tesco drew attention to itself by moving back into the high street. The takeover of convenience store chains like T&S in 2002–03 was seen as yet more evidence of Tesco's insatiable appetite for market share. It seemed that having profited from killing off countless high-street retailers, the company was now using its growing economic muscle to reoccupy the shopping parades.

Groups lobbying on behalf of small shops, like the Association of Convenience Stores, complained to the OFT that Tesco's move was anti-competitive and called for an inquiry. Initially, the OFT refused, saying that convenience stores were a different sector, despite the fact that people bought identical milk, bread, tea and coffee in them. Following a legal challenge, and pressure from the campaign group Friends of the Earth the OFT was forced to back down and admit it had been wrong, and referred the sector to the Competition Commission for a full inquiry (see below).

From Supermarket Sweep to Hypermarket Hurricane

The growth of convenience stores seemed to be the next big threat from Tesco. Quietly, though, the store was probably pleased at the furore over its return to the high street, which was proving to be a perfect example of misdirection. People were understandably preoccupied by the visible fate of their neighbourhoods, but they overlooked the fact that Tesco's real plan is to achieve still further huge growth by expanding and regrading its large supermarkets into massive hypermarkets.

When asked directly about its ambitions, Tesco is reluctant, evasive and unforthcoming. A parliamentary committee investigation into the future of Britain's high streets organized by the All-Party Small Shops Group called Tesco to the witness stand. It initially declined the invitation, saying it was too busy and that no one was available. Repeated efforts finally brought Tesco's corporate affairs director, Lucy Neville-Rolfe, in front of the committee. Questioned about the company's growth plans, all she could manage to say was, 'It depends on how well we do, how our customers feel about it and what the competitors do.'[14]

In going down the hypermarket path, Tesco follows in the footsteps of Wal-Mart, which morphed over a decade ago from general discount stores into 'super centers'. Like the Martians in H. G. Wells' *War of the Worlds*, Tesco's plans have been carefully laid. For at least half a decade, all of its new stores have been designed so they can be substantially extended. Shy or not though the company might be, those carefully laid plans are leaking out.

If all its current plans for the UK are allowed to come to fruition, Tesco will double in size at home. According to insider City analysis (the sort that finds its way into the public domain in unmarked plain brown envelopes), Tesco is set to end up taking £1 in every £4 spent by UK shoppers.

The company has already re-engineered itself so that, even when compared to Asda, the UK arm of the undisputed king of 'big box', Wal-Mart, more of its business is done through hypermarkets. At home at least, Tesco appears to be out-Wal-Marting Wal-Mart.

More than 100 Tesco Extra hypermarkets are already in business since first opening in Pitsea, in 1997. There are plans, and Tesco already has the sites, to develop and convert another 300 stores into hypermarkets. If Tesco succeeds, its sales area will double over the coming decade. Operating on that scale means more cost-cutting, which in turn typically means reducing the ratio of staff employed for every £1 of goods sold. It represents an idea of economic efficiency that views staff as an inconvenient cost, necessary only until a new innovation can be designed to make them redundant.

At the end of this process, the City expects Tesco to be earning an overall margin of about 7 per cent, well above the international average for the sector. For the food retail business, this is a huge amount of profit and clear evidence, I would argue, of how its market power enables it to escape from anything like real competition. It is also the result of Tesco's notorious abuse of power in squeezing the supply chain.

Tesco currently uses four basic formats: the hypermarket known as Tesco Extra; the supermarket; the high street or Metro store; and Express outlets. In under five years since early 2001, the share of space of all UK Tesco stores accounted for by the hypermarket format rose from less than 10 per cent to over 25 per cent by 2005, covering nearly 7 million sq. ft of floor space.

In effect, Tesco is relocating its beating business heart into the body of a vast, soulless warehouse. Unless regulators act to restrict the monopolistic instincts of Tesco, you, the shopper, will be spending six months of your life in the warehouse with them, filling baskets and trolleys.

In the US, Wal-Mart has stores of around 200,000 sq. ft. Tesco Extra outlets haven't reached that size yet, but they are moving in that direction. With stores as large as 120,000 sq. ft already, the company is thought to want to increase the scale of future hypermarkets by at least another 20,000 sq. ft. To conduct its quiet retail coup d'état, Tesco will need to continue being as successful at manipulating the planning game in the future as it has been in the past.

The company is growing rapidly around the world, but currently around 80 pence in the £1 of its sales and profits still comes from the UK. There are around 2,000 stores in the UK, complemented by over 800 – and growing – abroad (see Chapter Six). But why is Tesco so effective at capturing and keeping customers?

Figure 3: Watch It Grow: Tesco in the UK in 2006[15]

Tesco UK total	Number of stores	Sales area (million sq. ft)	Planned store openings 2006–07 (including acquisitions)
	1,897	25.9	153

	Number of stores	Sales area (millions sq. ft)	% of UK space
Extra	118	8.0	30.9%
Superstore	445	13.9	53.7%
Metro	163	1.9	7.3%
Express	654	1.4	5.4%
'One Stop' fascia	517		

(Figures for end of 05/06 financial year, UK & ROI: 26 Feb 2006)
(Source: Tesco)

Demanding Loyalty

When fifty-one-year-old Lynn Pierce, a grandmother thirteen times over, opened her door in Anglesey, the last thing she expected to see was a policeman. Two days earlier she had been to the Tesco in Holyhead to buy flowers for her mother's grave. Unknown to her, that visit had been carefully monitored. Someone operating the in-store CCTV security system thought they had seen something suspicious. At one point in her shopping trip, Mrs Pierce stuffed her scarf into her bag. Watching at the bank of CCTV screens, Tesco staff thought she was stealing an item from the store. What happened next reveals a link between convenience and surveillance that many would prefer to forget.

Staff members were too slow to confront the innocent Mrs Pierce in the supermarket, but she had used her Tesco Clubcard when paying. That gave them all the information they needed. Her address was traced from information contained in the Clubcard file and was passed on to the police, who knocked on her door two days later. However, almost immediately, the police realized that a mistake had been made. Closer inspection of the CCTV footage showed Mrs Pierce entering the store already wearing her scarf, and there it was, sitting on a sideboard in her home. 'All I did was put my scarf in my handbag while I was looking for my glasses, and they accused me of stealing from the store,' said Mrs Pierce to the *Daily Mail*. 'I'm disgusted that information from my storecard was passed on to the police and used in this way.' The supermarket apologized, but Mrs Pierce rejected their offer of £50 worth of Tesco coupons in compensation. A spokesman for Tesco said it was 'normal policy to use loyalty card accounts to trace suspected shoplifters'.

We have come a long way from the Green Shield Stamps Tesco introduced in 1963, not long before I was born. I can just about remember them from childhood. Licking them and sticking them into books that slowly filled up appealed to a small boy's instinct for obsessive collecting. There was something of the wartime ration book about them. Having no disposable income of my own, I would mentally trade in our books for every 'gift' available in the catalogue. The Co-op was a bit different, with the 'Divvy', or dividend – a modest but genuine share in profits with which you built up an account. Later, the Co-op also turned to stamps. I remember a vague disappointment when Green Shield Stamps were discontinued, but I needn't have worried. The concept of rewarding customer loyalty was set to return with a vengeance, and when it did it would revolutionize retailing in general and the fortunes of Tesco in particular.

This time, though, technology meant that in return for a few pence off your shopping you would have to sell virtually your whole life story to the supermarket. Safeway and Tesco both introduced loyalty cards at around the same time, in 1995. Sainsbury's followed later. Safeway's scheme was called the ABC card, and Tesco's the Clubcard. Initial euphoria about their potential benefits to the retailers was dampened when the sheer volume of data they delivered about the individual's shopping patterns was simply too much for computers at the time and the software then available to make sense of.

Today, shoppers use the Clubcard in eight out of every ten trips to Tesco. There are around 25 million in existence, representing 14 million households. Perhaps 10 million cards are in active use. This creates an extraordinary eventuality. Shortly before its fall, the German Democratic Republic – East Germany, one of the most famous police states in the world – only had a population of around 16 million people. That means Tesco almost certainly holds more files on British citizens than the East German state ever held on its own people. When shoppers use the Clubcard, they willingly if unknowingly paint a self-portrait in data. As a result, Tesco probably ends up knowing more about a cardholder's comings and goings than the holder's husband or wife. How many people, I wonder, realize the level of detail about them that Tesco keeps on file?

The Clubcard enables Tesco to keep a record of each holder's name, age, address, telephone number and email. The company knows your dietary requirements and the makeup of your family. It keeps track of exactly everything you've ever bought from it, and which stores you've bought from. The precise date and time of each purchase is held, too. From the data, Tesco can make pretty good guesses about whether you had a sad bachelor night in with a meal for one on Wednesday night, or threw a party at the weekend. It is certainly able to tell if you have a bit of a drink problem, or if you're a junk food addict, or whether you have an undue fondness for tinned pineapple. In at least one case that we'll come to in a later chapter, one man's Clubcard actually created an obsession with bananas.

The card also enables Tesco to tell which coupons and vouchers you've used, and when and where you used them. It will also keep a record of any complaints you have ever made, any additional market research you have taken part in and any other direct communication you may have had with the store.

The profile Tesco builds up with all that information allows it to typecast people in a number of ways. First, it analyses which 'life stage' you are at, whether you're a student, have a young family or are retired. Then it assesses how much you're worth to the company, how much you spend and how 'loyal' you are on a scale from 'uncommitted' to 'premium'. Next, it builds a picture of your lifestyle. Are you 'upmarket', 'market' or downmarket (or, as it euphemistically calls this category, 'cost conscious')? You are then 'segmented' by what you buy on a graph with axes for age and affluence, so Tesco knows what's likely to be dropped into your trolley.

The ability to do this has helped Tesco become the UK's dominant retailer. The facts about you that it keeps in its virtual information warehouses are as much covered by the Data Protection Act as any other commercial operation. Yet there is something inescapably – what is the right word? – *unsettling* that crawls out from under this pile of digital profiling. It's something that darts out of view just as you try to look at it. This sample profile, typical of what a Clubcard can deliver, is taken from a presentation made by Tesco's own data crunchers to show proudly what the system is capable of:

Mrs Smith is a <u>young adult</u>

She is a Premium shoppers. [*sic*]

She uses Watford Hypermarket for major monthly shops and Covent Garden Metro for daily requirements.

She often shops late in the evening and buys <u>upmarket products</u>.

She is particularly <u>loyal</u> to her cat food brand and fine fabric washing powder.

She buys <u>Hello</u> magazine and sometimes <u>Country Life</u>.[16]

Add Mrs Smith's address and mobile phone number – also available from Clubcard data – and all that is missing for a neighbourhood stalker is her hair colour and the location of her spare house key. Uncomfortably, you sense that by pressing the right buttons, by looking at her purchase of hair care products and with a little correlation, Tesco could work that out, too. The convergence of different types of data that companies hold on you adds another dimension. Imagine if you also have a Tesco mobile phone and bank account. A record will exist of all your movements; every conversation you have with friends and every company and service you call, and when, where and for how long; everything you buy with a bank card; and every service you pay for.

Yet another development is set to become commonplace in supermarkets: radio frequency identification tagging (RFID). RFID is designed, ostensibly, to improve stock control. But the technology also has the potential to be used as a security and anti-shoplifting measure. Tesco is gearing up to use it. At the time of writing, around forty stores had been made RFID-ready. However, an inadvertent consequence of the new monitoring technology is that, on top of all the things Tesco already knows about the illustrative Mrs Smith, RFID means that should she purchase a tagged product it would be perfectly possible for the supermarket to follow her with a tracking device, wherever she went.[17] During early trials it was made clear that tagging can 'locate the product, tell when it goes out of date, if it has been paid for and even if it has been recycled by a customer after use'.[18]

A darker twist to such surveillance technology emerged when the UK government let it be known that it planned to link proposed compulsory biometric identity cards, designed to help control immigration, to the data contained on supermarket loyalty cards. The idea floated was to allow two-way data traffic between the government and major corporations like banks and supermarkets. Information contained on the national identity database, set up to underpin the ID card scheme, would be made available to companies for a price. In the other direction, the police could be alerted the moment someone who was the target of an inquiry made use of a loyalty card or cash machine.[19]

Having Tesco's Baby

'The scheme is driven by this simple piece of plastic, but every time you shop with us we record all there is to know about you.'

Sarah Baldock, Manager, Marketing and
Communication for Health and Beauty with
'special responsibility for the baby category', Tesco[20]

The actress Sheila Hancock is being interviewed for a television programme called *Grumpy Old Women*.[21] It's a spin-off of an almost identical programme called *Grumpy Old Men*. She talks about her irritation at being asked at shop checkouts if she has, or would like, a loyalty card. Loyalty, she explains, is what she feels towards the people she loves – her friends, dear colleagues, family and children. She does not reserve feelings of loyalty for chain stores, she says, visibly appalled at the prospect of a commercial invasion of a personal emotional sphere.

But invade they do. Occupying armies of marketing professionals and data gatherers set up camp in the landscapes of our family lives. They take positions from which they can commercially exploit the hopes, fears and insecurities we hold for the people we love. Nowhere is this more brazen than in the successful application of the Clubcard to the marketing of baby products. It also reveals the aggression and tactics that Tesco uses to target its ever-declining competitors.

It is surprising how much people or firms will reveal about themselves when they are proud of what they've done. In a conference presentation by Tesco staff called 'Creating an emotional bond with customers', some of the reasons for the company's commercial success become a little clearer.

Concerned in 1997 that it was 'underperforming' by taking only about £1 in every £7 spent in the 'baby market', Tesco decided to launch Baby Club with the rationale that 'the baby and family customer . . . are the entry point to earning lifetime loyalty'. Just a single 'market share point' of young families' shopping is worth £114 million of turnover, according to Tesco. So the trusted high street chemist, Boots, became its target. Boots had been, up to then, the first port of call for young mothers and mothers-to-be. Tesco noted enviously that 'even key opinion formers such as midwives and health visitors would recommend Boots'. But not for much longer, if Tesco got its way.

> 'We have managed to create a single customer view of what it is to have a baby with Tesco.'
>
> Sarah Baldock, Tesco

Something horribly funny happens when real life passes through the filter of corporate management-speak. A mangling occurs that, despite sullying all it touches, also achieves a hilarity composed in equal parts of morbid fascination at its sheer awfulness plus quite real nausea. With the spectre of the appalling manager character David Brent from the television comedy *The Office* watching, Tesco feels able to comment:

> Not only were we threatened from a baby perspective but as these mums were also able to fulfil their health and beauty needs [at Boots], at the same time there was a much greater risk to our potential growth in total H+B [health and beauty].[22]

No retailer bent on market domination can afford to be 'threatened from a baby perspective'. It would have to stop. Tesco concluded that it needed 'a totally different positioning for our baby offering'. In working out how to capture more of the 'baby perspective' (help, please make it stop), the store demonstrated a level of self-awareness that never makes it into its 'You shop, we drop' advertising campaigns. Trips to the supermarket, they conceded, were 'tortuous' and 'daunting', especially for young mothers.

Clubcard's information warehouse allowed Tesco to create Baby Club, and through it to target hundreds of thousands of expectant and young mothers via sophisticated direct mail. The mailings include seven different magazines for each key stage, from pregnancy to toddler. Through these, the company thinks 'long and hard about the emotional need of mums and commercial need for Tesco'. Every issue, of course, promotes a carefully chosen range of Tesco products.

Tesco's joy at the arrival of Baby Club was undoubtedly only enhanced by the fact that it successfully persuaded its suppliers to meet many of the costs. Not only does the company get help from suppliers to pay for some of the costs of running Baby Club, it appears to have co-opted health care professionals and otherwise independent organizations to help it promote the scheme.

Young mothers get to hear about the club from a range of magazines and in-store promotions. But that's not enough. Tesco says, in an echo of the controversial marketing practices of baby-milk manufacturer Nestlé, that 'even your midwife might tell you'. Tantalizingly, the written transcript of the Tesco conference presentation that was passed to me promises at this point to 'explain in a moment how this happens' – but doesn't do so in writing.

Tesco boasts, however, that the kind of endorsements from health care professionals they had long sought, word of mouth promotion through organizations like the Independent Midwives' Association and others like the National Childbirth Trust (NCT), are now 'part of the scheme'. Health care professionals 'now recommend Tesco ranges and Tesco as the place to go', says Sarah Baldock. Academics and media personalities are also used in calculated fashion to add credibility.

Baby Club acquired over half a million members and achieved what it set out to do, knocking Boots from its commanding position in control of the 'baby perspective'. Now Tesco had around a quarter of the market and sold more nappies, baby food and milk than anyone else. Quick to milk a winning formula, it went on to create Toddler Club, recruiting 200,000 members in its first seven months. Like a scene from the dystopian science fiction film *The Matrix*, Tesco appears to be creating a kind of shopping dependency in which life at every stage is always viewed through the sliding doors of one of its shopfronts.

Please Swallow This

It's easier to understand the Tesco phenomenon by looking at how the company moves into new areas of business. After food, the thing people probably care most about is their health. Moves by the supermarkets to further envelop health care professionals look set to go much further still. The government is discussing with retailers the possibility of general practice surgeries opening inside supermarkets. At the British Medical Association's annual meeting in 2006, representatives reacted to the idea with horror. 'The notion that nicotine and alcohol may be sold where primary care services are to be delivered is anathema to the medical profession,' said one GP.[23] With several supermarkets already operating in-store pharmacies Tesco's strategy is straightforward, even if not immediately obvious to the casual shopper.

The company needs to grow to keep City investors happy, but is now so large in the conventional grocery market that even laissez-faire regulators have taken notice. Consequently, Tesco needs to find other ways to grow their earnings. Its most obvious options include further overseas expansion; extracting more profit from suppliers (though with so many struggling for subsistence already, that scope is limited); and setting out to capture a greater share of the public sector. That means the NHS, and legislators are already worried – including Lord Borrie, former head of the OFT:

> The ambitions of supermarkets to dispense prescriptions may have a seriously adverse effect on local pharmacies, to the detriment of the sick, in general, and the elderly sick, in particular.[24]

Tesco management must have been sad to see the departure of the former NHS chief executive Nigel Crisp. He was such a fan of the supermarket that he thought NHS foundation trusts should emulate Tesco's techniques to promote the 'new choice-based NHS market'.[25] The loss of one enamoured senior civil servant is unlikely, however, to change Tesco's business strategy for the sector, which is to treat as many low-risk, high-profit conditions as possible. It seeks volume and turnover in the health market just as it seeks it in magazines, music or milk. By teaming up with giant pharmaceutical companies like GSK, Tesco will seek to capture the market for selling non-prescription drugs and use its in-store pharmacies to grow its share of the prescription drugs market as well.

A feature from *Tesco Magazine* under the heading 'Summer Wellbeing' makes the company's intentions only too obvious. The in-store pharmacy, the article says, is 'more than a place to pick up prescriptions'. It offers services for repeat dispensing, reviews of your prescription, treatment for smoking addiction and also a 'minor ailments service'. That last item echoes how private-sector health providers target health services that are high-profit and low-risk. Private hospitals open to those with health insurance are happy to promote themselves favourably against the NHS as being 'clean', but will often quickly refer patients with acute conditions to the NHS, relying on it to treat serious illnesses. Tesco boasts that its in-store pharmacies are able to treat 40 per cent of people who visit their GP, promising only that you 'can rest assured you will be referred . . . if it is thought necessary'.[26]

There are several disturbing problems with this approach. At least superficially, it chimes with a Department of Health desire to relieve the work burden on GPs. As such, it gets officially welcomed. But the reality, motives and economics of Tesco and the disregard for the upkeep of broader social and economic infrastructure mean that the store's aggressive move into dispensing is like a wolf barging its way into the puppy litter of community pharmacy. First and foremost, Tesco exists to shift product and make profit. This is its undisputed reason for being. That means, in terms of health service, it has an interest in selling its drugs, leading to a risk of over-medicating the nation.

In October 2006 the drugs watchdog Medicines and Health-care Products Regulatory Agency (MHRA) forced Tesco to withdraw a 'two-for-one' in-store promotion on painkillers. Restrictions on inappropriate drug promotions were introduced in 1998 to reduce the chances for abuse and accidental poison-ing. The new rules led to 'a significant reduction in suicidal deaths and liver toxicity'. That's why Tesco's selling practices were judged 'not acceptable' by the regulator. The MHRA's Director of Vigilance and Risk Management of Medicines said of Tesco, 'When it comes to safety issues, the MHRA will not tolerate irresponsible promotion that undermines public health.'[27]

Take another seemingly innocuous promotion from *Tesco Magazine*, concerning an uncomfortable condition called Irri-table Bowel Syndrome (IBS). A little general information is given on lifestyle changes to combat the problem, but only after you've been sold the drug Buscopan, which is helpfully 'available on the shelf in Tesco'. The article does say it's a Tesco promo-tion, but what readers might not realize is the article is adver-torial, so might have come from Buscopan rather than Tesco. The maker of Buscopan is Boehringer Ingelheim Ltd, which describes itself as one of the world's twenty largest pharmaceu-tical companies with global sales in 2004 of €8.2 billion. Among other things, it manufactures a range of lucrative, so-called 'lifestyle' drugs for the treatment of fatigue and depression.

Conveniently, this piece sits alongside a reassuring article by a 'GP and busy mum', neatly validating Tesco's health credentials at a stroke and hitting its target shopper demographic at the same time.

The same magazine promotes treatments ranging from a wide selection of anti-allergy sprays to pills and solutions for tackling the complaints of modern life (of which Tesco is simultaneously both a large part and architect). There are painkillers, slimming pills and slimming programmes – although the supermarket's shelves are also heaving with multi-packs of chocolate, ice cream, cake, alcohol and cigarettes.

In the world of pharmacy more than anything else, Tesco's innocent offer of 'Every little helps' masks an almighty, strategic effort to re-engineer the fabric of our communities and essential services in its own profit-focused interests. Unlike food, where Tesco is thought to average margins of 7 per cent, with the sale of drugs (legal ones, at least) the scope for profit margins can hit 30 per cent. This is why, in early 2003, Tesco was about to welcome with open arms the latest thinking of its favourite regulator, the OFT.[28]

A Lethal Prescription?

The day after the publication of the nef report 'Ghost Town Britain' in 2002, the phone rang in my office. On the line was a senior NHS administrator. He congratulated us on our launch, but had something confusing to say about a delayed report from the OFT. The caller advised us to find out more. It was then that our attention turned to the future for community pharmacies.

It turned out that the OFT was on the verge of launching proposals for the full-scale deregulation of pharmacy, with the inevitable consequence that supermarkets would do to community pharmacies what they had already done to bakers, grocers and all other kinds of food shops (and were planning to do to newsagents and convenience stores).

But our report had gained so much negative publicity for the supermarkets that someone within the OFT obviously concluded it was not a good time to suggest undermining one of the few remaining bastions of the high street. 'Ghost Town Britain' didn't examine the case of the UK's 12,250 local pharmacies. We left them out for the reason that everything seemed calm and happily functioning in the world of community pharmacies. People were pleased with the service they provided, and the government spoke of enhancing their role in line with an NHS plan.

Regulations introduced in 1987 meant that only those pharmacists who convinced health authorities that their services were 'necessary or desirable' for a local area were allowed to provide NHS prescriptions. This situation made local pharmacies viable because around 80 per cent of their income is derived from NHS prescriptions. An assortment of cosmetics and bathroom products makes up the rest. But the situation irked the OFT. It thought that such 'market regulation' was effectively blocking new pharmacy businesses from entering the market, and was limiting competition.

The OFT waited until the post-Christmas lull in January 2003 before recommending that the government should deregulate and, in effect, hand the sector on a plate to the major supermarkets. By then, the first wave of concern about ghost towns had died down. Tesco immediately urged 'ministers to act quickly and positively on the OFT's recommendations'.[29] It looked like the depressing dynamic of Ghost Town Britain was set to repeat itself with community pharmacies.

If pharmacies followed other local retailers and services at the hands of the supermarkets, they would decline at the rate of 4 per cent a year, losing more than one pharmacy a day. The OFT pointed out that there was scope to open pharmacies in over 3,000 medium-to-large supermarkets. But over 6,600 pharmacies were located within the catchment area of two or more supermarkets, placing them under particular threat.[30]

Most disturbingly, in the areas where community pharmacies were under threat from supermarkets, between a fifth and a third of the populations in regions such as England's north and north-west are defined as 'most deprived' by the official Index of Multiple Deprivation.[31] Community pharmacies, it seemed, were most under threat in precisely the areas where people with the least mobility lived. Demands on health services are also much higher in deprived areas than in affluent ones. According to the Office of National Statistics, low-income households pay twice as many visits to the doctor as affluent households.

Another dimension not properly addressed by the OFT was the clear knock-on effect when services close. For example, when the last bank and post office branches close in a given area, other local businesses see drops in trade of between 10–30 per cent. The loss of local pharmacies, which have been able to withstand the onslaught of supermarkets because of their unique relationship with the NHS, almost certainly has knock-on effects too.

Community pharmacies fulfil important social functions that escape the radar of the market regulators. They are, for example, the launch pad for many Department of Health initiatives. Hemant Patel, President of the Royal Pharmaceutical Society, believes that people study pharmacy with an ethic of public service. 'It is an idealistic job to do,' he says. 'When I qualified, what I most looked forward to was working in the community, face-to-face contact with patients.' However, he sees that the emergence of big chains is leading to people leaving the profession and to an erosion of service:

> A community pharmacist needs to be a trusted local figure, and one of the ways this happens is by continuous service. Supermarket pharmacies tend to be run by locums, as a result of which there isn't any continuity of service. Any sense of a face-to-face relationship is completely lost. Large chains also have profit-driven criteria for remaining in an area, not a commitment to the people that they serve.[32]

Each community pharmacy serves, on average, 50 patients with diabetes, 150 patients with asthma, 10 patients with mental health problems, 750 older people and 50 patients recently discharged from hospital. They provide services such as controlled methadone for drug users and emergency contraception. Undermining community pharmacies jeopardizes such vital services and benefits which, in any case, sit uneasily alongside shelves stacked either with alcohol or salad and sandwiches.

The OFT report flew in the face of the government's own stated aim of 'joined-up thinking'. The Department for Trade and Industry and the Department of Health were effectively working against each other, supposedly to deliver choice in health care. The OFT, on the other hand, meant to be the consumers' champion, was making proposals that would actually reduce accessibility and choice for most people.

The National Pharmaceutical Association, representing 11,000 community pharmacies, argued that the proposals would leave rural and deprived areas particularly vulnerable to becoming health care deserts. Its chief executive, John D'Arcy, argued that, 'The only winners from [the OFT recommendations] will be the shareholders of the large, better-resourced players, whose main concern is profit rather than patients' health care services.'[33]

The OFT's own analysis showed that an astonishingly high 86 per cent of people were satisfied with local pharmacy provision. Given the old adage, 'If it ain't broke, don't fix it', the suspicion was that either the OFT had succumbed to behind-the-scenes supermarket lobbying, or it was behaving in an exceptionally ideological way, offering a solution to a problem that didn't exist. An unresolved tension had emerged between those who wanted pharmacies to operate like straightforward retailers, almost inevitably killing off small, independent community-based operators, and those who saw pharmacies with a broader community role supported by an appropriate regulatory environment.

Noel Baumber is a practising pharmacist in Grantham, and founder of the Independent Pharmacy Federation. 'We visit ninety people a week, providing health care,' he tells me, explaining how the Federation also provides a free collection and delivery service and even helps with dressing people's infections and injuries where appropriate. At the local hospice, Noel also helps to provide a general, supportive palliative care service. Scornful of the supermarkets, he thinks all they want is 'footfall' in their stores, and are unconcerned about the real life of the community. Events involving Tesco that were to unfold in another small town would seem to support his view.

We, the Neighbourhood

Working within the law as it stands, Tesco continues to increase the number of pharmacies in its stores. In 2006 it persuaded the NHS to allow it to open a pharmacy in its superstore in Dereham, Norfolk. The argument it used to win its case as a 'necessary and desirable' addition to local health service provision was, 'There are currently no pharmacies in the neighbourhood.' On these grounds, the Norfolk Pharmacy and Dispensing Committee, on behalf of Southern Norfolk Primary Care Trust (PCT), granted a contract.[34] But the argument was, to say the least, misleading.

Under examination following several appeals made against Tesco, the 'neighbourhood' mentioned in the application actually turned out to be the store itself. Tesco, situated on an industrial estate accessible largely only by car and not 'designed for pedestrian access', was justifying opening an in-store pharmacy that was likely to seriously undermine other local, community-based pharmacies on the grounds that there was a neighbourhood desperately lacking a pharmacy – but the neighbourhood was itself. The Norfolk Local Medical Committee disagreed, but the decision was approved by a panel on appeal. If Franz Kafka and Joseph Heller had been left in a room to write a play about local planning decisions, this would have made an admirable opening scene.

Tesco now operates over 200 pharmacies. Its equally innovative approach to planning law and the acute financial management that gives the company a huge supply of cheap capital to invest in expansion are both looked at in the next chapter.

Just one example of Tesco's relentless rolling back of retail frontiers is its move into catalogue shopping. Doing so will put it in direct competition with Argos, the UK chain store whose operation is built around its catalogue. But other targets are likely to include the upmarket retailer John Lewis and the department store Debenhams. For Tesco, a catalogue business will allow it to diversify into more non-food items like furniture. The range of clothes and electrical goods on offer will also probably increase. It will complement its shops' income with a new stream of money, and with so many stores it already has the base from which to promote a catalogue.[35]

In another case of restless retail ambition, Tesco's whole approach to business seemed set to redefine our access to justice itself.

The Law According to Tesco

In July 2003, government plans for radical changes to the way law firms operate created headlines in the national media. Lord Falconer, Constitutional Affairs Secretary for the Labour government, proposed removing a range of checks and balances originally put in place to secure the independence of the legal profession. Under the new system, law firms would be allowed to attract profit-hunting investors by floating on the stock exchange, and to enter into joint business ventures with non-law firms.

It was the beginning of a move in favour of big business that, three years later, the *Financial Times* would describe as making Britain potentially 'one of the most deregulated environments in the world'.[36]

So deeply has Tesco come to be synonymous with a particular laissez-faire approach to business that a single remark by Lord Falconer at the outset led to his initiative being permanently associated with the supermarket. He said, '. . . if we can get to the point where there is "Tesco Law", we think that's probably something of interest to the consumer.'[37]

An official review followed the announcement and gave birth to a draft legal services bill, although the tag 'Tesco law' stuck firmly. A steady murmur of dissent broke out into open confrontation in 2006 when a joint committee of the Houses of Lords and Commons condemned the proposed 'Tesco law' parliamentary bill for threatening the legal profession's independence and creating potential conflicts of interest. It could, of course, be seen as pure coincidence that Tesco became associated with the proposals. Yet the fact that conflicts of interest also echo around Tesco's encroachment into health services, its stalking of the media, control of the food supply chain and general desire for world domination, throws such happenstance more into the category of 'the truth will out'.

Lord Hunt, chair of the parliamentary committee, criticizing 'Tesco law', observed, 'The legal system must not only be independent; it must be perceived as being independent.' The government's proposals also came under fire from the Law Society.

Tesco, in the meantime, saw no reason to wait for the outcome of a complex debate over principle and the independence of the law. It dived into what it saw as a lucrative market and set up Legal Store (strapline: 'DIY legal solutions at great value prices'), offering triple Clubcard points on its Last Will kit.[38]

Of course, the company doesn't stop at seeking to extract a little extra profit from your plans for the afterlife; it'll also help you seek compensation, buy a property, sell your own, take on your employer, get divorced and confront a noisy neighbour.

With the power of Clubcard to analyse the lives of Tesco customers, this creates some fascinating opportunities for cross-selling. Remember, 60,000 different customized promotions go out with Clubcard mailings. Should the computer notice that Mr Smith is buying a lot of condoms when Mrs Smith seems to be away (indicated by a break in her regular shopping patterns), and Mr Smith appears to be buying flowers and lingerie when it isn't Mrs Smith's birthday, it's perfectly imaginable that Mr Smith's next Clubcard mailing might include a money-off voucher for the Tesco Divorce Pack. This would, after all, be simple, customer-driven market logic. From Baby Club to getting divorced and making your Last Will and Testament, Tesco will be there to take a slice of all of life's (and death's) key moments.

End of the Nightly Miracle

Every night in the UK, in the time it takes to doze through an average evening's worth of television, 14 million newspapers and 45 million magazines are delivered to 54,000 retailers. It's some-thing that the Freight Transport Association, perhaps amazed at the performance of its own members refers to as 'the nightly miracle'. But the miracle is more than just an impressive logistical feat. This system guarantees delivery of a full range of titles, without discrimination, to everyone from the smallest newsagent to the largest supermarket. It means everyone gets ready access to a diversity of news and points of view. It's an important part of an otherwise not very healthy democratic system. The reason it can do this is because of a particular system of exclusive, regional wholesale distribution agreements.

UK magazine publishing is astonishingly diverse. But you could never guess that by browsing the small range of mostly dismal copycat titles generally for sale in supermarkets. In fact, there are approximately 1,800 weekly magazine titles and 1,500 monthlies produced in the UK. One of the great advantages of magazine publishing under the present system is that there are low, so-called 'barriers to entry'. It's relatively easy to set up a magazine, and because there are so many small, independent newsagents backed by the exclusive regional distribution system, it means that the publications are also easy to get hold of.

'I will always get you the title you want,' says Colin Finch of the National Federation of Retail Newsagents. 'Try going to Tesco and asking for *Railway Modeller* and they will laugh at you. You might not need a specialist magazine today, but you might in the future, or your children might.'[39]

For some time, however, supermarkets have lobbied to break the system up and assume greater control of press distribution. They figure that substituting their own distribution system would save them money. There are other economic motivations too; although magazines represent less than 1 per cent of supermarkets' turnover, they are an important product because the top-selling, fast-turnover titles bring people into the store. Once there, the supermarkets assume they will stay do the rest of their shopping. The problem is that a terrible imbalance is built into the trade.

Remember the 80/20 rule? Supermarkets are disproportionately influential because, although the range of magazines they stock is small, they sell the large-circulation titles in huge volumes. Supermarket magazine sales represent around 36 per cent of the total market.[40] But, says Finch, 'No part of the supply chain should be more important the chain itself.'

Publishers also argue that allowing the opt-outs sought by supermarkets would fatally undermine the economics of guaranteed, universal distribution. It would threaten the easy access we have to a free and diverse press. Allowing supermarkets to control press distribution could threaten nearly one-third of magazine titles produced.

The OFT decided to investigate. Even if the system was working, the very idea of an exclusive agreement insulted an orthodox economic devotion to deregulation. Then, in the middle of what became a major review of how press distribution operated, on one of at least two occasions the relatively new head of the OFT appeared to intervene inappropriately in an investigation of which the OFT was part. Toby Hicks of the Periodical Publishers Association (PPA) pointed out:

> Very unhelpfully, the OFT's chief executive, John Fingleton, has stated he would welcome national distribution driven by the major supermarkets – a comment which PPA regards as completely inappropriate given the reliance the Press places on having a route to market free of potential censorship (commercial or otherwise) by powerful supermarkets.[41]

Even small changes that had the effect of strengthening the supermarkets, he warned, could create 'a domino effect, with the whole system potentially collapsing, only to be reformed with a new Tesco own-label set of chips'.

Changes in line with Fingleton's comments stood to have a double impact, hurting both small retailers and the choice of magazines available. According to Paul Dobson, Professor of Competition Economics at Loughborough University, up to 12,000 retail newsagents could be put out of business, and 1,000 magazine titles might be lost as their distribution became economically unattractive. Once again, action promoted under the rhetoric of choice and competition stood to destroy both. When 'winners' like Tesco emerge, who is there left to compete with? Too narrow a definition of 'consumer interest' on the part of the OFT then results in a smaller range of products available and in a more restricted and less diverse range of outlets: one more step down the road to greater cultural impoverishment.

The next chapter looks at more keys to Tesco's success: how it manages to get the land and planning permission to build stores, acquire the capital to invest and obtain goods on the cheap.

The Rise of the Supermarket through the Eyes of Tesco

1919   Jack Cohen starts selling surplus stock on a market stall in London's East End, and so Tesco begins.

1924   Tesco Tea becomes the first own-brand product.

1929   The first Tesco store opens in Edgware, north London.

1934   Tesco acquires land (illustrating the adage 'start as you mean to continue') in Edmonton, north London, for a new headquarters and warehouse, allowing centralized stock control.

1939   Tesco has around 100 branches.

1947   Tesco Stores (Holdings) Ltd goes public by floating on the stock exchange.

1956   Tesco's first self-service supermarket opens in Maldon.

1959   Tesco has around 400 stores following several mergers and acquisitions.

1960   Tesco buys a chain of 212 stores in northern England, and expands rapidly up to 1965.

1961   Tesco's store in Leicester becomes the largest store in Europe.

1963   Green Shield Stamps arrive on the scene allowing the store to offer discounts that avoid the rules of Resale Price Maintenance.

1968 The new Tesco store in Crawley, West Sussex, is referred to as a 'superstore'.

1974 Tesco has 771 branches, but many are small outlets and stores in poor areas are set to close. Tesco also opens its petrol stations at major sites for the first time.

1979 Store sales reach £1 billion.

1982 Store sales pass £2 billion.

1987 Tesco has 377 stores – many fewer than before, but each is much larger.

1987 Another twenty-nine stores are to be added in a £500 million building programme.

1991 Tesco becomes Britain's dominant independent petrol retailer.

1992 The first of many Tesco Metro stores opens.

1994 The first of many Tesco Express stores opens.

1995 Tesco Clubcard, the innovation set to transform the store's fortunes, and track its customers is launched.

1995 Tesco arrives in Hungary, twenty-nine years after Soviet tanks entered Budapest.

1995 Tesco becomes the biggest food retailer in the UK.

1996 Tesco spreads to Poland, the Czech Republic, Slovakia and Northern Ireland.

1996 Tesco opens stores for twenty-four-hour trading.

1997 Tesco moves to capture share of loan and personal finance market.

1997 Tesco spreads to the Republic of Ireland.

1997 The first of many Tesco Extra hypermarkets opens.

1998 Tesco spreads to Taiwan and Thailand.

1999 Tesco moves to capture share of the mobile phone market.

1999   Tesco moves into online bookselling and online banking.

1999   Tesco spreads to South Korea.

2000   The online business Tesco.com goes live.

2002   Tesco starts promoting Airmiles through its Clubcard.

2001   Tesco spreads to Malaysia.

2002   Tesco has 730 stores in the UK.

2003   Tesco launches home phone service.

2003   Tesco spreads to Japan and Turkey.

2004   Tesco enters music-download market.

2004   Tesco becomes broadband provider.

2004   Tesco spreads to China.

2005   Tesco makes profits (not sales) of £2 billion.

2006   Tesco announces plan to spread to the US.

2006   Tesco has 1,879 UK stores, including many acquired from the T&S chain of convenience stores as well as former Cullen's, Hart's and Europa outlets, plus many new Express and Metro outlets.

2006   Tesco controls about one-third of the UK grocery market and has enough land and assets in the UK to further double in size.

(Adapted from information available at www.tescocorporate.com and other sources.)

CHAPTER FOUR

Land, Money, Goods –
and How to Get Them

'We work with the grain of national planning policy.'
Sir Terry Leahy, Chief Executive, Tesco, 10 May 2006[1]

*'The characteristic Tesco attitude where it bid for and secured a new
site was to ignore planning regulations. Regulations from wherever
they emanated, like all kinds of rules, were regarded by Tesco as a
nuisance.'*
Andrew Seth and Geoffrey Randall, *The Grocers:
The Rise and Rise of the Supermarket Chains*, 1999

'Lock down', A Man with a Plan

Location is everything. That's why supermarkets want more and
more of them – many more, in fact, than most people think is
right. A David and Goliath struggle is going on at the local level
across Britain. On one side are the big supermarkets and on one
other, communities and local authorities. Compared to the bib-
lical myth, however, this time Goliath has a huge legal department, a big bag of tricks and inducements and a campaign team
that would humble the operation of a US Presidential hopeful.

Today, when a supermarket wants to win a planning application, it goes much further than filing its plans in a brown paper
envelope and hoping for the best. Nothing is left to chance;
sophisticated political strategies are used including door-to-door
canvassing, polling and letter-writing campaigns on the supermarket's behalf. Councillors and planning officers are put under

intense pressure. Local authorities often have to question whether they can risk the cost of long, drawn-out legal battles against much better-resourced, giant chain retailers.

A leaked Tesco 'battle plan' was obtained by the *Daily Telegraph* newspaper in late 2005.[2] It presented 'strategic advice on how to best promote developments and Tesco's interests to all local, regional, national and UK governments'. Techniques reportedly included how to build networks locally where stores were proposed, as well as advice on writing press releases, letters and petitions. Everything was designed to 'sell' Tesco and its new stores to local communities. It also revealed that 'as soon as [a planning] application is submitted all political channels lock down'.

Even when supermarkets are rejected, they often turn their planning applications into wars of attrition, constantly resubmitting proposals in an attempt to wear down local opposition. As a result, the 'big four' supermarkets now sit like occupying armies in the land of UK retail. But, as we will see later on, signs of resistance are growing. In playing the planning system, Tesco is merely carrying on a game that has served it well for many years.

Tesco won an ugly reputation during the 1980s. The rash of new out-of-town supermarkets and shopping centres drove the store's growth. Unfortunately, it also began the long-term cull of independent town centre shops. Tesco built stores while Conservative Prime Minister Margaret Thatcher's big business sun shone. Tesco walked over planning authorities, simply paying whatever fines it couldn't avoid. Even the multiple's supporters note that the store became 'known as the most cavalier and irresponsible of the operators'.[3]

It was after Thatcher lost her job as Prime Minister in 1990 that things became harder for rampant out-of-town developments. As previously mentioned, a new mood and a new environment minister in John Gummer introduced some curbs with new planning rules. Tesco, however, was able simply to sidestep the restrictions, because it had already 'banked' enough land to be able to keep growing.

Here was a well-established track record of running rings around both the planning authorities and the company's less cavalier competition. It seemed odd, consequently, when in 2006 the OFT begrudgingly conceded to investigating anti-competitive practices in the grocery market. It settled down with a particular focus on how the big supermarkets and Tesco in particular manipulate planning procedures and land acquisitions. It was as though the regulators had stumbled across a new and unexpected scam. Having consistently refused to look seriously at what everyone could see was happening, their surprised reaction to the results of their initial investigations carried a disingenuous whiff. When they finally looked properly, this is what they found, expressed in the stilted tones of officialdom:

> There are a number of features of the market that can reasonably be suspected of distorting competition and, in the case of at least some of those features, the evidence suggests that consumers may be being harmed as a result:
>
> There are reasonable grounds for suspecting that the land holdings of the large supermarket multiples may reinforce their existing market position in some local areas. The OFT has also found evidence of practices that could have an anti-competitive effect, including the use of restrictive covenants in relation to sites sold by the big supermarkets.[4]

At the same time, the OFT conveniently remembered that back in 2003 it had observed an imbalance built into a market dominated by just four retailers. 'The high market shares of Asda, Sainsbury's and Tesco,' it pointed out then, 'give these companies correspondingly greater strength in competition for new sites.'[5] But even this state of affairs masked a greater distortion. Tesco, because of its size and financial assets, was able to consistently outbid other retailers for potential sites – on average, by 48 per cent more than the next highest bidder. This led to rising rents and land prices in a given area, making land prohibitively expensive for smaller players. Again, the winner was taking all. Sometimes land was bought not with the intention of building a store at all, but merely to prevent a competitor doing so. The OFT found evidence of sixty-nine sites involving the 'big four' supermarkets where restrictive covenants were used. In one case, restrictions placed on the land after purchase were to last for 125 years.[6]

The campaign group Friends of the Earth conducted a forensic analysis of how supermarkets play the planning game, looking at 200 ongoing disputes. Ranging across the country and a wide variety of cases, its investigations kept coming back to Tesco. They found a weak planning system that supermarkets had little problem in circumventing. Sometimes supermarkets worked in collusion with local councils, against the spirit of the law and against the wishes of local people. Lobbying is used to overcome democratic procedures at the local level if votes go against supermarket planning applications. Tesco was found to own a 'land bank' of at least 185 sites, to be used either for developing its own stores or to prevent others from building in competition. The research found that Tesco's land acquisition appeared to be having 'a negative impact on Local Authorities' aspirations for new housing and essential facilities like doctors' surgeries'. The report concluded, 'The key questions here are not about illegal activity, but about an erosion of democracy; the inability of local authorities to make a decision against supermarkets.'

Tesco owned some land near Hadleigh in Suffolk, and applied to build a store there in 1999, but it was rejected both nationally by the government and locally by Babergh District Council. The council's original local plan did not accept a need for major new retail sites in the area. Then Tesco got to work. After concerted lobbying by the supermarket, not only was the local plan changed in 2004 to provide for new retail development in the Hadleigh area, but the precise piece of land owned by Tesco was specified.[7]

When the council in Carlisle, Cumbria, left a Tesco application undecided because it contradicted the council's vision for the city, the store wrote to councillors at their home addresses. The MP Eric Martlew called it 'just another example of Tesco using its massive power to bulldoze its way through. It is turning from a giant into a monster.'

In September 2005, Tesco opposed an Asda/Wal-Mart store for Bangor town centre, in Gwynedd. The council argued it would harm local shops and be detrimental to the town centre. Tesco then promptly opened its own hypermarket outside Bangor two months later.

In a now celebrated case in Sheringham, Norfolk, Tesco allegedly negotiated a secret deal with planning officers without the knowledge of councillors. This had the effect of smoothing its own planning application, restricting other retailers and tying the hands of councillors who wanted to reject Tesco. At the time of writing, the case is still under legal dispute.

In Newcastle, Tesco used a special website to promote its case for building a 120,000-sq. ft hypermarket in an area where the council believed there was only need for a maximum of 30,000 sq. ft of new retail space. The tactic of creating special promotional websites was also used for proposals in Suffolk and Dartford.

It's not always just local people who don't want Tesco. The High Court rejected Tesco's plans to build a store in Bridgnorth, Shropshire, but even that didn't stop the company pursuing further legal objections.

The investigative BBC radio programme *Face the Facts* looked into what Tesco was up to in Scunthorpe. John Hayes, chair of Scunthorpe's local chamber of trade, found his initial fears were realized about the prospect of Tesco opening at the edge of the town. 'Well, it's turned out disastrous really for the local retailers,' he said. 'They now, I think, have something like 40 per cent [of the] white goods [market] and 60 per cent [of] food. How they can say it doesn't have an impact?'

Following a public inquiry, a condition was placed on Tesco's planning permission, meaning that only a quarter of the store would be allowed to sell so-called 'comparison goods'. These included things like televisions, DVDs, white goods and clothes. But, the programme claimed, Tesco ignored the condition, 'made no effort to deny' what it was doing and simply submitted a retrospective planning application to legitimize what it was doing anyway.

Tesco brought its resources to bear on a new planning inquiry, which was run at the expense of North Lincolnshire Council taxpayers. Such procedures are a huge burden on councils, costing on average £250,000, lasting months and taking up the time of 'dozens of council officers'. Tesco got its way.

In Stockport, Tesco built one of its largest-format stores, a Tesco Extra hypermarket of 120,000 sq. ft. But it only had planning permission for a smaller store. Stockport Borough Council had insisted on a smaller size 'in the interests of road safety' and 'to protect the vitality and viability of existing centres'. After building had already begun, Tesco retrospectively applied to amend its planning permission, presumably hoping that the council would see the oversized store as irreversible and just accept it.

Speaking to the BBC, Stockport's planning committee chairman, Councillor Kevin Hogg, saw things differently. 'When Tesco actually brought it to our attention, which was after the store had been built, I was actually very, very surprised,' he said. 'They are a major retailer in the country and you would think that they would abide by the planning rules that are set down or were agreed.'[8]

The programme reported that the store opened in November 2004, and in May 2005 the council stated that 'at the present time the whole store is unauthorized and as such does not have a valid planning consent'. In response to a resident's complaint, Tesco wrote 'There was never any attempt . . . to bypass the planning system or mislead the council . . . the Council were aware that we were building the store to the larger size whilst we sought planning consent, a very common procedure across the whole construction industry.' Councillor Hogg said that the council didn't know that the store was 11,000 metres and was only asked to vary the conditions when the store was on the verge of opening. He also said that he worked in the construction industry and as a councillor on the planning committee for sixteen years and this was the first time he came across this 'common procedure'.

Lucy Neville-Rolfe, Tesco Group Corporate Affairs Director, dismissed what happened in Stockport to a Parliamentary Committee as 'a bit of a one-off'.[9] But what about the Friends of the Earth report that found other, similar cases of Tesco playing fast and loose with planning permissions in Bury St Edmunds, Suffolk, Gunness in Lincolnshire, and the Wirral in Merseyside.[10]

In Morton on the Wirral, Tesco was in breach of seven planning conditions and was fined for five of them. But according to Chris Blakeley, the Conservative councillor for the ward, the fines were too small to make a difference. 'They were fined for breach of five conditions, costs to the council; the total bill to Tesco's was £1,843,' he told the BBC, calling the punishments 'daft'. 'Tesco's know that even if the council take them to court the fine they're going to get, the slap on the wrist, is going to be worth absolutely nothing to them; it's peanuts, it's pennies.' Tesco's community action plan sits oddly next to its actual behaviour at the local level. It's something councillor Blakely struggled to reconcile:

> The chief exec, Sir Tony [sic] Leahy, a Liverpool lad – local lad – wouldn't you think he'd have a lot more concern about local communities? He's grown up in a local community, he's made the big time, he's done a real good job of that, but let's have a feel for our communities and not profits. And if Tesco's are going to build a store, then let's build it appropriately, let's stick with the planning conditions that are put upon us and let's be good neighbours.

No one can claim Tesco lacks ingenuity. Sometimes it can achieve results to equal Doctor Who's small-on-the-outside but big-on-the-inside spacecraft, the Tardis. For example, how did Tesco manage to get a 60,000-sq. ft store on to a site in Manchester for which Morrisons, until it was outbid, only planned a store of 35,000 sq. ft? The answer shows Tesco's cunning in getting around any seeming obstacle to growth thrown into its path. It simply built the store on stilts, in a stroke increasing the car parking and shelf space it could use to cram customers in.

In still other examples used by Friends of the Earth campaigners, it has been what Tesco *doesn't* do that can be harmful.[11] By sitting on large amounts of land and, in effect, blocking other kinds of development, Tesco puts its own needs before those of the community. In Rye, East Sussex, the local council ran into problems with its plans to build housing and premises for a doctor's surgery. In St Albans, Hertfordshire, Tesco sat on land that councillors wanted to develop for housing. There were similar problems in Sunderland. In Glasgow's West End, Tesco was in the way of plans to develop public transport.

In the village of Cam in Gloucestershire, parish council plans to regenerate the village around a new village square ran into a Tesco-shaped obstacle. The company held the covenant on a car park that formed part of the council's plans. Tesco refused to release the land from the covenant, leading Liberal Democrat councillor Dennis Andrewartha to comment, in a mixture of frustration and resignation:

> We've reduced our ambitions; we're leaving part of the site that they have effectively got control of, through covenants, unattached; they are in business to make money. Let them say that clearly and honestly and not pretend to deal with communities in an amicable and friendly way, because they don't.[12]

Tesco has become very good at playing the planning game. It is better than its commercial rivals, better than most councils and better than most communities. Gareth Morgan of the Royal Institution of Chartered Surveyors pointed out the regulatory failure and harsh imbalance of the current system to the BBC: 'It is a battle which many councils and local authorities feel that they're losing. Tesco's understand the law specifically in relation to the planning system far better than even many local authorities do.'

The anomaly between Tesco's newly stated commitment to communities and the reality is Orwellian in tone and scale. Lindsay Mackie of nef was present when Tesco launched its 'good neighbour' policy. More community consultation was high on its agenda. But when Terry Leahy was asked what Tesco would do if, after consulting communities, it was told that a store wasn't wanted, he replied that the company would have to seek out the silent majority which *would* be in favour.

Size provides Tesco with an automatic advantage when it comes to planning, partly because it can outbid and out-campaign anyone in its path. The reason Tesco has such a big battle fund couldn't be more ironic. Many of Tesco's beleaguered suppliers probably don't even realize that it is *they* who are largely paying for the supermarkets' creeping expansion and growing market domination.

How to Borrow £2 Billion for Free

'We are sensitive to both the opportunities and concerns raised when we invest.'

Tesco website

A refrain frequently heard from defenders of Tesco is that the company is tough, but fair. Criticized for its hardball tactics in driving down prices paid to suppliers, the excuse is that it is driving efficiency gains and passing on the benefits. Since Tesco's recent very public conversion to corporate social responsibility, it now promises to 'listen' more, even if only to catch problems before disgruntled suppliers go to the media to complain.

Investment advisers, regulators and friends in the big business community all seem to echo the view that the company might negotiate hard, but that it is a model of efficiency, sets an exemplary standard for the market and wins by playing within the rules. But rules can be blurred, or be made up along the way. Rules can be written by, or on behalf of, the people they are meant to keep in check. Is Tesco really so profitable because it is a better-run company (remember the now-certainly-superseded profit of £2.2 billion), or is it playing a dirty game, littered with professional fouls?

Britain's leading business paper the *Financial Times* certainly seems to think so. In a major investigation of how the big supermarkets managed their finances, the paper discovered that they, and Tesco and Asda/Wal-Mart in particular, were increasingly relying on a remarkable accounting trick. It was a way of handling how they paid suppliers that left the supermarket with hundreds of millions extra to invest in their own growth, and also left especially their poorer suppliers more hard up.

Because of the way that Tesco negotiates terms and conditions, it had managed in effect to borrow – and here's that number again – yes, £2.2 billion from its suppliers. It happens because of the way shops work. Tesco, however, managed to set the rules in such a way that it ended up profiting much more than similar businesses in the US or mainland Europe. Because retailers like supermarkets do not pay up front for stock, and turn stock into cash the moment they sell it, in the gap between selling goods and paying their suppliers they get, in effect, a loan. The larger the volume of stock they turn over in this way, the bigger the effective loan. All retailers do this to some degree, but the difference with Tesco and Asda/Wal-Mart was that their suppliers seemed to be providing them with 'large and increasing amounts of finance', so large, in fact, that the amount Tesco held in credit from suppliers – £2.2 billion – was equal to its soon-to-be-announced annual profits.[13]

We Know What You're Doing

> 'The supermarkets have pretty much got an armlock on you people . . .'
>
> Tony Blair addressing a public meeting
> of farmers, March 2001

Investment analysis firm Citigroup says, in relation to Tesco's track record with its suppliers, that 'repeated investigations have not found any evidence against Tesco'. This is a line repeated by the supermarkets' trade association, the British Retail Consortium, and countless supermarket executives. It is, however, unequivocally wrong.

Regulators have found Tesco, and most other top supermarkets, guilty of multiple malpractices. What gives rise to the confusion, and explains why the sector thinks Tesco has been let off, is that regulators − somehow spellbound by the market's biggest player − merely choose not to take any effective action against it. The list of official charges is, though, almost exhaustingly comprehensive.

Given the growing furore over supermarkets and the difficulty in calling them to account, it's worth taking a little time to see what the government and regulators already know about them, and have known for some time. The following revelations come from a major investigation into the big supermarkets at the start of the millennium, after which no meaningful action was taken.[14]

The Competition Commission investigated the supermarkets' manipulation of the prices and their treatment of suppliers. In the market for 'one-stop shopping' the inquiry found that five supermarkets − Asda/Wal-Mart, Morrisons, Safeway (since taken over by Morrisons), Sainsbury's and Tesco − all had 'power' over the market. It found that three pricing practices 'gave rise to a complex monopoly situation' and that two of those also 'operated against the public interest':

1. Tesco, among others, 'engaged in the practice of persistently selling some frequently purchased products below cost'. This was seen to undermine smaller stores that were often relied upon by 'the elderly and less mobile'. This, they repeated, 'operates against the public interest'.

2. Tesco, among others, used 'price flexing' – 'the practice of varying prices in different geographical locations in the light of local competitive conditions, such variation not being related to costs'. In other words, supermarkets charge what they can get away with once the competition is killed off, or when there wasn't any there in the first place. This, the Commission concluded, 'operates against the public interest' because customers end up paying more.

3. Tesco and others, in spite of persistent claims to super-markets being 'hotly competitive', in fact 'adopted pricing structures and regimes that, by focusing competition on a relatively small proportion of their product lines, restrict active competition on the majority of product lines'. Not such a competitive sector, after all, then. In practice what this means is that the stores were tempting people in by offering a few popular products cheaply (the cost of the offer typically being met by the poor supplier, not the supermarket), but once inside, everything else was for sale at top prices. It should be noted that this is a travesty of how market forces are supposed to work. 'Perfectly in-formed' consumers are supposed to switch between sellers item by item. But in a supermarket, the kind of compar-ison shopping that you can do in a real market, like a street market, is, conveniently for the supermarket, impossible. The Commission concluded that 'this distorts competition in the retail supply of groceries'.

The Commission found that Tesco in particular paid suppliers consistently 4 per cent below the industry average. But then, having recognized a whole series of problems, the regulators suffered some sort of brainstorm or loss of nerve and, extra-ordinarily, chose not to act. They were even aware at the time exactly how peculiar their response was, commenting, 'We recognize that it is unusual, although not unprecedented, for the CC [Competition Commission] to recommend no remedy for identified adverse effects.'

Two rather odd excuses were given: first, that the market was 'generally competitive'. Looked at from the point of view of smaller, and independent stores, however, the tactics identified by the regulators demonstrate exactly the opposite. They are anti-competitive practices, examples of how the supermarkets have rigged the grocery sector, abused their power and manipulated the consumer. The second odd excuse was that any action would have to be 'proportionate'. Given the vagueness and flexibility of the term, the Commission never explained why it couldn't find a more 'proportionate' action than no action at all. But that little list of bad behaviour was just a warm-up to how Tesco and some of the other big players have treated their suppliers. Take a breath.

In spite of what the Commission described as a 'climate of apprehension' among suppliers fearful of losing contracts, a list of fifty-two alleged abusive practices was put to Tesco and the other main supermarkets, despite the fact that 'most suppliers were unwilling to be named, or to name the main party that was the subject of the allegation'.

The Commission's legalese often hides how the supermarket's behaviour, in economic terms, has brutally undermined their livelihoods. The allegations included 'requiring or requesting from some of their suppliers various non-cost-related payments or discounts, sometimes retrospectively' (translation: demands for cash); 'imposing charges and making changes to contractual arrangements without adequate notice' (translation: further demands for cash); and 'unreasonably transferring risks from the main party to the supplier' (translation: making suppliers walk in front through the economic minefield).

Figure 4: Treatment of suppliers by Tesco

● = reported by suppliers and denied by Tesco
➤ = reported by suppliers and conceded by Tesco

● [Tesco] required or requested payments from suppliers as a condition of stocking and displaying their products, or as a pre-condition for being on [its] list of suppliers.

➤ [Tesco] required or requested suppliers to give [it] an improvement in terms in return for increasing the range or depth of distribution of their products [in its] stores.

● [Tesco] required sole supply of a product (other than retailer's own-label), i.e. that the supplier did not supply the product to any other retailer or multiple.

➤ [Tesco] required or requested a financial contribution from a supplier in return for the supplier's products being promoted in the store during the year (described by some suppliers as 'pay to play' or 'TAA').

● [Tesco] required suppliers to give overriding or 'in anticipation' discounts.

● [Tesco] sought discounts from suppliers retrospectively, which reduced the price of the product agreed at the time of the sale.

● [Tesco] debited suppliers' invoices or otherwise claimed from them without their agreement.

● [Tesco] required or requested suppliers to make payments to cover product wastage.

● [Tesco] required or requested suppliers to contribute specifically to the costs of store refurbishment or to the opening of a new store.

> ➤ [Tesco] de-listed a supplier or caused a supplier to reduce prices at [its] request under threat of de-listing.

> ➤ [Tesco] suggested to a supplier that [it] would de-list a product and later withdrew the suggestion, having received a discount on an unrelated product or a general improvement in terms.

> ➤ [Tesco] required suppliers to purchase goods or services from designated companies, e.g. hauliers, packaging companies, labelling companies.

> ● [Tesco] instructed intermediaries (e.g. packing houses) not to allow goods to be handled or processed that were intended for delivery to other retailers, where those goods originated from producers with which [Tesco] had ceased trading.

> ➤ [Tesco] required or requested suppliers to make a financial contribution to the costs of bar code changes or reduced price-marked packs.

> ➤ [Tesco] invited suppliers to make contributions to charitable organizations (directly or by participation in events designed to raise money for such bodies).

> ● [Tesco] required or requested suppliers to make payments for a specific promotion (e.g. gondola ends, advertising allowances) where the payments exceeded the actual costs to [Tesco].

(Source: Competition Commission, 2000)

The point, which the Commission directly acknowledged, is that whatever Tesco and the other big players asked for, they got. Whenever a supermarket with 'buyer power' requested something, it was, in effect a 'requirement' over which the supplier had no choice. Crucially, though yet to be properly appreciated or understood, the Commission set the threshold for super-markets to be able to wield potentially abusive 'buyer power' at 8 per cent of the grocery market. Tesco, today, has over 31 per cent. It is worth quoting the Commission's conclusion to its deliberations in full. It found that Tesco, though not alone, had:

> . . . sufficient buyer power that thirty of the practices identified . . . adversely affect the competitiveness of some of their suppliers and distort competition in the supplier market – and in some cases in the retail market – for the supply of groceries. We find that these practices give rise to a second complex monopoly situation.

The consequences of the situation were so damaging to farmers and producers around the country that they would undermine investment and innovation, 'leading to lower quality and less consumer choice' – and they were instigated by supermarkets that promise, above all, consumer choice. The supermarkets' ruthless pursuit of profit was found to be undermining the system upon which they, and we, ultimately depend. Such can be the myopia of big business. A full twenty-seven of the abusive practices towards suppliers by supermarkets with above 8 per cent market share also operated 'against the public interest', concluded the Commission.

What do you think the regulators' response was, as guardians of the public interest? The Commission recommended a Code of Practice. As required by law, it was then passed to the OFT. There, with close involvement from the supermarkets them-selves, the code was first watered down and then – surprise, surprise! – never used because the suppliers were too afraid of reprisals from the retailers. This sorry situation led eventually to the supermarkets getting bigger, fewer, more powerful and to yet another investigation from the regulators.

Tesco might defend itself by saying that it was only doing the same things other big supermarkets were doing. This would be a strange defence, a bit like a mugger in the middle of a crime wave excusing his actions by saying that there's a lot of it about. The question remains: if all the big supermarkets were 'at it', what makes Tesco different? Buried in the notes and annexes to the Commission's report in 2000 are some fascinating clues that point to the different culture of the company.

All the supermarkets were asked by the Commission to respond to the complaints from suppliers. Most responses 'correlated' with the complaints, that is to say, the supermarkets recognized and acknowledged what they were being accused of.

But Tesco didn't. It refused, initially, to admit to the full list of abusive practices it was charged with. It responded 'on the basis of company policy' – rather than how its buyers were actually behaving towards their suppliers – which meant it wouldn't admit what it was doing wrong. When pushed by the regulator, Tesco admitted to four more abusive practices, but this still left an 'inconsistency' between charges and confessions.

Clearly mistrusting what they were being told by Tesco, the Commission put four sample complaints to the store for which it had documentary evidence. They included:

. . . a letter from Tesco sent to a packhouse instructing that produce from either of two growers that had previously, but no longer, supplied Tesco was no longer to be used in any facility used for Tesco produce. Failure would result in immediate suspension of the packhouse's business with Tesco.

. . . a general store in Tredegar had begun undercutting an adjacent Tesco store on the price of bread, supplied to both outlets by a local bakery. The Tesco store manager had allegedly threatened to cancel its contract with the bakery if it did not persuade the general store to increase its price. The general store has since ceased trading.

. . . a letter from Tesco to its suppliers in which it informed them that there were too many invoice queries due to suppliers not invoicing at the correct case cost. The letter said that, in future, if these queries continued after suppliers had been contacted, an administration charge would be raised to cover the costs incurred within Tesco. These charges were as follows: £1,000 for the same query two weeks running, and £1,000 for every week thereafter until resolved.

. . . a small supplier of ethnic foods, now in receivership, said that one of Tesco's 'Category Managers' had written to the company, in respect of a price-marking problem . . . to the effect that Tesco would impose fines of £10,000 per product.[15]

It's clear, rereading the Commission's report, that it felt other supermarkets had been more honest and cooperative with the investigation; it singled out Tesco for being unhelpful. Compared to how the other supermarkets responded to allegations, Tesco's reaction seems to have been, 'Wasn't me, guv.'

But give the company the benefit of the doubt. Leaping forward to 2006, and to a new investigation into the big supermarkets, surely there has been enough time to right all these wrongs, hasn't there?

After repeatedly refusing to re-examine the supermarkets' growing control of the grocery sector, the OFT gave in to a combination of legal challenges and public pressure. The Association of Convenience Stores won a legal appeal against the OFT, and advocacy from assorted groups ranging from the environmental campaigners at Friends of the Earth to my own organization, nef, pushed it to take action.

The result of its investigation was mixed. On one hand, it led to a fuller assessment by its sister regulator, the Competition Commission. On the other hand, it was seized as an opportunity to attack the very planning system that had been used, half successfully, to restrain the rash of out-of-town supermarkets that had been killing off town centres. The OFT's initial conclusions, six years on from the previous big inquiry, made interesting reading; nevertheless, it concluded, 'There are a number of features of the market that can reasonably be suspected of distorting competition and . . . the evidence suggests that consumers may be being harmed as a result.'[16] In particular, the OFT found evidence that the 'buyer power' of the big supermarkets had gone up since 2000; big supermarkets were demanding ever-lower prices from suppliers than those on offer to others, including smaller independents and wholesalers; greater concentration of power and market share in the hands of the big supermarkets was harming consumer choice because it undermined other types of shops as well as the viability of 'alternative business models including wholesale distribution to the convenience store sector'; the large supermarkets' use of below-cost selling and price flexing was distorting competition.

Of course, the biggest of all the supermarkets that these findings related to was Tesco. The important thing to remember is that these are not the accusations of hot-headed campaigners, but the conclusions of the government's official regulator. The baton was passed to the Competition Commission, and it started gathering its own evidence. To appreciate some of the complaints against Tesco means grasping the often-complex logistics of retailing, but here's a flavour of what is still going on, taken from submissions to the inquiry that began in 2006:

Brendan Barber, General Secretary of the Trades Union Congress, wrote in his evidence that 'below cost selling is having an even greater distorting effect now than in 2000', and that the supermarkets' anti-competitive behaviour would lead to 'an increasing number of small efficient retailers being forced to the wall and local price reductions leading to price hikes for consumers in the medium to long term.'[17]

The National Farmers' Union (NFU) reported an increasing number of complaints about the treatment of its members by the big supermarkets.[18] The sorts of complaints included:

keeping suppliers supplicant by insisting that they supply no other competitor; manipulating contracts to prevent suppliers getting big enough to have power to negotiate with the supermarkets;

imposing 'across the board price cuts with little warning and no discussion';

demands on suppliers to provide staff to the supermarkets to stack shelves;

suppliers being forced to pay the costs of audits that the supermarkets need to carry out;

suppliers being forced to pay the difference when a retailer fails to meet its profit target;

suppliers having to pay to win a contract and again a share of turnover to keep it (I cannot explain how this differs from bribery, or from the protection rackets run by organized crime);

suppliers, especially firms supplying milk and red meat, being forced to 're-tender' for contracts and in the process make further up-front payments, recently 'amounting to millions of pounds'.

The NFU apparently concluded that the supermarkets did not want greater transparency in the supply chain because 'a certain amount of "fog' is good for their business'.

Unsurprisingly, Tesco also does not pay its invoices within terms, either. According to a report published by *Accountancy Age*, Tesco only paid 67 per cent of its invoices below the value of £5,000 on time.[19] There also seemed to be plenty of evidence for Tesco using predatory below-cost selling. It's thought that superstores generally make a gross margin on what they sell of around 25–28 per cent. Discounts above that rate mean the supermarket is probably selling 'below cost'. It's one thing for large supermarkets to use such tactics against each other (apart from the fact that it will probably be the poor supplier footing the bill), but used against smaller independents it is a clear abuse of market power. The Association of Convenience Stores provided three sample cases of Tesco using below-cost selling between 2004–05, at Withernsea, East Yorkshire; Bellshill, near Glasgow; and Hull. Discounts between 33–40 per cent were being offered. In Withernsea, they were used to 'secure the competitive position of Tesco against a successful independent operator, Proudfoot'.[20]

The Forum for Private Business criticized Tesco's use of another tactic: phoney promotions, where prices are raised only in order for them to be lowered to create the impression of a price cut. This practice is lawful, but it can mislead customers. The 'most extreme' case involved alcohol. Tesco 'raised the price of a 24-pack of 330ml cans of Carlsberg Export lager from £11.98 to £24.99. Soon after, the price was 'cut' to £12.48, with the offer promoted as a 'half-price' sale.'[21]

Downward supermarket pressure on the price of cheap clothes (think of Tesco's famous £3 pair of jeans), led mostly by Tesco and Asda/Wal-Mart, has had serious consequences for workers overseas, according to leading international development groups:

> ... [A spate of] fatal industrial accidents in Bangladesh, an export market led by Asda-WalMart and Tesco, demonstrates the impact of supermarket buying practices such as squeezed prices, and the flight to China on working conditions across the sector.[22]

Treatment of Britain's favourite fruit, the banana, reveals how overseas suppliers can pay a high cost when they get caught up in price wars between supermarkets. In 2001 and 2005, following its rival Asda/Wal-Mart, Tesco slashed the price of bananas, but passed much of the costs on to suppliers. To save itself time and money, Tesco also insisted that its suppliers begin delivering the fruit on wheeled trolleys rather than the usual wooden pallets. Suppliers had to meet the cost of the new system, which, because fewer bananas could be loaded on to a lorry, also meant more road trips and higher transport costs.[23]

As if all this weren't enough, Tesco can also make the roof cave in – literally. The company obtained planning permission for a store at Gerrards Cross, outside London, against the wishes of local residents. It 'paid its way on to the high street', based on a promise to redevelop the town's railway station. This then went horribly wrong when a new tunnel being built to allow the store to sit above the tracks collapsed, causing huge delays and inconvenience to the town and commuters.[24] BBC Radio 4's *Face the Facts* programme revealed later how '27,000 tonnes of lumpy grey incinerator waste' that packed the tunnel walls before the collapse were dumped in the Buckinghamshire countryside without the necessary planning permission.[25]

Perversely, having called on the Competition Commission to investigate the supermarkets, the OFT then immediately appeared to undermine the inquiry. Along with suppliers, small shops are among those worst hit by supermarket power. As such, they are likely to be among those with the most to say. Yet no sooner had the investigation begun than OFT head John Fingleton 'urged smaller retailers not to get involved in the inquiry'. Speaking to *The Grocer*, he said small shops should worry more about attracting customers: 'My advice to them is to put their focus elsewhere.'[26] This intervention seemed inappropriate in an investigation of which the OFT was part.

In February 2005, Margaret Beckett, then Secretary of State for the Environment, said:

> Supermarkets have to realize they and their customers need a sustainable UK-based supply chain, and that it is not in their interests to squeeze suppliers to the point of elimination.[27]

But when market power combines with a singular focus on the bottom line, a kind of unwavering tunnel vision seems to blind companies to the impacts they have.

One company that stares those consequences in the face is Grant Thornton, a major UK financial services company with over 40,000 private and corporate clients, and part of an international group with member firms in 110 countries. It is a major player in its field but stands outside the four giant accountancy firms that service most of the largest UK corporations. In that sense, it holds a view of the economy that is slightly more independent of the influence of big business. Because one of the services it provides is helping companies face insolvency, it is in the embarrassing position of doing well when some of its clients do badly; income from its department dealing in 'corporate recovery and insolvency' went up from £44–£47 million in the year to 2004. But, almost uniquely, Grant Thornton is prepared to speak out and criticize the circumstances that increase its own business.

In 2005 Duncan Swift, who heads the firm's Food and Agribusiness Recovery Group, accused the OFT's weak handling of the supermarket code of practice of papering over the cracks 'of a food supply chain that is increasingly finding itself under major financial distress caused by the market power wielded by the major multiples'.[28] He then said, 'The code is toothless, and vague proposals to use it more effectively will not make it bite.' Swift went public to highlight that several major food groups had gone out of business in the previous three years, and that in his experience 'supermarket misconduct' lay 'behind more than one of these failures'. He called for much clearer contracts to be enforced to protect suppliers from the supermarkets' caprice, and for the government to create a new Supermarket Ombudsman to match the ombudsman that exists for the banking sector. Prophetically, he warned in August of that year, 'Failure to act will result in more failures within the sector and an impoverishment of the choice the market offers.'[29]

Sure enough, inaction led to exactly that result. In July 2006 Grant Thornton reported that the number of food, drink and tobacco retailers had nearly halved during the previous eleven years. During 2005 alone there were 45 per cent more insolvencies compared to the previous year.[30]

It's not only small firms that suffer. One producer that went out of business, losing 690 jobs, was Northern Foods' Trafford Park Bakery. Tesco was its main customer, and union fingers pointed at the supermarket as partly responsible. Northern Foods had been in trouble and, under its new chief executive, Tesco was told it was 'no longer willing to produce' at the bakery on Tesco's terms. The problem for the bakery was that three-quarters of its business lay with just five supermarket chains. It had become dependent, and had nowhere else to turn.[31]

CHAPTER FIVE

Parasitic Retail: Why Too Many Chain Stores Kill Communities

'Sidewalk contacts are the small change from which a city's wealth of public life may grow.'

Jane Jacobs, author of *The Death and Life of Great American Cities* and *The Nature of Economies*

It is easy to look at something and not see what is really there. In 1791 Captain George Vancouver led two ships, HMS Discovery and HMS Chatham, to chart the coastline of what is now British Columbia, the west coast of Canada (and, yes, they named the city and island after him). He was one of many early European explorers to be utterly perplexed and sometimes intimidated by what he saw on the water along the coastline. The indigenous Indian population had canoes 'passing and repassing' his ships. Neither the latest scientific aids to seafaring nor the rationalism of his worldview could explain the scene.

'The native craft were as inscrutable as water beetles in their multitudinous comings and goings,' writes Jonathan Raban in *Passage to Juneau*. 'Full of obscure purpose, they paddled out to an arbitrary point in midstream, stopped for half an hour, then paddled off at another angle.' The Europeans' incomprehension led them to the false conclusion that the people they encountered, who inexplicably and consistently failed to take the shortest, most utilitarian route from A to B, were either lazy, superstitious, stupid or about to attack them.

The truth to which the Europeans were blinded by their conceptual blinkers was actually quite straightforward. The indigenous people were as naturally at home on the water as the Europeans were on land. Instead of fearing the lonely expanse of ocean and, say, only venturing into it under force or due to necessity, that was the attitude they took to much of the land, fearing the dark forests full of predators, myths and unknown threats.

Along the many inlets and around the uncounted islands, according to Raban, 'the sea provided the Indians with a neighbourhood, around which they loitered, scuffed their heels, and traded small talk . . . the water's surface was a broad public arena on which most of daily life took place.' Had Captain Vancouver remembered the weekly market in his home town of King's Lynn, England, he would have recognized exactly the same seemingly random comings and goings, the 'advances, retreats, crossings-over, and deviations that sociable pedestrians practise everywhere'.[1]

It is easy to be deceived. It was easy for planners and local authorities across Britain to have believed that crowding their towns with instantly recognizable national and international chain stores could lead to vitality and success. Until recently, they certainly looked like success; they had an official stamp of approval. Glossy information packs for government conferences on urban regeneration carried pictures of the big supermarkets, making the two seem synonymous. It became competitive. A 'me too' shopping development factor came into play. Chain stores dangled their possible arrival or defection as bait to get the best deals from local authorities, most of whom were desperate to be the first in an area with a big brand, or to catch up with the next town that already had one. How quickly things can change. Today, one town being the clone of another no longer seems such a great idea. What were we thinking?

Fashions pass. Clone towns now seem as attractive as kipper ties, flared trousers, mullets, bad perms or Turkey Twizzlers. But there were other deceptions. Whereas locally rooted businesses tend to irrigate wealth around a community, remotely owned chain stores can suck money out like giant cash vacuum cleaners. The big supermarkets may have put tens of thousands of existing local shops out of business, but they didn't replace all their functions. You could buy food and drink in the new superstores, but it became apparent only slowly that they didn't stock the intangible ingredients that first built and then held together communities.

Josephine's Shop

Josephine ran my local shop. Its wares were basic: bread, milk, papers and magazines, some batteries, tissues and razors. Add sweets and a few tins, and the shelves were full. It was also small; more than three people at a time could make it feel crowded. It was typical of the sort of surviving convenience shop you can find in and around south London housing estates, just the sort of place that ambitious, image-conscious local councillors and planners dream of replacing with shiny, branded, chain retailers. But this was Josephine's shop. She cared about the people who came in, and what happened in the streets around her. At any time of day, elderly people from the surrounding estate would come in to swap news and gossip. Because of that, she would know who needed looking out for. If anyone's routine changed or was broken, she would check up on them to see if they needed help. She made connections that get designed out of the working lives of closely monitored chain store managers, and of their even more minutely observed shiftworkers.

Josephine had what I would call big-time religion. A Christian radio station always played in the background. When there were problems, and there were many, she would finish every sentence meaningfully, asking God to give her strength. Her windows and

door were often striped with tape, holding together glass cracked by assaults from gangs of local boys. She was resilient, and had to be, because she also had to compete with a huge, new supermarket on the nearby high street.

Once, when she had to close the shop for two weeks because of illness, I saw her regulars instead picking up their basics at that supermarket. It was striking – as though they had stopped taking happy pills. Instead of the animated quality they displayed when shopping at Josephine's, their shoulders were slumped. They seemed downcast and dejected. Instead of living the day, they seemed to be merely surviving it. At one checkout I saw an elderly man, a regular of Josephine's, hopefully, longingly, trying to engage the till worker in the kind of conversation he was used to having with Josephine.

But the queue was stretching back into the store. The woman at the checkout looked at him, tired and hassled. Checkout workers are trained for speed and turnover. They are, quite literally, given scripts to control their interactions with customers: you offer cash-back, draw attention to the special promotion and offer to pack the customer's bag. You do not fall into conversation about whether Mrs Brown from no. 36 has been in for her milk today, and if she has had her dressings changed on her sore leg. The till worker was thrown. Processing endless baskets of shopping and using a script like a corporate film extra to manage engagement with the wider world does not equip you for being spoken to as a human being. She looked at the man with mild panic, then gestured to the queue and grunted. Dismissed, he plodded off to the busy street with a lumpy bag of own-brand shopping and, I'm guessing, the sinking sensation you get from an elevator that moves too quickly.

Josephine had no assistant. She was literally a 'sole trader', as such businesses get called. But she was not afraid to confront the gangs of young men that gathered on the pavement outside, and she waded in to stop any bullying. She gave work to a local window cleaner rather than to a big contract-cleaning firm, and employed local boys to deliver newspapers, giving them a little independence, income and self-respect. Seeing her most days made me happy. In a big, alienating city like London, she recognized my face and asked after my family. It was a small, important connection.

Locally owned, independent shops relate to communities around them in a manner entirely different to retail chains. For a supermarket or pizza restaurant chain to open in an area, the local population's 'demographics' have to match carefully worked-out economic criteria. This also works in reverse, and means that chain outlets can be fair-weather friends: if depression hits and the flow of cash changes, don't be surprised to see the instantly recognizable, once longed-for shopfronts of the clone stores empty as quickly as they filled. In the US, for example, at any one time hundreds of abandoned Wal-Mart stores that have already killed off local shops sit empty as soon as the management decides it's time to move on.

Independent, locally owned stores, on the other hand, tend to be more strongly committed to the communities in which they're based. To weather hard times and stay open to serve the community, they are more likely to use up savings and go into debt, even if it causes them hardship. For similar reasons, there is often a time lag of two to three years between big supermarkets opening and small independent retailers going out of business. When the savings have gone and the supermarket's anti-competitive practices have done their work, the uneven retail playing field exhausts the small business, and it closes.

Josephine's shop closed. Only afterwards did I realize, or find the words to describe, the most important thing that her shop provided to the local community. It wasn't the bread, milk or cornflakes that really mattered. Josephine sold the social glue that holds neighbourhoods together. She was a key thread in the local community fabric, and when she went, it became weaker.

She saw her 'shareholders' constantly, walking, talking and living around her, unlike a big supermarket that has to please a faceless group of shareholders in the City who are unlikely ever even to visit the south London estate where Josephine worked. She listened to the troubles of local people, heard their jokes, looked out for them day-to-day and made them feel more at home in the world. She ran a business fused with social purpose, rather than one that creates human problems. Where the supermarkets bring boredom, stress, frustration and a feeling of being overwhelmed, Josephine brought interest, calm, satisfaction and a sense of being part of a community.

Consumer research shows that the benefits Josephine brought to her community are mirrored more generally by local shops. More than vicars and priests, and more than local councillors

and the police combined, nearly three-quarters of people iden-
tify local shopkeepers and traders as the 'heart and soul' of
community, and over half are prepared to change their shopping
habits to support them. Middle-aged people see the threat to
their local areas presented by the major supermarkets as second
only to that of crime.[2] Findings from the shopkeeper's point of
view are similar. Over half say that customers come into their
shops for conversation and local news as much as to buy things.
On average, a local shopkeeper will know seven out of every ten
of their customers.[3]

As Professor Ian Clarke of Lancaster University Management
School puts it:

> Supermarkets risk becoming accused of being instrumental in
> the reduction of choice and diversity, rather than the pioneers
> of it . . . people seem to be saying that they value the genuine
> diversity and local knowledge that smaller locally-owned out-
> lets bring to their communities, and they need to be protected.
> Let us hope such calls are heard and that urgent action is taken
> before such cherished diversity disappears forever.[4]

Compare Josephine's relationship to the community around her
with that of the Tesco Express stores in Sussex accused by the
police of acting as if they were 'above the law.' Jean Irving,
violent crime reduction manager for the police in West Sussex,
alleged that several outlets repeatedly sold alcohol to under-age
drinkers, and failed to show 'due diligence or any responsibility
to the local community.' As a result the police called on the local
council to revoke the stores' licenses to sell alcohol. 'We've tried
mediation on this but if it had worked we wouldn't be going to
review,' said Irving. 'I just wish they spent as much time training
against under-age sales and protecting our children as they do
on promoting their Clubcard.'[5]

So, if the purpose of our economic system is to give us all better lives, wouldn't it make sense to support the arms of businesses that are truly connected to the body of society, rather than subsidizing those businesses that leave us feeling poorer and more miserable?

Annexation, Not Regeneration: The Story of Queen's Market

Tough choices – it's what we're told government is all about. The same goes for local government, where decisions about life on our streets get made. So when a supermarket promises jobs, cheap food, investment and a community asset, it's hard for councillors and planners to say no. But do the claims add up? Or can the presence of a big supermarket lead to the opposite: fewer and lower-skilled jobs, food that costs more, a haemorrhage of money from the neighbourhood and an overall effect that dissolves community cohesion?

Just such a tough choice had to be made in Newham, a deprived part of east London. Visiting Newham in February 2000, Gordon Brown, as Chancellor of the Exchequer, said in a speech:

> Opportunity for all means a Britain where all have the opportunity not just to work, but to work their way up, to gain promotion, start a business, become self-employed, upgrade their skills and rise as far as their talents and potential can take them . . . And too little attention has been give to deprived areas, to women and ethnic minority communities.[6]

In 2006, Tesco's main competitor Asda/Wal-Mart wanted to build a store on the site of the popular, long-standing Queen's Market. Convinced by the potential benefits of having another new supermarket, Newham Council announced plans in association with a property developer to demolish the old market. But it soon emerged that the council, like many others, had taken many of the supermarket's supposed benefits on trust. In a statement under the heading of 'Regeneration', the council assured its residents that a new Asda/Wal-Mart store 'will benefit everyone'.[7] But the council hadn't understood the existing benefits of the current market, or the damage to the fabric of the local economy that a new supermarket could cause.

Queen's Market is one of around seventy such markets in London, and has been going for more than a century. You can walk around stalls heaving with everything from saltfish, spices and callaloo to apples and pears, pots and pans, exotic fabrics and beauty products. You'll hear Cockney slang being spoken, along with Romanian, Hindi, Bengali and 'Banglish'.

A study commissioned from researchers at nef breathed life into Joni Mitchell's musical refrain, 'You don't know what you've got till it's gone.'[8] It quotes local people describing the market as 'multi-cultural coexistence at its best'. The leading British poet Benjamin Zephaniah said:

> I have spoken to people who recall when the customers were all German immigrants and someone else who remembers when they were all Jewish. I go there sometimes and you see the white, middle-aged guys who sell to the Asian ladies and have learned a bit of Urdu.

The study, led by my colleague Guy Rubin, revealed that the market serves over 400,000 customers per year and sells food at less than half the price of another nearby Asda/Wal-Mart, based on a comparable basket of goods. (Supermarkets are more expensive in other areas, too. Research by the consumer magazine *Which?* revealed some of the growing range of supermarket banking services to be overpriced and poor value. For example, the annual interest rate on a Tesco credit card was found to be 12.9 per cent, more than double the rate available on a card from the mainstream account provider Halifax, at 5.9 per cent.[9]) Not only is the food cheaper, but the informal culture that allows bargaining over prices and sees food reduced in price towards the end of the day particularly helps shoppers on low incomes who can adapt their shopping patterns to get even better deals. In markets, some food is even given away for free around closing time rather than being thrown away as rubbish, as would happen at a supermarket.

This matters because half the council wards in Newham are designated as 'food deserts', meaning that affordable fruit and vegetables are hard to come by. Overall, the cost of food for Newham residents represents a much larger share of their income than the national average – around one and a half times as much.

Around eight out of ten people interviewed for the Queen's Market study also said that in addition to the usual range of goods, they could find special and ethnic foods unavailable at a supermarket. Because the market has evolved with the local community, what it sells mirrors what the community wants. Supermarkets, on the other hand, are parachuted in with ready-made lists of what they are going to sell, dictated with minor variations by highly centralized management structures and supply chains.

There are other, unexpected benefits of the local market. For people concerned about the environmental damage of fruit and vegetables being flown around the world, the local popularity of the West Indian leaf vegetable callaloo has led to it being grown locally, especially for the market.

Unlike any mainstream supermarket I have ever encountered, over two-thirds of the market's customers are attracted by its atmosphere and the ethnic diversity expressed in the range of food, textiles, clothing and artefacts.

So much for the cultural value of the market that provides the local community with a better shopping experience and more influence over the goods available (consumer power, much praised by free-market economists, usually remains mythical), the market also provides astounding economic benefits, too.

Compared to a mainstream supermarket store, the market creates more and better jobs. It employs 581 people, over 300 of whom live in the immediate area. For every square metre of space that the market occupies it creates more than twice the number of jobs compared to a typical food superstore such as Tesco or Asda/Wal-Mart.

Supermarket workers have to endure monotonous and rigorously policed tasks like operating checkouts and stacking shelves. In comparison, the skills developed by market workers are more diverse and allow for greater individuality.

There are other, invisible benefits to shoppers in the market that would not have shown up in the supermarket plans seen by the council. The market traders know much more about what they are selling; someone shopping at one of the stalls would be able to ask for advice on how to cook sometimes unfamiliar produce, and even pick up recipes.

None of this should have come as news to the council. These things have been understood by academics for years, as this observation from a decade-old textbook shows in a discussion of, in other words, de-skilling:

> The demand for the all-round grocery clerk, fruiterer and vegetable dealer, dairyman, butcher, and so forth has long been replaced by a labor configuration in the supermarkets which calls for truck unloaders, shelf stockers, checkout clerks, meat wrappers, and meat cutters; of these only the

last retain any semblance of skill, and none require any general knowledge of retail trade.[10]

The list of the advantages of the market goes on and on. Typically, the monopoly powers of the 'big four' supermarkets make it increasingly difficult for small food businesses to break into the grocery market. So-called 'barriers to entry' are impossibly high. People who come from black and minority ethnic backgrounds face even more obstacles. But Queen's Market helps provide an answer to both problems. Low market rents and site flexibility were the stated reasons for the great majority of the traders being at the market. Against a backdrop of rising chain-retail dominance, the market acts as a perfect nursery for independent enterprise and supports self-motivated entrepreneurs. All this happens without a single patronizing government scheme in sight, just by letting the market 'do its thing'. If the local council actually listened to the traders and invested more in developing the market's existing strengths, the benefits to the community and local economy could be even greater.

As though things couldn't get any better, Queen's Market also directly generates over £11 million for the local economy in a year, and by attracting extra custom it creates an extra £1.8 million worth of spending for other local businesses surrounding the market. This is in stark contrast to the way that large supermarkets take business away from small, competing shops.

Here is the power of the supermarket myth. Here you can see how those millions spent on advertising, on legal and planning expertise and on managing relationships with civil servants and elected representatives at the local and national levels can lead to perfectly irrational economic decisions.

Queen's Market provides more jobs and cheaper food than a supermarket, and it does so in a deprived area where both are sorely needed. It also provides local atmosphere and diversity as a buffer against the march of clone stores.

But, blinded by the hype, Newham Council was prepared to support a plan that would reduce the size of the market and its financial contribution to the local area; the range and quality of jobs available; the range of goods and services; access to afford-able fresh food; the number of opportunities for business start-ups; and the close links between local retailers and the local community. An independent inquiry by The East London Communities Organisation found 'almost no enthusiasm for the Council's plans'.[11]

The nef study suggested an alternative that could 'retain the distinctive nature of this thriving market' and recommended an investigation into 'other forms of social and community own-ership and management for Queen's Market' that would give both traders and the community more control.

The council's short-sightedness became clear in agreeing to plans that faced widespread local opposition, but it was spared blushing. In response to an increasingly high-profile campaign that saw the market feature in a major-release documentary film *Wal-Mart: The High Cost of Low Price*, Asda/Wal-Mart withdrew from the development, saying it could not 'make its store fit' the proposed site. Some thought this odd, as Newham Council originally announced that Asda/Wal-Mart had been chosen because it was 'good at adapting to the needs of a well-known urban environment'.[12]

Threats to the scruffy but historic, vibrant and successful Queen's Market are symptomatic and also ironic. Under the march of so-called 'market forces', real markets come under the developers' demolition balls when, in fact, the market forces themselves often turn out to be little more than a mask for the activities of hugely leveraged and subsidized big businesses, which happen to have friends in high places.

The issues that came to light around this one market in the East End of London – about jobs, real economic value and how different approaches to business can build or undermine community – are not isolated; they are to be found everywhere. They question the whole orthodox approach to reviving run-down areas, and could be as significant to rethinking economics today as Adam Smith's example of the pin factory was over 200 years ago.[13]

Stuck in the Marsh?

British cities sporadically go up in flames. When poverty and neglect form a large enough pile of combustible frustration, boredom and indignation, all it takes is a catalyst. In 1985 it was Broadwater Farm in Brixton, south London; in the summer of 1995 it was Marsh Farm in Luton. The housing estate in the Leagrave area of Luton burst into three days and nights of rioting. Fighting only stopped, reportedly, when someone local had the presence of mind to organize a rave so that the rioters had something else to do. After speaking to local teenagers, journalists from the youth media outfit Children's Express commented:

This is the worst drama I've ever heard. It's like something on *The Jerry Springer Show*. These kids don't care about anything because they've been on the estate all their lives, so they don't know any different.[14]

The problem is not that places like Marsh Farm are ignored by government; like Brixton after the riots there, it attracted attention. Money for regeneration was poured in. The problem is what happens to the money once it gets there. Invariably, it pours straight back out again. In microcosm, these focused attempts at reviving communities reveal the flaws of an economic system increasingly in hock to and owned by big business. Because while wealth in poor areas urgently needs to be well irrigated so everyone can benefit and the economy can thrive, big, remotely owned businesses are actually designed to do the opposite. They are set up to drain local economic canals of money flowing through them and redirect it first to head office and then to the shareholders.

Marsh Farm is made up of around 10,000 people in 4,000 households. After the riots, residents could see for themselves the many small ways in which their own cash, as well as money meant to benefit the community, wasn't 'sticking', leaking away instead. They worked to find the leaks.

It turned out that on the estate, more than half the residents had takeaway food delivered at least once a week, and nearly a third more than once. Nine out of ten people used supermarkets outside the estate to do their weekly shopping. One in five frequented cafes or restaurants. For a community that was already poor, each of these spending patterns led to scarce cash leaking out of the area. It struck the local people that these were all things they could do for themselves. The research concluded, 'A community supermarket, fast food delivery service and cafe-restaurant would ensure wages paid and profits made remain within the estate.'[15] There are five Tesco outlets within a 3-mile radius of Leagrave.

The plumbing analogy is deliberate. The residents saw the estate as a bucket in which the water was a combination of their own money, grants made for regeneration and other resources. But their bucket was full of holes. All their cash quickly turned into profit for people living elsewhere.

For example, after the 1995 riots, some local young people made a proposal to put their graffiti skills to positive use. They suggested decorating an agreed space in the community in order to 'discourage wanton graffiti'. A total of £26,000 in funding was found; but instead of supporting local skills from the estate, a professional artist from elsewhere was paid to produce the murals, which were painted on walls rendered by another company from outside the immediate area. The opportunity to develop community-building skills and harness the energy of local graffiti artists was lost.

If you lived on the estate, you didn't need an economics degree to see what was going on. A community newsletter on the 'leaky bucket' explained it very clearly:

> This is why 'community regeneration' funds never make any long-term difference to our lives, only ever improving things in a very short-term and superficial way. In fact, to be an unemployed painter and decorator sitting in your flat while a contractor from miles away is getting paid for painting the outside of your home can make things feel even worse. After all it is not as though we can't paint our own doors or bake and deliver our own pizzas, it's just that we don't have the resources to set up our own businesses.[16]

For money to really benefit an area, it needs many small channels to flow through the community. If grants or businesses aren't connected up to countless micro-enterprises embedded in the community, local people will barely benefit. But get the economics right and you can reduce crime, revive neighbour-hoods, enhance individual well-being and give people work, hope and a sense of purpose. In the case of Marsh Farm, it led to a simple, practical and yet quite remarkable and revolutionary new way to get some of the basics of day-to-day life. It's something we'll come back to in the final chapter.

The impact of supermarkets is more like annexation than regeneration: they are only weakly connected to the local community, and put small, competing shops more deeply embedded in the neighbourhood out of business.

How local resources get drained is quite straightforward. Take a look at the annual report of a supermarket. Most of its annual earnings go towards things like VAT, supplies, rent, profit and workforce wages (a *lot* more to some workers than others). Virtually everything spent on the first four items directly leaves the immediate neighbourhood. Then, even assuming that all the pay goes to local labour – which is extremely unlikely – it means, on average, that for every £1 spent in a supermarket, 90 pence leaves the area. Where Tesco is concerned, the figure is a little higher, because staff costs as a share of turnover are lower.[17]

A slightly more complicated assessment involves looking at what happens to money after it is spent. By following the trail that money leaves, like tracking water flowing through rivers, streams, hoses and pipes, it is possible to see the degree to which it recirculates and brings benefits more than once. This is called the 'local multiplier effect'. One study followed the fortunes of a Cornish vegetable box scheme based near Truro and compared it to shopping in a supermarket. It tracked what was spent and where, and then what happened when that money was spent again. It turned out that every £10 spent with a local food initiative like the box scheme was worth £25 to the local area; but the same amount spent in a supermarket was only worth £14.[18]

When the same principle was applied to a much larger area by Northumberland County Council, it revealed startling potential implications. Like all county councils, Northumberland's had a large budget and the choice of buying what it needed from either remote or local suppliers. But the difference in outcome was huge. Local suppliers spent much of the value of any contract with other local people and businesses, making the money more 'sticky'. Suppliers from outside Northumberland spent more outside the area, allowing potential benefits to leak away. On average, across a range of work, £1 spent with a local supplier was worth £1.76 to the local economy, and only 36 pence if spent out of the area.

As a whole, the council worked out that a 10 per cent increase in spending to procure things locally would leave an extra £34 million each year circulating in the local economy. Repeated in disadvantaged areas across the UK, this calculation suggests potential benefits running into billions.[19]

In spite of examples like these, government policy creates successive perverse incentives for the opposite to happen. One example is the cumbersomely named Local Authority Business Growth Incentive, set up to promote 'enterprise, employment and growth'. First announced in 2002, the initiative came into operation in 2005, and intended to reward local authorities that successfully encourage enterprise by allowing them to keep a portion of any increase in rateable value on property (where the level of tax is determined by the assessed value of the property). The basic assumption was that an increase in the rateable value is a good indicator of more enterprise and jobs.

But an early review of the scheme revealed that the whole notion was misguided.[20] Change in rateable value was found to be an 'unreliable indicator', 'poor' at saying much at all about enterprise or jobs. It was also, in any case, difficult to discern the fingerprints of the local authority in changes that did occur. Most of all, the 'overwhelming winners' from the scheme were local authorities that 'gave planning consent for new large retail, retail warehousing and distribution warehousing developments'. This happened simply because of the rise in rateable value that typically follows the granting of consent. Some rewards to local authorities were even influenced because their areas included large, coal-fired power stations. Their rateable values are nothing to do with jobs, enterprise or open-market values, but get set by a national formula.

Possibly the best example, though, is northeast Lincolnshire.

It won a grant under the scheme of £1 million, more than half purely because two new Tesco stores opened in Grimsby. The grant could hardly be described as a reward for best practice because the area performed 'so poorly as a local authority that it received "no star" rating' (that's very bad in local government circles) in its 2005 comprehensive assessment by the government.

Supermarkets Aren't Working

In the absence of adequate checks and balances on the power of supermarkets due to sleepy, unconcerned regulators, a more dynamic group of MPs stepped up to analyse the impacts on local economies of the big stores. Following an inquiry that involved interrogating every interested party ranging from me to Tesco, which only attended after initially complaining that it had insufficient staff available to do so, the All-Party Parliamentary Small Shops Group published a detailed and damning indictment of the supermarkets' domination of British retail.[21]

It estimated that over 3 million people were employed in retail, accounting for one in nine of all jobs. It pointed out that small, family-owned retail businesses create more jobs, in terms of sales than the big stores. Pound for pound, the figure was more than double. Calculations for the year 2004 showed that the convenience store sector, which employs over half a million people, only took £42,000 worth of turnover to create a job. Superstores, on the other hand, took £95,000 of sales on average to create a single job. The same year, Tesco, with a £29 billion turnover, employed 250,000 people while small grocery shops, with a lower turnover of £21 billion, employed double the number of people.[22]

Yet whenever a supermarket is fighting for planning approval, one of its first lines of attack is to point out the number of jobs it will bring to the area. It's a form of moral and economic blackmail used against the local council, the implication being that to reject the superstore is to deprive the local community of much-needed employment opportunities.

It's a debate that rests on your definition of economic efficiency. To the supermarkets and their controlling interests in the City, efficiency means driving costs out of the business, which also means driving jobs out, too. For supermarkets, doing more business with relatively fewer people is one of the main ways they can increase their profitability and defeat their competition. For example, Tesco's payroll accounts for only around 7 per cent of its total turnover.[23] The destruction of employment is intrinsic to their business model; but some would say that in a country where the Puritan work ethic is king and the unemployed are demonized, a better measure of economic efficiency would be how many more jobs for your pound you could create. The Group's report supported the conclusion of older, telling research.

A study by the National Retail Planning Forum showed that new superstores have, on average, a negative net effect on retail jobs. Researchers monitored what happened in a two-year period following the opening of new, out-of-town superstores, looking at the impacts within a radius of 10 miles from the new stores. The results were striking. They calculated that in food retailing alone, there was an average loss of 276 jobs. But the real figure is likely to be even larger, because the impact on other outlets, such as newsagents, florists and clothes shops was not measured.[24] Although there have been academic squabbles over how to measure impacts (there always are),[25] the negative effects not only seem well grounded but also the logical consequences of the supermarkets' business model and price squeeze.

Evidence from the most recent and quite sophisticated research in the US shows that Wal-Mart, Tesco's global rival and

UK competitor through its ownership of Asda, has the same impact on jobs as well as driving down wages in its own back yard. In the US, a county is much smaller than in the UK (typically, it has the population of a small-to-medium-sized British town). In detailed research, Wal-Mart was shown to reduce the number of retail jobs at the county level by 180. For every Wal-Mart post created, one and a half jobs were lost elsewhere. Yet its impoverishing effect was worse than that. Where big chain retailers are concerned, the best chance a local community has to capture and keep a share of benefits is through the wages of staff. Most of the rest of the money spent by consumers in-store tends to quickly leave the area. But when a Wal-Mart store opens, the average amount of money taken home by retail workers across a county drops by $2.5 million.[26]

Over the last decade, planning rules introduced in the mid-1990s to prevent town centres turning into ghost towns have restrained the excessively rapid expansion of out-of-town retailing. But now there is a simultaneous attack on the planning regime coming from the supermarkets themselves; from the Treasury, via an inquiry known as the Barker review; and, as mentioned, from the OFT, meant to be the supermarkets' own regulator (for reasons reviewed later, the Office of Fair Trading has earned the nickname 'the Office in Favour of Tesco').

In planning terms, the Barker review, published in December 2006, was a throwback to the 1980s. The wind of chaotic market forces blew through its 226 pages. There were recommendations to weaken safeguards on green belt land and do away with the ability of local authorities to assess whether there were too many or too few shops in the local area. Amazingly, it also encouraged business to make more 'direct community goodwill payments on a voluntary basis, when this may help to facilitate development'.[27] Planners swiftly condemned the last proposal as tantamount to bribery. Robert Upton, Secretary General of the Royal Town Planning Institute, was reported as saying:

> The planning system exists to establish what development should take place in the interests of the wider public, not to allow deals behind closed doors to give developers a quick and dirty permit.[28]

What the review failed to grasp is that the planning system exists precisely to compensate for market failure. Without rules to balance people's interests, developers would cover city parks and country beauty spots with office blocks and leisure parks in an instant. To argue for weaker planning rules must be to assume that the market is working better, and therefore that less guidance is needed. A quick glance at supermarkets alone tells us exactly the opposite.

Even where small shops are not entirely put out of business, they frequently have to adjust. When large superstores open on edge-of-town or out-of-town sites, local speciality shops and convenience stores lose anything from one-fifth to three-quarters of their market share, either forcing them to close or to lay off staff.[29]

Much of this loss and impact, however, remains invisible to decision-makers and partially explains their seeming indifference. Nearly all local shops employ fewer than fifty people – the minimum that requires a business to report to the Department of Employment. When they close, consequently, their passing doesn't register directly on the nation's employment figures. So deep changes in our commercial landscape go unrecorded by central government – though it's not even about just the number of jobs affected by supermarkets, but about their quality too.

Pick Your Own

One of the hardest tasks is holding supermarkets to account for abuse that happens remotely, lost along complex supply chains. Because such things happen at several steps removed from the company, it can dismiss its responsibility by using the old political technique of 'plausible deniability'.

Tesco and Sainsbury's are the two biggest customers of the company S&A Produce, which accounts for one in three of all strawberries sold in the UK. S&A Produce was accused by the Transport and General Workers' Union (T&G) of creating conditions for its largely migrant workforce akin to 'modern-day slavery'. Based on the testimony of the workers, the union described as typical fourteen-hour days with barely any breaks; cramped, unhygienic and unsafe living conditions; and the refusal of important medical care. It was also alleged that workers had to pay fees of over £300 for the privilege of working at Brook Farm in Herefordshire. This wasn't the first time the strawberry grower had been in trouble. Previously, Herefordshire Council accused it of riding 'roughshod' over planning laws.[30]

After presenting evidence to the firm, being rebuffed and not being allowed direct access to the workers, the union's Deputy General Secretary Jack Dromey, said:

> Workers have told us of their appalling abuse at the hands of S&A Produce. They are being treated like modern-day slaves, exploited for profit at the very bottom of the food supply chain. S&A Produce has refused to act, despite repeated appeals.

Both supermarkets were called on by the union to boycott the firm, although neither did, pending further consultations with the supplier.[31]

Tesco's cool response to the union's whistle-blowing is more easily understood in the light of its special relationship with S&A Produce – a company that helps Tesco to be among the first to get English strawberries on to its shelves each season. The supermarket is so proud of S&A Produce, in fact, that it claims, 'Our supplier is generally considered to be the Michael Schumacher of the British strawberry world.' Tesco also boasts that its supplier 'has been painstakingly monitoring the different climates and light levels that effect [sic] the growing of the strawberries'. Unfortunately, it seems that S&A Produce paid rather less attention to the working conditions of its staff, many of whom appeared to be living six to ten to a caravan. Something of a contrast to the perfectly regulated 'natural summer conditions in their modern computerized glasshouses' that S&A Produce created for the strawberries and that was so lovingly described by Tesco.[32]

Adding food insult to human misery, the catalyst for all this simultaneous abuse and adoration was a fruit variety that is infamously tasteless and synonymous with how supermarkets have sucked the flavour and variety from our diets and from the Elsanta variety of strawberry in particular. As one newspaper put it, 'As the supermarkets' power to dictate requirements to growers has increased, the range of almost all foodstuffs has diminished.' To meet supermarkets' requirements for yield and the ability to be transported without being easily damaged – so called 'shipping qualities' – the Elsanta has come to dominate the market. Unfortunately, its tastelessness has led to it being called 'the most firmly linked in the public mind with tasteless modernity'.[33] The blandness of the fruit is a direct, if unintended, consequence of the supermarkets' business model. As with many other products, the demand for volume and low prices puts pressure on suppliers to add weight with cheap ingredients. In the case of everything from strawberries to tomatoes and, more off-puttingly, meat, that means increasing the water content of the product. The higher the water content, the more diluted the intrinsic flavour.

On one hand, then, Tesco's praise for S&A Produce was inappropriate, and on the other, the suffering of the workers seems to have been for no good cause, unless you include the healthy profits of Tesco.

Let's return to a key theme: cheap stuff. Whether in food, clothes or homeware, supermarkets promise low prices. But in one important sense, there's no such thing as cheap; cheap comes from cutting costs and, as we've seen, when the supermarket 'drives costs' out of the retail system either jobs are cut entirely or by playing one supplier, manufacture or food processor off against another. A race to the bottom gets triggered in terms of standards, terms and conditions. Things are bad now, but the rise of 'deep discounting' stores could make things worse.

Jack Clarke is a senior researcher on retail issues for the T&G, one of Britain's biggest unions. He sees a creeping casualization of the workforce being pushed by the 'everyday low price' model:

> Employment status is the biggest area of abuse. Temporary status is a scandal. This is the result of price pressure. Even core workers have been casualized. Casual workers are taking the overtime of former permanent workers. It's dividing the workforce, generating racism [because migrant workers accept lower pay] and dividing communities.[34]

The workers on the strawberry farm are not alone. Another union, the GMB, accused the firm Katsouris Fresh Foods, part of the Geest Group that supplies Tesco and other supermarkets, of a safety record so bad that multiple accidents occur on a daily basis. Katsouris, which operates from sites at the edge of London, had seven notices served on it in a four-year period by the official Health and Safety Executive (HSE). Katsouris is in the business of preparing 'ready meals' for supermarkets. When two separate incidents happened close together in which workers had fingers severed, the GMB demanded action from the HSE and pursued recognition for its union among the 2,500-strong workforce.[35] According to the union, pressure on costs from the supermarkets meant that production lines were operated at speeds likely to cause accidents.

Although tragic in their individual circumstances, these examples are only symptomatic of wider trends in the world of work in an age of supermarket globalization, when the balance of power in the food chain is so unequal. In recent years, the profits of only six supermarket chains (since reduced to five) have been consistently above the profits generated by all the UK's 230,000 farms.[36] Welcome to the age of the new serfs.

The New Serfs[37]

Every feudal order has its serfs. In the kingdom of UK retail, they are the invisible labourers who, underpaid, unprotected and overworked, provide the muscle that moves the economy. They do much more than just grease the profits of a few retailers. Cleaning offices, building houses (then looking after both house and baby), waiting in hotels, selling sex, picking fruit, harvesting vegetables and digging for cockles, the disavowed ranks of migrants bear the burden of supporting our jobs and lifestyles.

Their serfdom is a particularly brutal modern variant, lacking any of the medieval sense of reciprocity and paternalistic responsibility. In the fourteenth century, serfs could enjoy up to eighty public holidays a year and take enough time off to go on pilgrimages. Fifteen weeks' work a year could secure a livelihood and, along with a little military duty, the protection of the lord.

Today, often sold into bonded labour through the cost of paying their traffickers, Britain's invisible and frequently illegal migrant workers appear to us in their full vulnerability only when we learn of their sometimes bizarre deaths: Zhang Guo Hua drops dead after working a twenty-four-hour shift in a Hartlepool factory putting logos on microwave ovens; three young men are killed in a van crushed by the 7.03 A.M. train from Hereford to London (variously reported as Kurds, Iraqis or Arabs, they were off to pick onions in the West Midlands); fifty-eight Chinese men and women are suffocated among boxes of tomatoes in the back of a lorry; a forty-seven-year-old Ukrainian man working as a cleaner in a swanky London restaurant is found dead in a broom cupboard (he slept there to save money, sending all he earned to relatives). Then, most infamously, twenty-one illegal Chinese immigrants working as cockle pickers drowned in 2004, abandoned by their gangmaster in the mudflats of Morecambe Bay on a miserable day in February.

It could be the opening interior dialogue for a detective film, as the investigator tries to work out the connection between these apparently unrelated deaths. Then the penny drops: a serial killer is at work. The murderer turns out to be our deep hypocrisy surrounding our cultural antipathy towards immigration on one hand and our enjoyment, on the other, of rock-bottom prices, of the fruits of these immigrants' labour.

Whenever criticisms are levelled at retailers like the 'big four' supermarkets, the first line of defence is to point to the cheap food they sell. But the rule of 'no free lunch' operates here, as elsewhere. We have merely evolved a system better at hiding or distancing cause from consequence. In the name of modern retailing methods, farms go out of business, communities collapse, jobs are lost, habitats for plants and animals get destroyed – and people die, too.

Migrant labour in all its forms, legal and illegal, is characteristic of economic globalization. There are an estimated 120 million migrant workers worldwide. Many travel between developing countries in Asia and Latin America. This workforce is increasingly female, and does work that is typically dirty and dangerous. But at the other end of the migrant labour flow, developing countries are losing between 10 and 30 per cent of their qualified workers and skilled professionals to countries like Britain, where they keep our hospitals and schools running.

Migrant labour in the UK increased dramatically in the last decade. Some of it is 'managed' through seasonal agricultural schemes, enabling workers to find jobs in labour-intensive, low-wage sectors such as tourism, domestic help, agriculture and meat- and fish-packing. In Britain, an estimated 3,000–5,000 gangmasters do the organizing and at least 1,000 have operated illegally, providing no protection to their workers. Altogether they control as many as 100,000 labourers. Long chains of subcontractors, commercial confidentiality and contractual obfuscation allow household-name retailers to hide behind plausible denials. As is so often the case, it is an imported trend that crossed over from the Atlantic. Wal-Mart was taken to court by a group of cleaners who were working illegally, and who claimed that the company knew their immigration status and conspired with the cleaning firm to keep pay low.[38]

In 2003, a Commons committee reported on conditions among migrant labourers. Workers were sleeping ten to a room and living in buildings with no toilets, kitchens or washing facilities. People working in packhouses producing supermarket ready-prepared food were being paid just above half the minimum wage. Unlike the slower pace of life in the rural, feudal Britain of long ago, a modern supermarket packhouse will keep going 364 days a year, 24 hours a day. The committee accused the supermarkets of taking a 'see no evil' approach, in effect encouraging illegal labour by driving prices to suppliers down to the point where legal workforces were unaffordable.[39]

When Tesco announced its record annual profits in April 2006, the investigative journalist Felicity Lawrence pointed out that the two things were connected:

> The supermarket sector, with its just-in-time ordering that requires casual labour to be turned on and off like a tap, and its new packhouse industries, has been one of the most prolific creators of demand for trafficked labour ... No, supermarkets don't employ abused migrants directly, the dozens I have interviewed who have been packing food for Tesco have been employed by subcontractors to contractors to Tesco. But its profit margins have undoubtedly been built on a system that only functions thanks to underpaid illegal workers.[40]

A typical example, exposed by Lawrence, of 'abusive employment at the hands of gangmasters' at one of Tesco's major suppliers, is Nature's Way Foods in Suffolk. The company specialized in prepared salads, and was set up 'at the suggestion of Tesco to supply all its branches with salad'. In its casualized workforce supplied by gangmasters, Lawrence found people lacking proper legal papers, receiving chronically low pay. Tesco was surprised by the allegations and replied 'We take our responsibilities in this area very seriously and while we don't pretend to get things right every time we always act swiftly if any issues are identified,' and denied poor practice.[41]

A licensing scheme for gangmasters introduced in 1973 actually existed until 1994, when the Conservative government dropped it. Then, following several tragedies involving migrant workers, Labour MP Jim Sheridan, with the support of the T&G, introduced a private members' bill to establish a new scheme. In the wake of the Morecambe Bay deaths, then-Home Secretary David Blunkett lent his backing. On 1 December 2006, the Gangmasters Licencing Act came into force. Now anyone supplying workers to either agricultural or food-processing industries needs to hold a licence. A jail sentence of up to ten years is waiting for operators caught without one.

Yet migrant labourers are still somehow seen as a burden. The truth is quite the opposite. Home Office research shows that in a single year migrants, including asylum seekers and refugees, contributed £2.5 billion more to the economy than they cost in taking up services.[42] In the US, the National Research Council has estimated that first-generation migrants cost the country $3,000, but the second generation gives back many times more to the national coffers – $80,000 over a lifetime. Even the Cato Institute, a right-wing US think tank, calls migrant workers the lubricant to our economy.[43]

Interestingly, in the UK, migration is one of the few social forces preventing the spread of ghost towns. Immigrant workers, therefore, not only help make profits for the supermarkets by picking and packing food for their shelves, but they are also the people who keep otherwise denuded local economies going.

As in the countryside, so in the towns and inner cities: immigrant labourers are prepared to work in places and conditions that others have given up on. In so doing, they often drive up local wages and employment. According to the Global Entrepreneurship Monitor, Asian people are twice as likely as white people to be involved in autonomous start-ups; Caribbean people three times as likely; and Africans nearly five times as likely. The reason is not just the discrimination that keeps migrants out of regular jobs, but the entrepreneurial mindset that it takes to establish a life abroad in the first place.[44]

But the highly politicized and often hysterically reported issue of immigration plays out in a much bigger historical picture. Decades of failed economic advice from financial institutions such as the World Bank and the International Monetary Fund have left many developing countries wrecked or creaking. On top of that, the global commodities trade has experienced market failure on an enormous scale (see Chapter Seven). Economic migration, then, can be seen as a logical search for opportunities denied at home. It is certainly nothing new. Lawrence James, in *The Rise and Fall of the British Empire*, recalls Robert Southey's imperial daydreams about Britain in which 'superfluous men and women, unwanted by reason of their poverty or criminality' travel east and west to make their living in new worlds. Most emigrants from Britain travelled willingly. The wealth they found or, more often, took, put the empire on its pedestal.

We may have to accept that the age of passports and border controls has passed its zenith. The passport, after all, is quite a recent invention. Things tightened up only with the First World War. Now, in the enlarging European Union, old national passports have been replaced with a standard member-state format. Passports designed for travel within trading blocs may become the model for border control. The issue then becomes not the policing of borders, but the collective protection of people's rights in their workplaces, wherever they happen to be.

It may be enlightened self-interest that finally persuades us to act. Once before, exposure of the 'gloom and horror' endured by European migrant labourers in Chicago's meat-packing houses led to a Presidential inquiry and a new law to regulate the trade. That was in 1906, and happened after Upton Sinclair's novel about the trade, *The Jungle*, was published. There was genuine sympathy for the exploited workforce, but the buying public had another concern: it was worried about the quality of the meat it was eating.

Back at the Local

Josephine's story, which began this chapter with the range of socially useful tasks she performed – mostly falling far beyond the 'core' business of small shops – would have sounded incredibly familiar to Jane Jacobs. In 1961 she wrote *The Death and Life of Great American Cities*, a classic work on why urban communities thrive or die.[45] In that book she wrote:

> One ordinary morning last winter, Bernie Jaffe and his wife Ann supervised the small children crossing at the corner [on the way to school]; lent an umbrella to one customer and a dollar to another; took custody of two keys; took in some packages for people in the next building who were away; lectured two youngsters who asked for cigarettes; gave street directions; took custody of a watch to give the repair man across the street when he opened later; gave out information on the range of rents in the neighbourhood to an apartment seeker; listened to a tale of domestic difficulty and offered reassurance; told some rowdies they could not come in unless they behaved and then defined (and got) good behaviour; provided an incidental forum for half a dozen conversations among customers who dropped in for oddments; set aside certain newly arrived papers and magazines for regular customers who would depend on getting them; advised a mother who came for a birthday present not to get the ship-model kit because another child going to the same birthday party was giving that; and got a back copy (this was for me) of the previous day's newspaper out of the deliverer's surplus returns when he came by.

Even though Jacobs was revealing the foundations of community life in New York in the early 1960s, the bias of policymakers towards large, remotely owned enterprises has accelerated up to the present. In many places it has reached tipping point. Local enterprises that provide much of the social glue that holds neighbourhoods together are enduring a mass extinction event, under the marketing onslaught and unfair competition of socially indifferent clone stores. Many could soon be a thing of the past, taking with them all their vital, but often invisible, social, economic and cultural benefits.

There is justifiable concern at Tesco's aggressive advance on smaller high street and corner convenience stores. But this is a useful misdirection for Tesco's management. Its real focus for grabbing more market share is the development of ever larger, out-of-town hypermarkets. This means being dragged inadvertently further towards the US model where, as Robert Spector writes, the traditional concept of 'neighbourhood' has been changed by the deceptively simple fact that we no longer walk through it but drive to it.[46] This may sound undramatic, but it has profound consequences. If the places where we live are, increasingly, no longer made up of living streets, there will be no more sidewalk contacts to provide the small change 'from which a city's wealth of public life may grow'. As a result, our neighbourhoods will be poorer.

CHAPTER SIX

A Global Plan: Why Scale Matters

'Countries . . . should be encouraged to remove any size limitations on individual stores, numeric limits on the number of stores in the country and geographic limitations on store locations in the country.'
Letter from Michael Duke, Executive Vice President
of Wal-Mart (Asda) to Robert Zoellick, US Trade
Representative to the World Trade Organization (WTO)
'requesting' that this position be adopted as official
US 'negotiating strategy', 1 May 2002

'I sympathize with those who would minimize, rather than those who would maximize economic entanglements among nations. Ideas, knowledge, science, hospitality, travel – these are things that of their nature should be international. But let goods be homespun wherever it is reasonable and conveniently possible, and above all, let finance be primarily national.'
John Maynard Keynes, 'National Self-Sufficiency',
The Yale Review, 1933

Like unimaginative monsters from a bad B-movie, in most sectors of our economy a handful of businesses have grown to dominate the marketplace. They consume each other and grow of their own accord. Waves of mergers are interspersed with quieter, more static periods but overall, the trend towards ever-greater concentration of economic power and market share continues. From food to publishing, accountancy and pharmaceuticals, fewer, larger firms control more of what we swallow, look at and listen to.

But for Tesco, it is not enough to dominate retailing in the

UK. It is already a large multinational retailer, with plans to continue expanding hugely around the world. As the company puts it: 'Since the mid-90s, Tesco has been investing in new markets overseas, seeking out new opportunities for growth and ways of generating long-term returns for shareholders.'[1]

Tesco already does business in thirteen markets outside the UK, in Europe and Asia, and is on the cusp of entering two other huge marketplaces, the US and India. Over half of Tesco's floorspace is outside the UK even though it accounts for a minority of its profits. Although it has some smaller outlets, the vast majority of Tesco's international business is done through huge hypermarkets.

Figure 5: Tesco Goes Global, and Grows and Grows . . .

	Year of entry	Number of stores	Sales area (millions sq. ft)	Planned store openings 2006–07 (inc. acquisitions)
Czech Republic	1996	35	2.5	44
Hungary	1994	87	4.3	30
Poland	1995	105	4.8	39
Rep. of Ireland	1997	91	2.1	8
Slovakia	1996	37	2.3	10
Turkey	2003	8	0.6	12
China	2004	39	3.5	12
Japan	2003	111	0.3	10
Malaysia	2001	13	0.9	4
South Korea	1999	62	4.1	47
Taiwan	2000	6	0.5	—
Thailand	1998	219	6.8	207
		2,710	58.7	576
		(includes UK)		(includes UK)

Correct to end of 2005–06 financial year (UK and ROI: 25 Feb 2005; international: 31 Dec 2005)
(Source: Tesco)

The figures in the above table are a snapshot of Tesco's known global presence early in the first decade of the new millennium.

But it is growing so quickly that these figures are like a single still image extracted from fast-spooling cinema reel – out of date almost as soon as they are published.

Tesco, for example, planned to open a further twenty stores in Poland during 2005–06 to add to the seventy-eight it already owned. (Poland's top ten retailers are all owned by foreign companies, including Tesco and France's Auchan and Carrefour.[2]) But in mid-2006 Tesco purchased another 220 small stores for £72 million from the French group Casino. By that time, the number of its existing stores had already grown to 107. Expansion into Central and Eastern Europe was clearly going better than planned.[3]

What motivates Tesco? It may be the biggest retailer in Britain, but globally it faces competition. Wal-Mart is in a different league in terms of size and sales. Other food retailers ahead of Tesco in the table of the world's biggest, however, are not, such as Carrefour, the Dutch Ahold, Germany's Metro Group and the US chain Kroger.

But as Tesco stalks its competitors in the global markets, none are standing still. As one leading trade journal asked:

> How big can a retailer get? Wal-Mart, Carrefour, and a few other global giants seem to be testing the limits, with no end in sight for growth via international expansion.[4]

The logical consequence of a handful of already-giant retailers using their leverage to expand still further is that more and more of the world's food system falls into fewer hands. Carrefour, Ahold, Wal-Mart and Tesco had combined total sales in 2003 of over half a trillion dollars – $520 billion. One prediction suggests that by 2010 there will only be ten major global food retailers. Once again, it's a winner-take-all dynamic.

Figure 6: The World's Dominant Food Retailers

(2004 ranking)

Company	Home country
1 Wall-Mart	USA
2 Carrefour	France
3 Ahold	Netherlands
4 Metro Group	Germany
5 Kroger	USA
6 Tesco	United Kingdom
7 Target	USA
8 Rewe	Germany
9 Costco	USA
10 Aldi	Germany

Source: *US Food Link* (published in association with *Progressive Grocer*)

Just thirty retailers already have captured one-third of the global food market, and their control is increasing. The biggest stores are growing faster than the market as a whole. Wal-Mart's global market share is nearly as big as the next five largest stores combined, and it has been expanding faster than the others. Tesco has achieved the next-fastest rate of growth among the biggest stores, driven both by its aggressive push to develop more giant hypermarkets, by sales of 'non-food' items and by its rapid international expansion.[5]

So why does this matter? To ensure that everyone's needs are met, every marketplace needs checks and balances. The lopsided accumulation of power tends to mean bad news for the powerless. Arguably, this might not matter if the goods in question were, for example, luxury hi-fi equipment or balloons. But this market concerns our most basic need: food. Just as importantly, it concerns the people who grow it.

If your life or livelihood depends directly on working in the food chain, and you either lose out or become entirely superfluous to the people who control it, you are in big trouble. This is a theme that will be glanced at here and returned to properly in the next chapter.

Growth, returns, mergers and acquisitions: they all cause enormous excitement in the City. Their details fill the hours, articles and broadcasts of business journalists. However, if you take the controversial view that the most important task of the global food system is to feed people and to do so securely, organizing that system primarily to meet the demands of investors is bad news. As long-term observers of the international trade system point out, concentration and rising market domination by the supermarkets 'has weakened the bargaining power of farmers and food producers and given enormous power to supermarkets to make deals to their advantage and abuse their dominant market position'.[6]

The driving force of global supermarket expansion by corporations like Tesco has been the removal of checks and balances on how investment swirls around the global economy, coupled with the stores' continual need to expand driven by the demands of investors. There are few things in government policy as elaborate and arcane as the rules governing trade and investment. But over time, a clear shift has happened. Governments in poorer countries were once able to set terms and conditions on foreign investors in order to make sure that some economic benefits stayed local, rather than merely allowing foreign multinationals to extract profits at will. Now, increasingly, rules are instead placed on governments, severely restricting their ability to manage foreign investment for local benefit. It is now much easier for so-called 'foreign direct investment' to behave in reality more like 'foreign direct extraction'.

One analyst describes how it happens in the case of the supermarkets (my note and emphasis added):

When [developing] countries liberalize supermarkets under GATS [*Note: this is a set of international rules, irreversible once signed, called the General Agreement on Trade in Services, which is overseen by the machinery of the World Trade Organization*] governments are bound to rules that prevent them from taking measures that they might see [as] useful when abuses and negative consequences occur. For instance, Art. XVI of GATS forbids limitations on the number of service suppliers or service operations in the form of numerical quotas. This means that governments cannot stop foreign supermarkets from rapidly expanding, by creating regulations that limit supermarkets to a certain market share or a certain number of outlets per supermarket.[7]

In different phases since the early 1990s, and after the end of the Cold War, controls on foreign investment have been removed in line with mainstream thinking – a particularly triumphalist version of market economics. Wherever controls have been removed, from the former Soviet Union to Asia, Latin America and Africa, the supermarkets have turned up. Since then, the lustre of financial liberalization has dimmed somewhat, owing to vast, investment-related economic crashes in – by extraordinary coincidence – the former Soviet Union, Asia and Latin America (Africa escapes purely because it fails to attract sufficient reckless investment in the first place in order to subsequently crash).

Generally speaking, supermarkets have embarked on a trail of expansion around the world, following demographic signposts that led them first to the wealthier places where more people live in towns and cities and where the roads, utilities and communications are best. In practice, this meant that the bigger, richer Latin American countries were first in line, quickly followed by East and Southeast Asia and Central Europe. Then came the less economically attractive parts of Latin America and Asia, before the supermarkets eventually got around to poor old southern and finally East Africa.[8]

All of this was lubricated, of course, by a flood of profit-hungry private investment. Perversely, the poorer the country in question, the higher the level of risk perceived by the investor – which means that for every dollar invested, investors expect a higher rate of return. In other words, poorer countries pay much more to attract investment. Commercial confidentiality makes figures hard to come by, but one World Bank study produced some fairly shocking statistics. In the 1990s, the level of profit demanded by investors from developing countries as a whole in return for their money was 16–18 per cent per year. But to invest in sub-Saharan Africa, the figure was 24–30 per cent.[9] These figures underlined a common characteristic of market economies: the poor pay more. The disbandment of State Trading Enterprises, which deal with importing and exporting, is a typical example of an economic policy foisted on to developing countries through rich country-controlled financial institutions. The idea was to open up markets and allow local enterprise to flourish, but, as Bill Vorley of the International Institute for Environment and Development points out, this 'does not create an open market, but replaces cartels with similarly one-sided markets, dominated by global agribusiness'.[10]

Figures from the Bank of England show that in recent years there has been a sudden upsurge in the amount of money leaving developing countries to sit in British banks. Although the reasons for capital fleeing countries of origin will differ in each case, where some very poor countries are concerned the removal of rules governing the movement of capital means that the amount of money leaving often dwarfs the volumes of aid these countries receive.[11]

Tesco is a major example of a whole sector that is currently washing around the world like an economic tsunami. Three waves have hit Central and Eastern Europe. In the mid-1990s, supermarkets spread throughout the Czech Republic, Hungary, Poland and Slovakia. They now control up to 50 per cent of the food market there. Then they moved into Croatia, Bulgaria, Romania and Slovenia, taking between one-quarter and one-third of the market to date, and they're still growing fast. In Russia, supermarkets have only one-tenth of the market so far, but the sheer size of the country makes it a major target for further investment.[12]

In the space of a single decade, supermarket control of food shopping in Latin America went from an average of just 10–20 per cent to upwards of 60 per cent. In Brazil, supermarkets account for a full three-quarters of all food sales. For a region as a whole synonymous in the Western imagination with violent military takeovers often leveraged in various colourful ways, two key things stand out: Latin America's food coup is both foreign-owned and highly concentrated in the hands of a few corporations. In most national markets, five leading chains tend to dominate, and around 70–80 per cent of these are foreign multinationals.[13]

As in the US and the UK, these companies are setting out to re-engineer how the food economy works, employing business practices that have enormous consequences for local people. At the heart of it is the centralization of purchasing and distribution. As elsewhere, the supermarkets work with only a small number of farmers and suppliers capable of operating on the same scale, thus 'pulling the market out from under the feet of thousands of small and medium rural enterprises' – enterprises that create and provide a huge variety of jobs, livelihoods and independence to millions of people in rural communities. In Brazil, Carrefour set up a single distribution centre to supply fifty hypermarkets that were roughly the size of 500 average supermarkets, and worked across three states to serve 50 million consumers.[14]

What is happening in Latin America is echoed in Central and Eastern Europe. Between 2003 and 2004 Tesco, for example, set up big distribution centres in the Czech Republic, Hungary and Poland.[15] But the Latin American experience is merely a template and a dry run for what is about to happen to the vast rural economies of Asia.

Although Tesco and others pounced on new opportunities in the former Soviet-bloc countries, and the likes of Wal-Mart, Carrefour and Ahold dominate in Latin America, it is the prospect of growth in Asia that really makes a manager's pulse race faster. Tesco has set up shop in Thailand, South Korea, Malaysia, China, Taiwan and also in wealthy Japan. In one small change of plan, Tesco appears subsequently to have abandoned Taiwan in a store swap with French retailer Carrefour. In return for six existing and two planned Taiwanese hypermarkets, Tesco was set to receive eleven in the Czech Republic and four stores in Slovakia. The full deal's long-term future was questioned, however, when Slovakian regulators blocked Tesco's local takeover complaining that it would make them too dominant and able to control the market.

Half the growth in global food shopping is predicted to come from a handful of so-called 'emerging markets'. Analysts can't stop talking about one country in particular; something to do with the fact that it's the world's most populated country and, to date, doesn't have that many supermarkets. India is interesting, but China is *irresistible*.

There are some obvious reasons why the supermarkets have been slower to enter China than other countries in Asia. It is a large, politically repressive country that is also strong enough to decide for itself the pace and nature of its engagement with the global economy. It is also relatively free to say when and how supermarkets can do business on its soil. But there are other issues, too.

The US Department of Agriculture (USDA) reported that

supermarkets and cloned chain restaurants 'had difficulty obtaining reliable supplies of standardized quality products from China's traditional system of small household farms geared towards producing food for home consumption' and, as a consequence, recommended that 'farms will have to adjust by specializing in a particular commodity, consolidating fragmented land holdings to achieve scale economies'.[16]

It's a fascinating insight into the mind of the global (American) policymaker. It lays bare the always-implicit assumption that, above anything else, the world must be readied and made acceptable for foreign investment (rather than foreign investment being made safe for the world). Unpick, for a moment, what has been written:

The USDA sees a country in which much of the population grows a wide diversity of food types, on their own land, primarily to feed themselves. But because this doesn't fit in with the needs of American- and European-owned supermarkets, the USDA thinks this should change; the supermarkets know better. Apparently what people actually want is a small range of identical foodstuffs that can be bought directly from them and, to achieve this consumer nirvana of homogeneity, local people will have to do two things: they should first stop growing that diversity of pesky, misshapen, locally adapted crops. Then they should give up their family plots of land, which provide them with moderate self-reliance, in order to create the big farms that supermarkets prefer to do business with.

Stripped of its blasé assertions and unthinking economic dogma that brooks no dissent, what the US government paper proposes, in effect, is a second Chinese cultural revolution, this one to cause potentially as much upheaval, if not more, than the first. To its minor credit, they are at least aware that there will be consequences. Hence, they observe that by 'forging stronger links with processors and retailers', farmers will be locked into a trend that is 'likely to continue and may profoundly alter the way food is produced in China'.[17]

It would seem, though, that the new cultural revolutionaries, with Tesco in their middle, are getting their way. Starting at a flat level in 1991, in just twelve years supermarkets had captured nearly one-third of the urban food market and were growing at between 30–40 per cent each year.[18]

The speed of change in Asian food markets will certainly be familiar to anyone who has lived through an actual revolution. In Thailand, which is one of Tesco's most important Asian markets, a combination of supermarkets and other new stores has been 'cannibalizing traditional outlets'. Their share of business shot up from under one-third to around half in just five years between 1998 and 2003. Even more dramatic is the change in Vietnam where, as recently as 2000, supermarkets had only a half of 1 per cent of the food market; their control is now expected to have hit 40 per cent in 2006.[19]

To date, Africa's relationship with supermarkets has been stronger as a supplier of luxury horticultural goods like flowers and produce like *mange-tout* than as a target for international store expansion. However, that is starting to change beginning with South Africa, which – along with Nigeria – is one of the continent's relative economic giants. By 2004, according to Thomas Reardon, an academic and observer of the supermarkets' global spread, South Africa had 1,700 supermarkets doing business equivalent to that of 350,000 small stores, known as *spazas*. From that base, they are spreading out around southern and East Africa. Kenya, Zimbabwe and Zambia all have growing sectors.

In all these global regions, it's possible to observe the same process that has happened already in Britain, the rest of Europe and the US. The big supermarket fish are getting bigger by swallowing the smaller fish and dining on their unequal, greater access to finance for further investment. Reardon points out that, 'Global and retail multinationals have access to investment funds from their own liquidity and to international credit that is much cheaper than the credit accessible by their domestic rivals.' This reinforces their initial head start and is hardly what you would call a level playing field. The 'asymmetry' is merely a mirror of wider inequalities in the global economy, where size alone can be enough to put you on the right side of a winner-take-all relationship.

And They're Not Finished Yet

'Tesco's plan for US expansion suggests it may have found its ideal second home in the relentless suburban sprawl of the southwest sunbelt.'

Financial Times, 18 May 2006

The UK business press sang its approval at Tesco's apparent ability to spot a new business opportunity. It had seen a gap in an otherwise saturated US retail market: plans emerged that Tesco was to target stores at a range of custom-built, new middle-class neighbourhoods that were being overlooked by domestic giant Wal-Mart. But praise from some quarters was faint, and the tone ironic. The *Financial Times* mocked the new outlets' suggested name 'Fresh and Easy', and its choice of adjectives stung. Tesco would, it said, fit comfortably in these 'anonymous' communities with homes built around *ersatz* village squares. The depressing banality of global supermarket living appeared to be dawning even among leading commentators who were heartily in favour of big business.[20] With friends like that, Tesco might not need its more obvious enemies.

If the problem were purely aesthetic, Tesco could shrug it off. The store has never, as it were, set much store in good looks. But it isn't. Being synonymous with, and a driver of, suburban sprawl, Tesco has entered into a romantic suicide pact with the cheap-oil economy upon which its own activities and the suburbs depend. As cheap oil becomes more expensive, the tightening, inescapable noose of peak oil (which we'll come to in more detail later on) will squeeze Tesco's market along with its channels for supply and distribution. One US commentator remarked that suburbia represents the 'greatest misallocation of wealth' in history. That may seem extreme, but it's not far out in relation to suburbia's greedy diet of neat fossil fuels.[21]

As the title of this book suggests, the sheer size of corporations is an issue in itself. It matters what you do when you are big, because it's easier to tread on others and more damaging when you do. But it also seems to matter *that* you are big. Why is that so?

Why Scale Matters

Scale matters. A single painkiller can calm a headache, but swallow a whole bottle and it will kill you. Whatever we do, the scale of our action is critical to its effect. Cut down a few trees and you can call it woodland management; clear-fell a forest and an entire ecosystem is destroyed. Whether something is beneficial or destructive can simply be a function of the scale on which it happens. Fireworks are fun, after all; a cluster bomb is not.

One of the biggest changes in the modern world is precisely our ability to do things on a massive scale. There have always been wars, but the destructive power of contemporary weapons mocks the most ferocious inventions of earlier ages. It is a long way from the longbow to the obliterating power of the cruise missile.

These simple if rather extreme examples are a commonsense indication of why big can be bad, but when it comes to the organization of corporations and the global economy, a completely different assumption applies. When we talk about how to do business, there is an expectation that, sooner or later, we should do it in a global marketplace. Ambitions to stride out on to a worldwide stage are as much a part of the senior corporatocrats's infectious culture as flying business class, staying in five-star hotels, reading the *International Herald Tribune* and watching CNN. If, as a senior manager you don't already have the global profile, it serves you well to grow one quickly, because conventional wisdom dictates that a successful firm gets bigger and bigger and takes over other firms, regardless of national boundaries. Why? This assumption has permeated so deeply into our consciousness, that few voices are even raised when it is brought to bear on previously exempt areas of our lives like health and education.

Richard Sykes, the former chair of the global pharmaceutical giant GlaxoSmithKline (GSK) – sometimes referred to as 'the Microsoft of the drugs market' – provides an insight into the senior management mindset of a modern multinational. He is a useful example because, at the highest level of corporate management, directors are expected to be relatively interchangeable. Rather like government ministers who randomly swap portfolios, say, from farming to defence, it is the management culture and boardroom skills the managers are wanted for rather than their knowledge of any issue in particular. Hence few commented when Terry Leahy's predecessor at Tesco, Ian MacLaurin, was given the top job in English cricket when he left the company.

Sykes, in particular, seems to have an issue with size. By doggedly pursuing a merger between two already-huge pharmaceutical companies, Glaxo Wellcome and SmithKline Beecham, he in effect created GSK. The interests of huge firms are frequently interwoven. Sometimes they fight; sometimes they dance. Today, as Tesco muscles into health care provision and grows the market for selling 'lifestyle' drugs to the worried well, GSK shifts a huge amount of product through the supermarket and its expanding list of in-store pharmacies.

In a rare example, for Sykes, of large being less attractive, within two years the merged company reportedly lost 15,000 jobs.[22] But lost employment was not the only thing for which GSK under Sykes was criticized. Oxfam estimates that 38,000 people in developing countries die every day from preventable diseases, and that illiberal patents restrict access to essential drugs. Beginning in 2001, the charity was severely critical of GSK for its pricing policies in poor countries and its restrictive approach to patents.[23] GSK was further criticized by the group Consumers International in 2006 for the irresponsible marketing of drugs to patients in wealthy countries.[24]

In 2003 he caused outrage when he told the *Financial Times* that small shareholders should be banned from company annual general meetings (AGMs), which should be saved for only large-scale investors. The little people, he thought, were disruptive timewasters. A queue of investment experts rapidly formed to denounce Sykes' view, pointing out that there was a clear relationship between a low turnout of shareholders at company AGMs, and bad corporate governance.[25] Big companies, it would seem, actually need the little people to keep them in order.

Sykes also sat on the board of the mining multinational Rio Tinto, and in 2001 was made Rector of the London-based Imperial College of Science, Technology and Medicine. (By coincidence, I encountered Sykes in an interview on BBC Radio 4's agenda-setting *Today* programme. nef had released a jointly authored report about how the government effectively subsidized a number of large oil companies by funding research and development through some of Britain's leading universities. Sykes appeared as the injured party and, as the argument drifted away from him, reacted in a manner reminiscent of Nikita Khrushchev, verbally banging the table with the repeated line of defence, 'But we dig holes in the ground, that's what we do!', almost willing that to be an adequate defence through force of assertion.)

When Sykes took over Imperial College, he wasted little time in pushing for yet another grand merger, this time between the

College and another of London's leading academic institutions, University College. Protests from staff and students and cold water poured from Graham Zellick, Vice Chancellor of the University of London – who said the outcome would be an institution too big to manage – led to the merger being called off a month after it was announced.[26] But why did Sykes assume it would be a good idea? Why did he think big would be better?

In spite of that blip, the trend is mostly one-way, and increasingly the 'big bias' is backed by law. If a country becomes a member of the WTO or the International Monetary Fund, it effectively signs away the freedom to ask: what scale of economic organization, what size of market, is right for the different sectors of its economy? By joining either institution, a country becomes committed to instant or creeping integration into global markets for either finance, goods and, increasingly, services (which are even more contentious because they include things like health and education). This obligation exists for countries regardless of whether it is right or productive for them to be exposed to such international pressures. Global institutions, underpinned by the agreements they forge and police, actually legislate against the freedom to question the appropriateness of economic scale.

Recent years provide plenty of evidence why this is a problem. The increased freedom with which money moves around the world creates the conditions for ever-bigger and more damaging financial crashes. After Mexico, Russia, Asia, the hedge fund crises and the current US bubble economy, even the bullish financial media occasionally cautions about a rising tide of economic instability. The more all parts of the economy become concentrated, ranging across banks, energy corporations, food retailers and accountancy firms, the greater the damage that will be caused by the failure of any single, major company. Such vulnerability is intensified by the instability that issues as a direct consequence of the rapid and increasingly unmanaged flow of information and finance.

Standard & Poor's, one of the world's foremost credit rating firms, assesses companies as investment prospects. In just the last two decades, its changing view of the stocks of the top 500 companies is evidence of a deep, unsettling of economic stability. In 1985 it rated just over one-third of stocks (35 per cent) as high-risk, and a higher amount (41 per cent) as low-risk. Move ahead to 2006, and the landscape of risk for investors has been fundamentally rearranged. By 2006 over two-thirds (73 per cent) were considered high-risk, and only around one in eight (13 per cent) low-risk.[27]

Global commodity markets display another downside of unmanageable 'bigness'. Developing countries are often heavily dependent for their export income on just a handful of products such as coffee, tea, cocoa, sugar and cotton (see Chapter Eight). These represent some of the most common, fast-moving, high-volume products sold by the supermarkets. Over the last few decades, these countries received bad advice from Western governments and people in places like the World Bank who should have known better. They were all told that exporting more of the same goods was the secret of economic success. The problem was that demand for these kinds of goods was relatively stable and, as their supply increased, prices started to fall. As everybody did the same thing, prices kept falling so that poor countries – hooked into global markets – were running faster to stand still.

Rashes on the landscape of single crops grown to the horizon are often monocultural legacies of colonial administrations, or more recently promoted by commercial agriculture. It is an approach that creates vulnerability. By reducing plant and animal diversity, food systems are more exposed to pests and diseases, and are likely to recover more slowly from disasters caused by severe weather events and climatic extremes. Large-scale, chemical-intensive farming also, typically, has fewer jobs to offer and creates less secure livelihoods as well. Mechanization, loss of land tenure, dependence on more casual, shift-based and seasonal work and the extraction of profit and surplus all lead to less resilient local economies and fewer economic benefits kept within the community.

So, scale matters.

Instability in the global environment is another consequence of our blindness to issues of scale. It is easy, for example, to stand up and defend the 'freedom' of everyone to own a car. But that freedom will never be extended beyond a wealthy global minority, and those relative few have bought into lifestyles whose dependence on fossil fuels is already driving global warming. This, in turn, conjures up a classic modern paradox of freedom.

The pursuit by a global few of their right to drive ends up denying the 'rights' of millions to live and work comfortably in homes and towns that are vulnerable to climate change. A similar paradox is to be found on our supermarket shelves. The supermarkets have created an expectation that we should be able to enjoy limitless out-of-season fruit and vegetables from January to December. The production and supply chains needed to fill supermarket shelves with exotic produce for twelve months a year are enormously hungry for at least two precious commodities: water and oil.

Whose freedom comes first when over-consumption by the world's wealthy middle classes is on a collision course with the needs of poorer communities? Is it the villager whose need for water is greater than the demand for *mange-tout* peas, or the London dinner party waiting for this vegetable side dish? Is it the person living on a low-lying, small island state, threatened by rising seas and climate change, or the parents who want to take their children to school and shop at out-of-town Tesco hypermarkets in gas-guzzling 4x4s? The limits are fuzzy, but they are there, and choices have to be made. Scale matters, quite simply, because it can be a matter of life and death.

So why have issues of scale been so comprehensively ignored, their importance misunderstood by mainstream economics? Open a typical dictionary of economics and, if mentioned to at all, scale is discussed only in the sense that firms can gain 'economies' from scale. In other words, they can make more money by being big.

Money is the single arena in which a major debate on scale has occurred. Economists have argued exhaustively over what the optimal geographical area is for a currency to function well – the almost mystical 'optimal currency zone'. Ironically, one result of that debate is that Europe now has the euro to challenge the dollar. In other words, the world now has two big currencies instead of one.

But, as the expert on alternative currencies David Boyle points out, what we really need are currencies working at lots of levels, from town to global. Currencies are not just for buying and selling; they also communicate information and emotion. Their flow indicates our likes and dislikes and tells whether we are feeling confident or insecure. The more flexible and adapted to particular circumstances they are, the better they are likely to be at doing their job. If you are in any doubt at all, look at the success of loyalty card schemes for supermarkets in general and Tesco in particular. Loyalty cards, as discussed in Chapter Three, provide a form of money that is incredibly effective for the supermarkets. It tells them all they need to know about your shopping patterns and guarantees that more of your spending is done in their stores. As any economist will tell you, if you have the power to issue money, a whole lot of benefits will flow in your direction. Also, now that supermarkets like Tesco and Sainsbury's operate conventional, if expensive, banking services, like all commercial banks they quite literally print money by lending it into existence. 'The process by which banks create money is so simple that the mind is repelled,' wrote John Kenneth Galbraith.[28]

We face complex and contradictory economic, environmental and social problems, ranging from climate change to ghost towns and clone towns. The evolution of new multiple currencies at the local, regional, national and international levels are likely to be needed (supermarket money sits in a different category) to create a dynamic and flexible monetary system capable of responding. It's another analogy for the under-appreciated need to retain diversity across our economy against the creep of scale and homogeneity and, in particular, in our food retail system.

Yet outside the community of orthodox economists, and mostly on the margins of intellectual inquiry, the debate about appropriateness of scale has raged. Some of its key concepts have emerged in unlikely places. E. F. Schumacher's book *Small is Beautiful* (a title that, although it has entered the language, the author is said to have disliked, and was forced on to him by his publisher Anthony Blond) is hailed as the classic analysis of scale and one of the founding texts of the green movement.

Schumacher modestly defers to the Catholic Church as the author of the notion of 'subsidiarity', the idea that things are always best done at the lowest practicable level. Although this may apply to some day-to-day questions of store management, the concept is very far from the corporately planned world of Tescopoly. Pope Pius XII described the 'principle of subsidiary function' in this way:

> It is an injustice and at the same time a grave evil and disturbance of right order to assign to a greater and higher association what lesser and subordinate organizations can do.[29]

By observing this principle, the encyclical says, 'the stronger will be the social authority and effectiveness and the happier and more prosperous the condition of the state'. Subsidiarity re-emerged in the early 1990s around Europe as a political pressure valve on the cooking pot of the project for a single Europe. Politicians could be seen struggling with the term on evening news programmes, not entirely certain of its meaning, trying to either explain or condemn it. Bruised by the experience, the concept retreated to the offices of Eurocrats and academics only to resurface now, much later, as the anti-globalization movement searches for the theoretical underpinnings of the different world order it seeks.

Even before Schumacher's book came out, another economist, Leopold Kohr, wrote the definitive attack on what goes wrong when things get too big. *The Breakdown of Nations* was published in 1957, still in the shadow of the Second World War. Kohr wrote that he was searching for a single theory to describe human activities and social organization. He saw his quest being as bold as the search by physicists for a single theory to explain the universe. The conclusion he came to was unequivocal:

> The result is a new and unified political philosophy centring in the *theory of size*. It suggests that there seems only one cause behind all forms of human misery: *bigness*. Oversimplified as this may seem, we shall find the idea more easily acceptable if we consider that bigness, or oversize, is really much more than just a social problem. It appears to be the one and only problem permeating all creation. Wherever something is wrong, something is too big . . . On a small scale, everything becomes flexible, healthy, manageable, and delightful, even a baby's ferocious bite. On a large scale, on the other hand, everything becomes unstable and assumes the proportions of terror.[30]

Today we could quibble with Kohr. We could say that things can also go wrong and can assume the 'proportions of terror' if they are also too small. Oppressive states can use minute surveillance technology to spy on their people; a Clubcard slips barely noticed into a wallet. In the wrong hands, the fingerprint of your unique life code – your DNA – could be used against you, for example, by insurance companies in predicting your susceptibility to illnesses, applying a kind of 'economic eugenics'.

Biotechnology and nanotechnology give us plenty of cause for concern, but again, the problem is one of scale. These processes manipulate life and matter at a level so small that the consequences are as hard to predict as the manipulations are to see. Every field trial of a genetically engineered plant is, effectively, the full environmental release of a new life form. Their impact is difficult if not impossible to predict. One bumper sticker called it 'giving pollution a life of its own'.

There is growing concern also in the scientific community that nanotechnology might create products that are impossible to control, ultimately working against human interests. But again, problems arise especially where these technologies are applied on a large scale – for example, in commercial agriculture. Nature is perfectly capable of crossing genetic information between plants and animals and among plants, but it does so on an occasional basis. It doesn't develop a new crop in a laboratory and then plant it abruptly in several million acres.

We now know it is not just about ideas of absolute size, it is about appropriateness. Schumacher's words describe why the lens of scale is under-used:

There is wisdom in smallness if only on account of the smallness and patchiness of human knowledge, which relies on experiment far more than on understanding. The greatest danger invariably arises from the ruthless application, on a vast scale, of partial knowledge such as we are currently witnessing in the application of nuclear energy, of the new chemistry in agriculture, of transportation technology, and countless other things.

Little has changed in the more than thirty years since *Small is Beautiful* was published. Some issues have got much worse. In Schumacher's day, global warming – a consequence of the scale of our consumption of fossil fuels – had been predicted, but was far from a major concern. But conservation was, and future generations will almost certainly look back aghast at the reckless squandering in the past three decades of Earth's fossil-fuel inheritance that took millions of years to build up.

It is a popular misconception that Schumacher thought everything should be small-scale. Actually, he thought that:

> The burden of proof lies always on those who want to deprive a lower level of its function, and thereby of its freedom and responsibility . . . they have to prove that the lower level is incapable of fulfilling this function satisfactorily and that the higher level can actually do much better.

I think the example of Tesco demonstrates that, in several important ways, the 'higher level' does much worse.

With no apparent sense of irony, Kirkpatrick Sale wrote a very large, heavy book of more than 550 pages and called it *Human Scale*. Published in 1980, it gathered together a huge body of evidence to show that things work better when they operate on a human scale. He looked at food production, waste disposal, the optimum size for convivial communities, transport, health, education and architecture among other things. He also looked at energy, following Ivan Illich's earlier *Energy and Equity*, which itself is a classic treatise on the question of scale in relation to energy – how we produce it and how we consume it.

Since these landmark works were written, many have tried to put their principles into action. Countless individuals, often derided for dropping out of society, have tried to live their lives also according to the ideas.

Yet all the time that this work was going on, two contradictory things have happened. The writers and activists have been proved right, but things have continued to get bigger. In the process, they have also often gone wrong. The global economy gets bigger, but so does the gap between rich and poor, and the share of the poor in the benefits of growth has also shrunk dramatically. Big, remote electoral processes and the centralization of power in Western democracies is killing the ballot box. People have voted, or rather not, with their feet. Turnout rates on polling day have crashed, hitting record lows in Britain and the US. People are disillusioned with one of the great human triumphs of the last century – electoral democracy. It is now clear that to restore vitality and participation in the democratic process the opposite must happen. Communities need power and control over issues that affect them. People need to believe that there is a point to becoming active citizens.

Corporations keep getting bigger, in spite of the fact that over two-thirds of mergers and acquisitions fail to bring business benefits, according to the accountants KPMG. As they grow, two things happen. Power concentrates in the economy and people lose their trust in business. Globally, land ownership continues to concentrate into fewer hands and intellectual property protected by law – ownership of which determines the distribution of benefits from economic activity – is largely held by a tiny global elite of corporations, governments and research institutes. One reason for the persistent failure of mainstream economics, even today, to address the question of scale is because the damages from 'bigness' – in terms of pollution, human alienation and social breakdown – fall outside the balance sheet. It is part of the equally persistent failure of economics to give proper value to the well-being of the wider system.

Yet one of the most important questions we can ask is: what is the right scale on which something can work best? At what level do we maximize economic, social and environmental benefits, and minimize the costs?

If local is the best level to do something, it will be different depending on whatever that thing is. For example, baking bread might happen on your street corner, growing food in a field 20 miles away and building trains somewhere else entirely.

Several years of anti-globalization protests may not have created checks and balances on corporations at the global level. But they have fed deep suspicions that big business has little interest in public well-being. Research shows steady decline in the number of people who think 'most companies are fair to consumers'.[31] As a result, business is polishing its public relations to deal with the alienation that has grown from its bigness, fat-cattery and ruthless ambition.

As concentration in various economic sectors increases, corporations lack the feedback mechanisms to warn that things are going wrong until it is too late. A spate of failures from such giants as the energy conglomerate Enron, the communications corporation WorldCom and the professional-services firm Arthur Andersen stand like dead, warning carcasses along the road of corporate hubris.

The reality of three or four huge firms controlling over three-quarters of a market is a long, long way from Adam Smith's vision. In his view, to operate in the public interest a market was supposed to be characterized by countless small firms competing with each other, there being no obstacles to setting up in business.

Figure 7: What are the ingredients?
Localization v. Globalization

Localization	Globalization
Distinctiveness	Uniformity
Nearness	Distance
Diversity	Homogeneity
Markets as a means to an end	Markets as their own end
Profits stay local	Profits go to remote shareholders
Benefits go to economically/ socially active	Benefits go to owners of finance
Rules to manage abuse of power	Deregulation and liberalization
Social cohesion a particular objective	Social cohesion not considered
Subsidiarity	Level dictated by the market
Optimizing economic activity	Maximizing economic activity
Something you do yourself	Something that is done to you

If Jack Cohen were starting out in business today under a different name, he'd find the equivalent of Tesco in his way, blocking the path to market. He'd face a thicket of anti-competitive practices by corporate retail giants, the manipulation of price and supply chains, unfriendly and overpriced leases for shop space. If he wanted to build his own store, he'd find most of the available land already in the control of his potential competitors – namely, Tesco.

CHAPTER SEVEN

Profiting from Poverty:
Shelves Full of Global Plunder

'Down the valley
Up the mountain
Tesco is our dear friend.'

> Song sung by children of plantation workers
> earning 1 penny for picking a pack of
> *mange-tout* selling for 99 pence in Tesco,
> whose parents were soon to go on strike.

'A poor man's field may produce abundant food, but injustice sweeps it
away.'

> Proverbs 13:23

Mange-Tout (Eat Them All)

It started with a small newspaper article about exotic food from
Latin America. Filmmaker Mark Brozel was looking for a new
project, and decided to make a modern fable following the journey
of a vegetable. The theory was that, as with fables, much can be
revealed by looking closely at some arcane detail of life. Mark had
no idea where it would lead; the journey wasn't like Joseph
Conrad's murderous *Heart of Darkness*, but it did reveal the cold
and counterproductive heart of the global marketplace, where
cash comes before common sense and human welfare. It led even
the conservative *Sunday Telegraph* newspaper to describe Tesco's
overseas supply chain as a form of 'neo-colonialism'.

Mark approached several food retailers to discuss making his
film. Marks & Spencer was too terrified to return his calls, and

Sainsbury's too disorganized. Meetings with Waitrose were cordial, but went nowhere. Hearing that Tesco was also being approached, a senior Waitrose manager gave the filmmaker a beguiling idea of what lay in store for him: 'You know, Mark,' he said, 'unlike some people, we're not bent on world domination.'

It took a further five months to persuade Tesco to take part. Brozel thinks the company took a calculated risk in agreeing to make the film. It didn't occur to it that onscreen, some things might end up looking quite as bad as they did. The farm in Zimbabwe growing the *mange-tout* that became the film's subject had, for example, a woman among its workers 'whose home had no running water and who had to walk over a mile with water on her head'.

According to the World Health Organization (WHO), lack of access to safe drinking water and a lack of basic sanitation kill at least 1.6 million children under the age of five every year. For some sense of scale, that is more than eight times the number of people who died in the great Asian tsunami of 2004.[1] It is, of course, much easier to get water if you happen to be a product likely to make a profit for a supermarket: 'Water was specially piped in to the farm to clean the *mange-tout*,' says Brozel, adding, 'I didn't start with a sense of rank injustice, but [I] probably finished with one.'

There is a growth market for the export of luxury horticulture from Africa, including everything from flowers to *mange-tout*. The problem is that these types of products are very thirsty crops and need huge amounts of water. Yet around two-thirds of African people already have to rely on water resources that are limited and highly variable.[2] Climate change is set to make matters much worse. The UK Meteorological Office's Hadley Centre for Climate Prediction and Research looked at the share of the Earth's land surface prone to extreme, severe and moderate drought. Its conclusions were genuinely shocking.

The percentage of the Earth's land surface that suffers from extreme drought has trebled from just 1 per cent to 3 per cent in less than a decade from 1998.

The future looks much worse. Their research then projects a continuing trend that will carry on until 8 per cent of land surface becomes susceptible to extreme drought by 2020, rising until no less than 30 per cent of the globe is affected by 2090.[3] Half the world's surface will, by then, be affected by at least one form of drought. In these circumstances, much more than the export market for thirsty exotic vegetables will need to be reconsidered.

Brozel's film set out to follow the journey of the *mange-tout* from a field in Zimbabwe to a table in Hampstead, north London. Its power came, I think, because it calmly revealed in a profound way how human beings scattered around the planet can be connected and interdependent in terms of natural resources, yet be terribly disconnected when it comes to understanding and responsibility. Somehow he portrayed a world growing smaller, and yet further apart.

Tesco staff from the UK were flown out to the farm twice a year, in business class, at the farmers' expense. Brozel says:

> When the twenty-six-year-old buyer arrives wearing blinkers, he doesn't see or enquire about whether the woman worker has water or whether children get to school, he just sees whether the pea is close enough to 70 mm in length, and he doesn't want to pay for the 'waste' that doesn't fit his requirements.

What would drive Tesco to insist on such onerous, even crippling, conditions? Brozel believes that it's nothing to do with 'consumer interests', as the supermarket claims, and all to do with the fact that standardization makes its business operations easier. Brozel recalls:

The farm manager said, 'Tesco call us partners but we're not. We do what they say', and these were white farmers used to ruling the roost. But there was this twenty-six-year-old buyer who was the new White Man.

Brozel described there being something militaristic about Tesco:

The visit was the visit of a king. They [the community] slaughtered animals. They roasted a lamb. The schoolkids rehearsed welcome songs for three days and gave Tesco presents. Tesco gave nothing back. The adage 'To those that have shall be given' came to me. Why would poor Zimbabwean children give presents to Tesco when they didn't even have a school on the farm?

Like many documentary projects, it ended in tears – Tesco tears. Although the company was immune to the generally bad light in which the film showed it, when the film was broadcast, it ended with two facts that upset the supermarket very much. First, it showed the pitifully small share of the *mange-tout*'s final selling price that actually went to the workers who grew and picked it. Second, it revealed that the workers went on strike because their pay was being slashed in response to Tesco's new demands on the farmer. Brozel says that Tesco's senior management believes he made up both accusations. Unfortunately for Tesco, this information was all on film. Brozel says:

What's amazing to me was that the only thing they objected to was when I revealed the workers had gone on strike, in effect because their wages were being pushed down by 40 per cent by Tesco.

This was the result of Tesco insisting on only paying for the peas that met its exact length requirements. The rest, the so-called waste, was fed to cattle. These were the best-fed cattle in Africa, according to Brozel. More disturbing still was that the Tesco buyers took it for granted when fourteen-year-old girls sang them songs of worship. Other farm workers assumed that Tesco was a country, and thought its staff was royalty.

Two days before broadcast Brozel was contacted at home; Tesco had seen the finished film. 'The head of corporate affairs got my home number,' Brozel recalls, 'screamed at me down the phone and threatened to sever their link with the farm if we didn't change the film.' Brozel refused, and faxed Tesco the transcript of the footage that justified his allegations but that hadn't been used in the finished film. Things went very quiet, and he heard nothing more from the company.

There is, however, a sting in the tale. The film was broadcast to huge critical acclaim. It won awards, and Brozel was told that he achieved insights in his fifty-minute documentary that academics had failed to communicate in decades of applied research. Since then, however, all the films that made up the documentary series have been repeated, except *Mange-Tout*. No evidence has come to light that Tesco has applied any pressure to prevent the film being shown again, but no reason has ever been given to explain the broadcaster's failure to repeat its award-winning film. 'It may sound conspiratorial,' says Brozel, 'but that's what happened.'

Britain had over 250 years of pertinent economic change to prepare itself for the arrival of Tesco. By comparison, the re-engineering of food and farming in Asia, Latin America and, to a lesser extent, Africa to accommodate the global supermarkets is happening virtually overnight. The last time change of this type, speed and scale was felt in the global South was in the late nineteenth and early twentieth centuries. One prominent social historian has described the consequence of that last great upheaval at the hands of the major European powers as the 'late Victorian holocausts'. [4]

The reason Tesco couldn't understand the fuss over the documentary is the same reason why defenders of 'business as usual' see nothing wrong with economic globalization. Both are blind to the consequences brought by an excessive imbalance of power. Key to mutual benefit arising from an economic exchange is the ability of both parties to negotiate. If only one has real power, it will impose self-interested terms on the other party.

It was obvious to the viewers of *Mange-Tout* that, as the smartly dressed village schoolchildren sang songs of praise to their neocolonial trading masters, that something terribly unjust was being played out before their eyes. It was a picture of a relationship between Europe and Africa that many of us believed in either hope or complacency had been consigned to history. At moments it was hard not to just stare, mouth open. The Tesco buyers, on the other hand, merely accepted their dues and screwed an even better deal from the farmer. Haven't we now, though, moved on to an era of general corporate social responsibility? Certainly, this is what the adverts tell us. But company habits, it seems, and historical patterns of economic inequality, prove to be remarkably resilient.

A Question from the Audience

The Queen Elizabeth II Conference Centre just off Parliament Square in Westminster, in central London, looks a little like an intergalactic space prison dumped by an advanced civilization whose design standards had recently and dramatically improved. It's big, alien, cold, slightly intimidating and not pretty. But it is functional. It was the perfect location for Tesco's Annual General Meeting in July 2006.

The event draws suited investors ranging from the big City institutions to the retired ranks of Middle England who pore over the ebb and flow of share prices each morning at breakfast. In the artificial lighting of the big conference hall, Gertruida Baartman stood out: aged thirty-nine, she is a single mother from South Africa with three children. It was good that she was noticeable, because Gertruida had a question. Her job was picking fruit for 38 pence per hour to be sold in Tesco stores.

She wasted no time getting to the point: 'I don't get paid enough to feed my children and I have to work with pesticides with my bare hands. I don't get the same wages as men even if I do the same work. I am here today to ask Tesco what it is going to do about my problem?' It was the kind of question that gives corporate event managers night sweats.

Nor was Gertruida's experience an aberration. Evidence gathered by the development group ActionAid, which invited her to London, showed that Tesco's profits were being 'made at the expense of thousands of women workers'. Moreover, one year since these problems were first brought to light, workers still 'were paid poverty wages, faced hunger and worked in hazardous conditions'. The group also gave voice to other workers:

[Tawana Fraser:] I get £32.50 every two weeks. I can't afford school fees for my daughters or go to school functions or buy school uniforms. We have no gloves or protective clothing and we have to climb wet ladders and pick pears from the trees while they're still wet from pesticides.
[Gloria Nzama:] I sleep on the floor on a plastic sheet . . . there's no water or electricity and the walls are made of cardboard.[5]

To make UK companies take responsibility for their international operations, several environment and development groups supported a Company Law Reform Bill. The bill would see that people overseas harmed by the activities of a UK company would be able to take action against them in a UK court (See Chapter Ten).

After Gertruida raised her question, Terry Leahy personally promised to look into the problem. This would be reassuring if it wasn't for the fact that every time such abuses are exposed, companies like Tesco promise to do the right thing and ensure that the problem never happens again; but it always does.

In the mid-1990s, I was invited with my colleagues from the development agency Christian Aid to Tesco's head office in Cheshunt, Hertfordshire. We'd recently published a fairly damning report called 'The Global Supermarket: Britain's biggest shops and food from the Third World'. In it we exposed a litany of appalling pay and other conditions affecting the people upon whom we – and the supermarkets – depend to fill our fridges, vegetable racks and fruit bowls.

None of the big supermarkets came out well. I'd gone to investigate conditions on pineapple plantations in the Dominican Republic. The giant fruit company Dole dominated the export market, and most of the pineapples ended up in Europe. We found the fruit looking exotic and oddly out of place on Tesco's shelves. Local people in the Dominican Republic, however, didn't eat them often – sometimes just for cultural reasons, others because they were just too expensive on the local market.

The day of a plantation worker coerced into doing long hours of overtime could start at 5 A.M. one day and finish at 2 A.M. the next morning. At the time we visited, the workers were paid the equivalent of £2.48 for the day shift plus 32 pence per hour for overtime. Getting to and around the plantations meant long drives in the heat, being shaken over unmade dirt roads. Frequently, the journeys to work for the pickers involved being crammed like cattle into the back of a seat-less company truck called a *carreta*. People would hang on to each other in order not to fall. One worker, said his colleagues, did in fact fall; the truck ran over his leg, which had to be amputated in the company dispensary. According to his former colleagues he received no compensation, had to buy his own prosthetic leg and ended up unemployed. In the field, the work was hard, with no protection from the sun and inadequate protection from the widely used chemical pesticides.

While fruit conglomerates like Dole profited from controlling the export trade and paid pittances to its workers on the plantations, small-scale farmers could barely scrape a living. 'I would grow even fire to sell if I could get a good price,' one farmer told me, in the poetry that often flows effortlessly from the experience of people in poverty, an angry rebellion against a life he felt was imposed by distant decision-makers. More such terrible experiences percolated up in discrete conversations held in back rooms with frightened workers. It was the same for people who struggled to make a living in the tax-exempt export-processing zone, where cheap clothes and electronic goods were made for sale in 'big-box' stores in the US.

The report and subsequent campaign eventually led to the creation of the government-endorsed Ethical Trade Initiative. Soon after we published our findings, Tesco wanted to engage with us.

We went to see them. Brozel had told me that if you go to Tesco HQ, in the waiting room there are 'UK suppliers sitting like ten-year-olds waiting to see the headmaster', and that he hadn't realized 'how ruthless and cut-throat business could be'. But we sat in a room with several senior managers, and one by one they promised earnestly that whatever the problem was, they would deal with it. They would throw staff and resources at preventing abuse along the supply chain, and because they were Tesco, they would do it bigger and better than anyone else.

Ten years later, either Gertruida had managed somehow to

slip through a gap in the space-time continuum, landing with peculiar coincidence in the middle of Tesco's AGM, or nothing was being done differently. A shower of new codes and guidelines had been swept up and filed, and nothing had changed.

The Shirts Off Their Backs

Clothing is one of the areas of shopping where Tesco sees room for growth. It has already become the nation's third-largest clothing retailer.[6] The store often gets publicity when it manages to source 'label' goods such as Levi's jeans on the so-called 'grey market', and sells them cheaply. But just as it has done with food and other goods, Tesco sees the advantage of developing its own-brand labels. Florence and Fred, or F&F, is one of those.

Tesco calls the label 'a design-led capsule wardrobe of carefully conceived essentials for men and women in sumptuous fabrics'. An investigation for Channel Four television news called it 'child labour'. Researchers tracked down two suppliers in Dhaka, Bangladesh, called Harvest Rich and Evince. Bangladeshi children under the age of fourteen are not supposed to work. Ethical Trading Initiative members, of whom Tesco was a founding participant, are not supposed to employ children under the age of fifteen, or knowingly buy from companies who do, and all workers are to receive a 'living wage'.

The journalists interviewed a twelve-year-old girl working for Harvest Rich who said she earned £9 per month. A boy said that, when asked about his age, he told the factory he was eleven years old; it didn't complain, and the boy commented that he thought there might be another 200–300 child workers at the factory. Both Bangladeshi suppliers denied that they employ children. Tesco made its own inquiries and refuted all the allegations. It found no evidence of any use of child labour at any of the factories visited for the programme. Tesco said that all its suppliers must demonstrate that they meet their ethical standards on worker welfare which are closely monitored.[7]

Then more evidence emerged of what happens when there is systematic downward pressure on prices. Interviews with sixty workers at six different textile factories in Bangladesh revealed subsistence pay and poor working conditions. The factories supplied cheap clothes to Tesco, Asda/Wal-Mart and Primark. Sewing machine operators toiling for eighty hours a week for pay of 5 pence per hour were not the worst off. Free-marketeers rushed to defend what was for them only 'relative' poverty, and an inevitable step in economic development. The fact that pay in Bangladesh's textile and garment sector halved in real terms in the 1990s was conveniently overlooked; and, for a sense of perspective, the equivalent of 5 pence in Dhaka will buy you one and a half foreign cigarettes, a bus ticket or a hairband.

Other workers worked up to ninety-six hours per week, and some took home as little as £8 per month. Forced overtime and the loss of holidays were common. A combination of bullying within the factories and poor audit practice meant the abuses carried on. But even where buyers did insist on improvements following factory inspections, their simultaneous demand for low prices made raising standards hard or impossible to implement. Mohammed Lutfor Rahman, Vice President of the Bangladesh Garment Manufacturers and Exporters Association, was interviewed when the research was published and said:

> But who pays for these things? The buyers' profits are going up. But if we ask for more money for improvements they say China is very cheap. It is a threat to move the work somewhere else.[8]

According to the researchers, their findings highlighted the 'plight of millions of garment workers around the world, and especially those supplying low-cost retailers such as Asda/Wal-Mart, Tesco and Primark. Workers are condemned to work more and more so that UK shoppers can buy for less.'[9] In response, Primark said, 'As members of the Ethical Trading Initiative we are fully committed to the campaign to improve working standards in Bangladesh'. Asda conducted 13,000 factory audits worldwide to ensure workers were not being exploited.[10]

The lack of overall progress is quite easy to understand. There are small ethical fish swimming against a floodtide of conventional economic forces and unbalanced trading relationships. We shouldn't be surprised that a system designed to deliver one-sided benefits to the most powerful players does what it is intended to do. We bite into that inequality every time we enjoy the nation's favourite fruit, the banana.

Bananas

In January 1997, twenty-eight-year-old Phil Calcott bought nearly half a tonne of bananas from Tesco. He likes bananas, but wasn't that hungry; he bought them for a different reason. Because of a special Clubcard promotion, Phil calculated that for every 3 lb bunch of bananas he bought, Tesco was actually giving him money. He was earning the equivalent of £1.25 in Clubcard points for every £1.17 spent on the fruit at the Worcester store where he shopped. His living room became home at one point to approximately 3,000 bananas, and he racked up 7,850 Clubcard points. Phil became known as 'the banana man of Worcester'.[11]

Considering how much we love them, and how the future of whole economies rests on their slippery yellow skins, it's odd that the banana is the most comic of all fruits. Britain is the world's fifth-largest importer of bananas. In 2004 we scoffed an extraordinary 855,000 tonnes of them. Since 1998 it has been our favourite fruit, overtaking the apple. They arrive on ships from all around the world: Cameroon in West Africa, Colombia in South America and St Vincent and the Grenadines in the Caribbean.

In St Vincent the banana plantations are a short distance from an old-fashioned botanical garden. The garden has a breadfruit tree allegedly grown from seeds brought by Captain Bligh of *The Bounty*. Many very poor countries in the Southern Hemisphere still depend on just a handful of export crops to earn foreign currency. It's a hangover, both from colonial times and from the bad advice given by international financial institutions since. Bananas account for over one-third of all St Vincent's exports. When there is trouble in the banana market, it means trouble for that whole country; and, it seems, there is always trouble where bananas are concerned.

To a European, the sight of a banana tree symbolizes the exotic (though strictly speaking it is not a tree at all, but part of

Credit: Tom Pilston

Workers carry bananas on a small farm
in St Vincent in the Caribbean

the herb family). Perhaps due to global warming, in recent years the more hardy varieties have become increasingly common in British gardens. I planted one myself (an inedible variety) in solidarity with my friend Renwick Rose, a hard-working, enormously patient and enduring advocate for the small-scale banana farmers of the Windward Islands in the Caribbean. To Renwick the banana tree does not symbolize anything 'exotic'. It stands for the struggle to survive.

For two decades or more Renwick, based in a small office in Kingstown, St Vincent, has followed the international power plays of world trade negotiations. In that time the fate of the banana, and hence the economic future of his country, has been knocked backwards and forwards between Europe and North America. Bananas got caught up in intractable disputes about trade quotas and market access at the WTO. The reasons behind this are long and complex, and needn't detain us. What should, though, is what has happened to the price – and the growing power of the supermarkets.

Over the last forty years, the price of bananas in real terms has more than halved.[12] As well as satisfying our demand for an easy-to-eat fruit, bananas make tasty profits for supermarkets. They have become the highest-value grocery item sold and an incredibly important part of the companies' 'offer' to consumers. Petrol and lottery tickets are the only items that generate higher sales, but the profits on these are small.[13]

It's often said among observers of international development (or the lack of it) that poor countries lose out because they sell mostly raw commodities. The real money, they point out, is to be made processing them to 'add value'. For a variety of reasons, however, that tends to happen in wealthier countries. Yet even with bananas, which barely need any processing, the split of the proceeds is atrocious, and goes something like this: For every £1 worth of the fruit, the retailer – in this case the supermarket –

takes 40 pence; the international trading company gets 31 pence; the firm that ripens and distributes the bananas gets 17 pence; the plantation owner, 10 pence; and finally, the worker toiling in the plantation takes just 2 pence.[14] In total, this leaves the producing country with only 12 pence from every £1 worth of bananas sold.

But it can get worse than that. Supermarkets have exacting requirements to do with the cosmetic appearance of the fruit they sell – remember the precisely measured *mange-tout*. Banana skins naturally acquire black, pitted markings, but supermarkets want to sell perfectly yellow fruit. Anything that doesn't make the grade is rejected and goes to waste. On St Vincent there are stations where the growers take their fruit to be weighed and checked by agents for the exporters. Whole truckloads, representing weeks of hard labour by local small-scale farmers on their plantations, commonly get waved away by the agent acting under instructions that flow down the supply chain from the supermarkets.

The retailers, their trade associations and even their regulators commonly argue that the sector is highly competitive. In fact, supermarkets frequently compete only on a small range of high-profile products, like bananas. When the stores engage in a typical price war, it is usually the producer who takes the hit. In 2001, following a move by rival Asda/Wal-Mart, which dropped the price of bananas to 94 pence per kg (from £1.08), Tesco slashed its price too. While Asda/Wal-Mart cut its own margin to sell at a lower cost, Tesco protected its profits by forcing its suppliers to provide the fruit much more cheaply. The same thing happened again in January 2005,[15] but this time the price was lowered even more, to 66 pence per kg.

Banana Link is a UK-based group that works to get decent terms and conditions for banana farmers. Its view is that:

No company can continue to pretend to be promoting ethical trade along its supply chains when it slashes supplier prices to the point where growers who pay a living wage, treat their workforce with respect and make environmental improvements, are cut out of the market.[16]

Costa Rica is the second biggest exporter of bananas to Britain. In 2004, unions from the UK teamed up with Latin America banana workers unions to

> . . . reverse the 'race to the bottom' in the banana industry, a 'race' in which companies increasingly source from those countries with the lowest wages, the worst social conditions and the weakest environmental protection.[17]

In April that year, a delegation visited the Bribri banana plantation in Costa Rica, owned by a local consortium called El Ceibo Ltd, which, according to a report by Banana Link, had a 'history of aggressive anti-union behaviour'.[18] El Ceibo's bananas were sold via an independent British importer through Tesco's stores across the country. According to the plantation workers at Bribri, none of them earned a 'living wage', and some did not even earn the legal minimum wage. This all happened long after the promises that followed the Christian Aid campaign of 1996, and in contravention of the Ethical Trade Initiative code, which committed Tesco to ensure that free trade unions could organize and collective bargaining take place in its suppliers.[19]

It is an inconvenient truth that there is no such thing as cheap food. Edwin Laurent, former Ambassador of the Eastern Caribbean States to the European Union, had this to say on the matter:

> How can you grow bananas on the other side of the world, under very difficult circumstances, and sell them so cheaply

in the UK? It is because you have exploitation of labour and the environment. Then production moves to where exploitation is easiest, and large plantations push small ones out of business.[20]

To Renwick, at home in St Vincent, the reality is tinged with sadness. Falling prices not only undermined banana farming, they created social upheaval. In a once God-fearing, strongly Anglican community, the drugs trade has taken root. With its particular climate and soil, St Vincent has limited options to grow other things. But one high-value crop for which there is always a market – cannabis – grows easily. The island's position between South and North America also, unfortunately, makes it a convenient trans-shipment point for harder drugs. With that comes crime and violence. Renwick's own daughter was attacked. Some local farmers who can no longer make a living, however, feel they have little choice.

It's too easy to forget that cheap food for relatively wealthy British consumers means less pay for poorer producers and feeds into a growing, general culture of poverty.

Figure 8: Bananas as % of Total Merchandise Exports

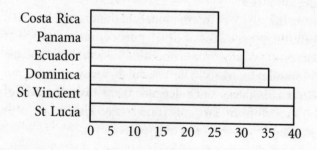

(Source: The Food and Agriculture Organization [United Nations])

Commodities

When you look at changes to the prices of the things we depend on to get us through the day, like tea, coffee and sugar, it's easy to see why the gap between global rich and poor has grown dramatically. Although the price on the packet might have risen, the 'real' price, allowing for inflation, has plummeted. Overall, across all farm products, prices have fallen by nearly half in the last forty years, and the price of some key products has fallen even more. To make things even more confusing, and making life harder to plan for millions who live on the edge of sub-sistence, prices also surge and then crash unpredictably.

As many as forty-three poor countries rely on a single commodity for over one-fifth of their export earnings. They tend to be among the poorest countries in sub-Saharan Africa or Latin America and the Caribbean, where the national income per person is under $900 per year. Everyday products like sugar, coffee, cocoa, cotton and bananas are most commonly relied upon to support local livelihoods.[21] According to the UN's Food and Agriculture Organization (FAO), the long-term downward trend in the price of farm products 'threatens the food security of hundreds of millions of people in some of the world's poorest developing countries'.

Following the advice of international aid donors and financial institutions, the populations of developing countries have been drawn increasingly into cash economies vulnerable to volatile global commodity markets. The reason so many of them are under threat is because, once dependent on cash, the sale of crops for export from farming (universally known as 'cash crops') frequently becomes the only source of it.

In real terms, the price of coffee is less than a quarter of what it was thirty years ago, and it fell 70 per cent between 1997 and 2001. The price decrease threatened to wreck the livelihoods of around 25 million people in several African and Central American countries, and was a catalyst for several food emergencies. Cocoa, the source of our multiple chocolate addictions, has a similar story to tell. In four decades from 1961, the price fell to less than one-third of its original level. The same thing happened to tea. Overproduction and huge stockpiles had a similar effect on the price of sugar. Over thirty years from 1971, sugar fell in value as an export crop to less than one-quarter of its former price.

This represents market failure on a global scale, but one that affects rich and poor very unequally. The difference in what you earn from imports and exports is called your 'terms of trade'. While terms of trade for farm products have got much worse for the poorest countries, according to the FAO, rich countries have escaped any similar long-term trends or major price fluctuations.

Coffee shows the unbalanced outcome. In the early 1990s, coffee earned producer countries around US$10–12 billion, for a product that sold mostly in rich countries for about $30 billion. Since then, income for rich-country retailers more than doubled to over $70 billion, while the share of income to the producer countries halved to $5.5 billion.[22]

Much of the crisis was predictable. For decades, Western economic advisers told poor countries to export their way to success, but many of the countries grew the same crops, flooding markets and pushing prices down. The ultimate betrayal, considering how wealthy consumers have benefited from cheap, imported food, is found in the circuitous logic of the advisers: Instead of growing food to meet your own needs as a priority, you should grow things to sell on the international markets. This earns you cash, which you can then use to buy food or spend on something else.

But poor countries have run faster, not even to stand still, but to slip back. Growing more for less, they have come to 'depend on commodity exports to finance food imports', according to the FAO. The decline in price leaves millions in poor exporting countries in a trade trap and going hungry.[23]

Oxfam estimates that if the price of the ten most important farm exports from developing countries had simply kept up with inflation since 1980, the exporters would have earned $112 billion more in 2002 than they actually received – more than double the total amount of aid given worldwide. Instead, not only are prices down, but producers the world over are being left with less of the value of what they grow compared to traders, processors and retailers. This is even the case in the US, where, in 1900, farmers received around 70 cents from every $1 worth of food bought. Now, under the rise of increasingly powerful retailers, that has shrunk to between 3–4 cents.[24]

Figure 9: Real Terms Commodity Prices

	1961–63	1971–73	1981–83	1991–93	2001-02	2000	2001	2002
Bananas	43	25	29	24	22	17.5	23.5	20.7
Cocoa	114	125	143	56	38	36.3	42.5	32.8
Coffee	n.a.	188	196	66	40	56.9	39.2	40.4
Cotton	146	158	128	70	40	52.3	41.3	38.7
Sugar	n.a.	25.28	18.11	10.15	6.56	7.24	7.44	5.68
Tea	266	159	138	95	88	96.1	89.1	86.0

(Source: FAO, 2004)

Notes: Prices are deflated by the United States Consumer Price Index (1995 = 1). Basis for prices for individual commodites: Bananas (Ecuador) US cents/lb; Cocoa (Ghana) US cents/lb; Coffee (United States) US cents/lb; Cotton (United States) US cents/lb; Sugar (London and New York) US cents/lb; Tea (Sri Lanka) US cents/kg.

The shift and concentration of power has two faces. In some areas (e.g. horticulture or coffee), retailers like the supermarkets dominate. Working often directly with large-scale suppliers, they set exacting terms and conditions for the product (if not the workforce). Big traders, on the other hand, tend to dominate the market for bulk commodities like grains and cereals, where their controlling power enables them to drive down prices. For example, Cargill, ADM and Bunge control approximately 90 per cent of the global grain trade.[25] In the face of such acute concentration of power, producers have little say over prices and virtually no choice over with whom to do business.

The irony is that under the rhetoric of 'free markets', the WTO and Northern governments restrict the freedom of poor countries to manage how they do business with the rest of the world. Stealthily, over years, the world agricultural markets have fallen under the control of a handful of giant firms. It is these firms, insulated from competition, and not the markets, that have the power to set prices. At the global level there is no regulator to prevent the emergence of monopolies or Tescopolies. Amidst all these power plays and the great shifts in the global economy, it is small-scale farmers in developing countries who get hit worst. Because of the enormity of family farming in poor countries, that means a lot of people.

Family Farms Under Threat

One of the great unforeseen and potentially devastating consequences of the rise and rise of the supermarkets is how their re-engineering of the global food supply chain will affect small-scale farmers. In Britain, this is still an important issue, but it is tempered by the fact that only a tiny percentage of the country's population depends directly on farming for its livelihoods.

The vast majority of farmers in the global South, however, operate small farms. Quite literally, billions of the world's poorest people depend on the rural economies underpinned by these farms. There are approximately 400 million known small farms worldwide. Nearly nine out of ten of those are to be found in Asia; most of the rest are in Africa. China alone accounts for almost half of the total at 193 million, followed by India, then Indonesia, Bangladesh and Vietnam. Africa has over 30 million small farms, accounting for eight out of ten farms on the continent. Most of Europe's remaining 16 million small farms are found in Central and Eastern Europe. Russia, too, has a significant number.

In Africa and Asia, the average size of farms was just 1.6 hectares in the late 1990s. Farms are also getting smaller as land gets subdivided. In Latin America, where gaps between rich and poor are starker, the average is 67 hectares. Unsurprisingly, one of the biggest social campaigns in that region is the landless movement, campaigning for redistribution of land.

Unequal distribution means that smallholdings, which numerically make up the majority of farms, occupy a minority of actual farming land. Family farms account for eight out of ten of the total number of farms in India, but only occupy a little over one-third of the land. Roughly three-quarters of Uganda's farmers are smallholders, but they have only around one-quarter of farmland. In Brazil, where one in five farmers is a smallholder, they have less than 1 per cent of the land.

Despite all the factors weighed against them, small-scale farmers are remarkably productive. In India they dominate dairy and livestock, and in the early 1990s were producing 40 per cent of foodgrains. Up to 90 per cent of farm production in Africa comes from small farms.[26]

Regardless of their importance, small farmers tend to be either ignored or undermined by policymakers. Their amazing knowledge about farming often goes unacknowledged. Their effort and disproportionately positive contribution to feeding the poorest people goes unsupported and underfunded, especially compared to the official backing given to commercial agribusiness. (I once asked a UN official at the launch of a report on 'food security' what future she saw for farming and rural people in a massive country like India. She painted a picture of shiny commercialization and increasing mechanization operating on large farms. But what would happen to the family farmers, I asked? She replied that such a process of change may create more 'flexible factors of off-farm production'. Confused, it took me about a minute to realize that she was saying her vision for farming in the developing world would result in millions of unemployed farmers. If lucky, they might get work as low-paid wage or migrant labourers, their life and death incomes vulnerable to the whims of employers and the global markets. Oh, yes, there's nothing like official euphemism to hide the brutality of economic dogma, inflexibly applied.)

Disingenuous promises litter mainstream development. The science writer and global agriculture expert Colin Tudge argues that in total, over half of the four billion people living in the so-called Third World survive by working the land, most as subsistence farmers. He calls 'fanciful' the suggestion that their future lies in following a Western development model, by abandoning the land to make way for supermarket 'efficiency' and then living in cities and working in factories and service industries. India's success at information technology is often held up as proof that people in poor countries can safely turn their backs on agrarian lives, but Tudge estimates that while 60,000 people may currently work in the IT sector in India, the country has 600 million farmers in India – 10,000 farmers for every individual IT worker.

Although highly productive, many in number and lacking support, small-scale farmers are considered to be 'among the most disadvantaged and vulnerable groups in the developing world' alongside the landless and urban poor.[27] Over half of smallholdings in Kenya, three-quarters in Ethiopia and nearly all in Mozambique are below the poverty line. One-third of farmers in India who work on less than half a hectare go hungry. Already held back at home and abroad by lack of resources, official support, information, power and infrastructure, the spread of supermarkets is set to knock back smallholders still further.

The Power to Bargain

The United Nations Conference on Trade and Development (UNCTAD) is a specialist arm of the UN dealing with the relationship between trade and human development. Inevitably, that means it has to analyse the balance of power between transnational corporations (TNCs) and developing countries. Rubens Ricupero is the Brazilian former Secretary General of UNCTAD. In 1999, as the meeting of the WTO famously collapsed amidst mass protest and clouds of tear gas in the US city of Seattle, Ricupero underlined why mistrust of transnational corporations was at the heart of the WTO's crisis of legitimacy.

Their impact, he argued, 'depends significantly on how well the host economy bargains', but '. . . the capacity of developing host countries to negotiate with TNCs is often limited'. The problem, he added, was that 'weak bargaining . . . can result in an unequal distribution of benefits or abuse of market power by TNCs'.[28]

The Dutch-based Centre for Research on Multinational Corporations (SOMO) studied the activities of supermarkets in developing countries and found farmers and producers to be in an almost impossible position. Because supermarkets have become so dominant, they represent the only possible outlet for many to sell their goods. In terms of classical economic theory, that represents market failure. Put another way, supermarkets have got poor producers and poor countries over a barrel. SOMO's Myriam Vander Stichele writes:

> For fear of losing their business, many farmers and producers accept some of the low prices offered by supermarkets, and sell with low or no profit margins. In contrast, supermarkets often take very high margins on the fresh fruit and vegetable products they sell.[29]

Supermarkets are control freaks. As we have seen, they like to avoid wholesalers and instead develop direct relationships with 'preferred suppliers', generally only large farms who must meet the scale and regularity of supply wanted by the supermarkets. They have to be able to produce fruit, vegetables and exotically named 'luxury horticulture' (i.e. flowers) to the precise colour, shape and size requirements that the companies have decided are necessary to look good in-store. These are criteria that lead to appallingly high levels of good food being wasted. 'Preferred suppliers' will often have to sign exclusive contracts with the supermarket, making their entire livelihoods dependent on keeping on good terms with the buyers. (That is why the school-children sang their welcome to Tesco on the farm in Zimbabwe.)

Once on a list of preferred suppliers, the threat of 'de-listing' is the reason most often given by producers to explain why they don't speak out against the abusive practices of supermarkets. It takes little imagination to see how the great majority of small-holders will be disadvantaged by a global food chain increasingly dominated by supermarkets. One-sided trade liberalization that opens poor country markets but not rich ones, coupled with the dumping of cheap imports into poor countries, already under-mines local small-scale farmers. They are left with little bargaining power, either against new indigenous supermarkets or when a Tesco or Carrefour come in from abroad. When they do arrive, producers face the same old bag of supermarket tricks that they use in their domestic markets, for example, having to pay to be on the supplier's list, dealing with threats of de-listing, paying for supermarket advertising, special offers and fitting out new stores, etc. etc. ad infinitum.[30]

Centralization proceeds in steps, according to retail expert Thomas Reardon. It begins with single stores sourcing what they sell and shifts to the use of distribution centres that handle first 'a zone – then a country, then a region, then globally'. With the restraint characteristic of academics, Reardon concludes that in developing countries, 'a relatively unambiguous picture appears to be emerging of exclusion of small processing and food-manu-facturing firms' all along the supermarket supply chain, and that 'the forces leading to exclusion seem to aim in just one direction'.[31]

In one case in Beijing, China, a retail chain cut its number of suppliers from 1,000 to 300 in the space of one year – as soon as the chain's new distribution centre was opened. Similar dy-namics have affected dairy farmers in Russia and livestock farmers in Central America. Small and family farms find themselves in a lose-lose situation. If they do business with the new supermarket players, they find themselves at the very weak end of a power relationship just like farmers in Britain, Europe and the US, but worse.

Meeting supermarket standards is expensive, and supermar-kets are experts at passing on their own costs to suppliers. These are costs that poorer farmers usually can't afford. In this situation many small firms and farms have gone out of business over the last decade. This dynamic, in turn, drives further concentration in the food sector as larger firms take over. On the other hand, not doing business with the big retailers means these suppliers are squeezed out of the marketplace.

Reardon points to a 'general tendency' for supermarkets to only want to deal with wealthier farmers. As supermarkets increasingly capture the market for food in towns and cities, this also cuts off an economic lifeline for small-scale farmers who once supplied the urban population through smaller stores and open-air markets.

None of this is surprising. It is the supermarkets' model. They centralize their purchasing and distribution, as Reardon puts it, to 'drive costs out of the system'.[32] It's just that the 'costs' being driven out happen to be the livelihoods of millions of family farmers and small businesses. The whole process triggers a negative redistribution of wealth on a wide scale. The rich get richer and the poor, relatively poorer. Economists love to defend economic globalization by saying that wealth trickles down. Yet a defining characteristic of the global economy in recent years has been the opposite trend, a flood of wealth from poor up to rich, where the current is flowing ever faster.

In the 1980s, for people in the world whose income was less than $1 per day, every extra $100 worth of global economic growth sent $2.20 in their direction. The 1980s was meant to be a bad decade for international poverty reduction. Everything went wrong: there was a debt crisis, interest rates went through the roof and commodity prices collapsed. But the 1990s got much worse, even after the promise of a 'peace dividend' from the end of the Cold War. During that decade, the slice of the economic growth pie that went to the poorest people shrank from $2.20 in every $100 to a miserable 60 cents.[33]

Worse still, the high environmental costs of growth such as climate change are falling disproportionately on precisely that same group of people who have the fewest resources with which to protect themselves (see Chapter Eight). People defined officially as living in extreme or 'absolute' poverty are therefore getting none of the benefits of growth, but are paying its costs.

Economists say that growth, like a rising tide, lifts all boats. To mix metaphors, something which they are inelegantly prone to do, they ask, why share the cake more evenly when we can bake a bigger one? But now sea levels really are rising as a result of global warming, driven by the pollution from economic growth, and millions of the poor have no boats in which to rise. The last time I looked, the massed ranks of orthodox economists have yet to find the ingredients, or even a recipe, to bake a spare planet to share among the world's population.

Oxfam sees the spread of supermarkets putting small and family farmers in an impossible position, increasingly excluded from both local and national markets. It calls them the 'outsiders', left as 'residual suppliers to low-priced' commodity markets and wholesalers. Fair-trade schemes offer some hope, but while they remain a niche market their impact is limited. Ironically, if they do grow, there is a different problem: if large supermarkets move in, Oxfam fears the market could then demand 'levels of scale and traceability that exclude small farmers'.[34] Some argue that the spread of supermarkets in poor countries makes an important contribution to 'market development'. The trouble is that the markets they develop then turn their backs on the poorest people.

There's also another big problem. Something rather important doesn't register properly in the supermarkets' profit and loss accounts. With them as our suppliers, we've grown accustomed, in Britain, to having what we want from wherever we want, at any time of year that we want it. The retailers are part of an economic system that recognizes only one constraint on what we consumer: the ability to pay.

Even then, access to credit enables us to live beyond our financial means. In all of this, it's easy to forget that the economy is a wholly owned subsidiary of the environment; the bigger problem we face is that we are living beyond our *environmental* means. Floating in the bubble world of supermarkets, we seem to want to have our planet and eat it too.

CHAPTER EIGHT

How Much is Enough?

'And before you finish eating breakfast this morning, you've depended on more than half the world.'

Dr Martin Luther King, Jr,
'A declaration of interdependence'[1]

Before Tesco came along, how many people among the British general public had heard of the Himalayan goji berry? 'We found out about the berries while we were researching functional foods,' said David Cooke, in charge of buying wholefoods for Tesco. 'Functional foods' refers to the pharmaceutical and food industries' efforts to combine drugs or 'supplements' with what we eat. Goji berries, says Cooke, 'have remained one of the area's [i.e. the Himalayas'] best-kept secrets because of the remoteness of the region.'

The fruit appears to be enormously nutritious, a product of the 'unique conditions' climate and altitude in the Himalayas. Our indigenous fruits, all packed with goodness – the black-berry, blueberry, raspberry, strawberry, blackcurrant, redcurrant and so on – suddenly seem old-fashioned and second-best compared to the exotic newcomer. Which is all very well, but there are consequences to extending the reach of our consumption across geographical and seasonal boundaries. Tesco is a product of the way we live in modern Britain, but it has also helped to create that way of life. It has brought within our grasp vast possibilities for consumption that were beyond the imagination of previous generations. Supermarkets like

Tesco have trained us to believe that nothing apart from our purses should constrain what, when or how much we consume. As a result, we have forgotten that we live on an island planet, and although our individual demands may be unbounded, Earth itself is subject to blurred but very real limits.

One of the defining features of life in the UK, the world's fourth-largest economy, is the sheer scale of our material consumption and the ease with which we ignore the burden that it distributes around the globe.[2] This reveals itself in our growing, one-sided, global interdependence.

A clear demonstration comes from looking at the day in a typical calendar year when, in effect, we stop relying on our own domestically available natural resources to support ourselves and start to live off the rest of the world. The moment we begin living beyond our environmental means is what can be called our *ecological debt day*. At current levels of natural-resource use in the UK, the average person goes into ecological debt around 16 April. As consumption grows, the day moves ever earlier in the year. Back in 1961 it fell on 9 July, then advanced to 14 May in 1981 before arriving in mid-April today.[3]

But the nation's high-consumption lifestyles are only possible because the rest of the world supports us with large supplies of its own natural resources. The way we live also sets a model of materialism that people in much poorer countries understandably seek to emulate. No individual country has to be entirely self-reliant, of course. We trade what we can't produce locally, and positively enjoy exotic goods that come from all around the globe. But the world as a whole does have to be self-reliant, because – so far at least – our trade relationship with the rest of the universe is yet to yield much capable of filling our supermarket shelves. As a whole, the world is living beyond the capacity of its ecosystems to regenerate. Globally, we currently go into debt

The open-veins of the global economy - how Britain depends on the rest of the world to live beyond its environmental means. The lines on the map represent resources flowing into the the UK using a standardized measurement that shows the size of their ecological footprint.

If the whole world consumed at the average rate of people in Britain we would need the equivalent of 3.1 planets' worth of resources.
If the US was the model the figure would be 5.3. We currently break even at the consumption level of people in Mauritius.

Country	Number of planets needed to sustain whole world at that level of national consumption	
US		5.3
UK		3.1
France		3.0
Germany		2.5
Russia		2.4
Brazil		1.2
Mauritius		1.0
China		0.8
India		0.4
Malawi		0.3

(Source: nef, 2006)

around 9 October. After that date we are, in effect, running down our natural capital.

In a striking example of what that means, research reported in the journal *Science* showed that fish stocks had collapsed in nearly one-third of the world's sea fisheries. At current rates of decline in marine biodiversity, the researchers warned that by 2050 there would be little left to fish from the seas, with enormous impacts for humanity.[4]

Looking back, if the whole world had wanted to share UK lifestyles in 1961, when Tesco's dream of national domination would have seemed comical, the Earth would just have managed with its available resources. One planet would have been enough. Today, if the whole world wanted lifestyles like those enjoyed in the UK, we would need 3.1 planets to support them. That means that to live within our overall environmental budget and give people around the world a chance to meet their needs, the UK will have to reduce its levels of consumption and the burden its lifestyles create.

Understanding the impact of ecological footprints sometimes means having to visualize long and complex supply chains. Take, for example, one environmentally significant product that is invisible to most consumers, but is an ingredient in a huge range of things they buy: palm oil. The UK imported over 700,000 tonnes of it in 2004.

Palm oil is a key ingredient for cheap chocolate. Oil and wax from the palm kernel tree are used to add bulk and shelf life to a variety of products ranging from food to cosmetics. Tesco admits it stocks a 'wide range of products, both own-brand and branded, many of which have palm oil as an ingredient'.[5] The products include bread, chocolate spread, mixed nuts, margarine, oatcakes and more. Palm-tree plantations make good money in Southeast Asia, where the trees grow quickly and plantations are expanding rapidly; but their spread, and the way they are grown in vast monocultures, is creating serious problems. The destruction of rainforests and other unique ecosystems and the generation of local pollution and social conflicts rooted in the increasing power of agribusiness have all been reported.[6]

Early in 2005 Friends of the Earth wrote to Tesco, asking it to trace its palm oil and adopt minimum production standards. By the end of the year the campaigners accused Tesco of inaction, saying, 'Their failure to act means that Tesco shoppers are unwittingly contributing to rainforest destruction and the extinction of Asia's only great ape.'[7] Following consistent pressure Tesco finally agreed to join the Roundtable on Sustainable Palm Oil.

So, oddly, there is a thread connecting chocolate spread to palm trees and shrinking rainforests in Southeast Asia – but that the thread is difficult to see. Examples like this are growing in size, number and complexity as the world becomes ever more interdependent.

Peaking Too Early

Since the mid-1970s, international trade has made up a growing share of our national income and now accounts for nearly half. In other words, for the last three decades our economy has grown increasingly interdependent with the rest of the world. In the four decades from 1964 to 2004, imports to the UK increased by an enormous 257 per cent, and they keep rising by over 3 per cent per year.[8]

A similar pattern is repeated at both the European and global levels. Interdependence is growing. The widening veins and arteries of economic globalization, though, depend on the oil that flows through the system to keep it alive. Projected problems with the supply of oil in the medium-to-long term introduce a key frailty to the system, a kind of fossil-fuel sclerosis. A range of projections suggests that the moment when global oil production peaks and begins a long slow decline can occur at any time between now and 2020 (sooner is more likely than later). The phenomenon has become known variously as 'peak oil', the 'topping point' or 'the Hubbert Peak', after geologist King Hubbert who, in the 1950s, accurately predicted the moment two decades later when North American oil production would peak.[9]

When the peak happens, the gap between supply and rising global demand will cause a huge spike in the price of oil. In the 1970s, we experienced two 'oil shocks' when the oil-producing nations gathered under OPEC took control of the global market. Rationing, blackouts, debt, recession and a huge push for energy conservation followed. Back then, however, there were so-called 'swing producers' outside the OPEC block that softened the blow to the world economy, acting as a buffer for supplies.

The oil shocks of the 1970s will seem like nothing compared to the crunch of global peak oil. Our deepening lines of interdependence fuelled by oil will, instead of fostering economic cooperation, transmit economic distress signals. The lines of fossil-fuel addiction that connect the supermarkets to their globalized supply chains, and which link the network of vast hypermarkets to endless housing estates of suburban sprawl, will be broken.

A permanent dilemma for poor countries is what balance they should strike between using land to grow crops for sale in the casino of the global commodity markets, and what should be used for growing food for domestic consumption. Another emerging clash that will be intensified by the imminent peak and decline of global oil production is between land for food and land for crops to produce biofuels. These conflicts stand to divide poor consumers from wealthy consumers, and further divide rich countries and poor countries.

There is huge hype surrounding biofuels as a solution to rising fuel prices, but such crops demand huge swathes of land. According to the Department for Transport, Britain only has enough available land to provide one-third of its transport fuel needs from crops by 2050 (a figure others consider over-optimistic).[10] With current and growing levels of demand, more will have to come from elsewhere. It's all too easy to foresee wealthy owners of vast 4x4s driving with a smugly ethical aura because the cars are powered by biofuels, forgetting that the land to grow them was probably switched from growing food or created by forest clearance. Following the example of how the Amazon rainforest has been slashed to provide land for the growing global demand for soybeans, there will be unavoidable new pressures on forests and farmland due to biofuels just as the land and forests are needed even more for food and to regulate the atmosphere.

As the UK's reliance on trade has grown, its traditionally high level of food self-sufficiency has dropped. The trade gap for food, animal feed and drink widened in 2003 to £11 billion, as we imported more than we exported.[11] UK food self-sufficiency has been falling steadily since the mid-1990s. According to the most recent statistics available (and allowing for changes in the way the government calculates its figures), our domestic pro-duction of indigenous food now appears to have hit its lowest point for half a century.[12] Our dependence on the rest of the world's ecosystems to feed us is growing.

Lorries Passing in the Night: Ecologically Wasteful Trade

Rarely heard in the rush to praise international trade as a panacea for all our economic problems are the many often nonsensical examples of lorries passing in the night, loaded with almost identical goods heading in opposite directions. The environmental impact of petrol, diesel, aircraft and shipping fuel is not included in their price. Although there is a large environmental impact from freight transport, there is little economic incentive to reduce it.

The consequence is that orthodox economists don't even raise an eyebrow at figures showing that the UK both exports and then re-imports half a million kg of gingerbread in given year. In a world of interdependence where what we do is set within unavoidable environmental limits, this is not the bristling competitiveness of a successful European economy – it is ecologically wasteful trade.

The twenty-first-century equivalent of shipping coals to Newcastle appears to be not the exception but the rule. For example, in 2004 the UK imported 17.2 million kg of chocolate-covered waffles and wafers and exported 17.6 million kg; we imported 10.2 million kg of milk and cream from France and exported 9.9 million. The figures for the same trade with Germany were 15.5 million kg and 17.2 million. Germany sent us 1.5 million kg of potatoes and we sent them, yes, 1.5 million kg of potatoes. We imported 43,000 scarves from Canada and exported 39,000. Drink is also swilling around the international markets; the UK imported £310 million worth of beer in 2004 and exported £313 million worth. For spirits, the figures were £344 million and £463 million respectively.

Just as we imported 44,000 tonnes of frozen boneless cuts of chicken, we exported 51,000 tonnes of fresh boneless chicken. From an environmental perspective, it would seem that some-one somewhere is pulling a chicken's leg.

Food Costs the Earth

We spend less of what we earn on food in Britain today than we have for decades. In one sense, food is now very cheap. Just 16 pence in the pound of what we spend goes on food and drink, excluding booze. But we haven't been paying the real price, and that could all be about to change.

In the space of three months from May 2006, something strange happened to the price of food at Tesco, the supermarket so proud of its aggressively low prices. The cost of butter went up 21 per cent; milk, 11 per cent; bread, 7 per cent; and instant coffee, over 6 per cent. Across a huge range of products, the price of a basket of goods busted the background rate of inflation, which never crawled much over 2 per cent.[13]

Heavy rains in Vietnam helped push coffee prices to a seven-year high, while poor weather drove wonderfully named 'orange juice futures' to a sixteen-year price high. Early summer heatwaves led to poor wheat yields and early harvests in Britain. In the Ukraine, Russia, Hungary, Slovakia and North America, crops were hit by bad weather. In Poland, Minister of Agriculture Andrzej Lepper feared that up to 20 per cent of the country's entire harvest would be destroyed by drought if the heatwave continued. According to the European Commission, droughts were driving up both demand and price for cereals.[14]

All this, added to the third consecutive year of rising fuel costs, led two of Britain's biggest flour millers, Rank Hovis and ADM Milling, to increase the price of flour by around £29 per tonne – meaning knock-on price rises of between 15–20 per cent for producers who use a lot of flour.[15] According to the National Association of Master Bakers, small craft bakers stood to be hit particularly badly. As with so many things in an age dominated by the rise of big phenomena like the supermarkets and global warming, it's the little guys who get it.

Tesco conceded that shoppers would be paying more for food because of the extreme global weather conditions: 'Obviously poor harvests and changes in market conditions can have an effect on availability of produce.' Even fruit, which we might imagine happily bathing itself to ripeness in any amount of sun, suffered in the heat. Yields were down, and with southern Europe (a 'default supplier' when crops fail at home) also in trouble and not able to provide, prices went up.[16] This could, of course, be dismissed as merely a stumble in the food system, attributable to normal seasonal variation, but there are some inconvenient and important voices in the background suggesting otherwise.

One of them is President of the American Association for the Advancement of Science, Professor John Holdren. In one of his first public statements in this role, he said global warming was already happening, and much faster than previously thought:

We are not talking anymore about what climate models say might happen in the future. We are experiencing dangerous human disruption of the global climate and we're going to experience more.[17]

Even more worrying was the conclusion of a conference specially convened by the Royal Society in 2005 to look at the impact of climate change on how we grow food. Results were presented of a series of large-scale field experiments on a range of staple crops including maize, rice, soybeans and wheat. They showed much worse impacts on food production than the pattern of global warming predicted by the Intergovernmental Panel on Climate Change (IPCC). Increasing temperatures, drought and ground-level ozone concentrations 'will result in substantial reduction in crop yields'.

Several people, if not sceptical about the fact of climate

change, have argued that its impacts will not be as bad as many fear – and even that the prospect of growing more tropical plants in British back gardens means we should welcome it. Based on controlled laboratory experiments, many believe that with more carbon in the atmosphere, plants would have more of what they need to photosynthesize, grow more and possibly even produce 'bumper crops'. But research revealed at the Royal Society conference showed that negative impacts are likely to far outweigh any positive consequences.

The difference between the hoped-for outcome and what actually happened was down to the intrusion of the real world. Professor Steve Long of Illinois University reported:

> Growing crops much closer to real conditions has shown that increased levels of carbon dioxide in the atmosphere will have roughly half the beneficial effects that were previously hoped for in the event of climate change.[18]

Experiments were carried out in the US, China and Japan. Increased temperatures in a warming world are likely to lead to more smog of low-level ozone. One reason for pessimism is that when the ozone levels were increased in the field trials, crop yields collapsed. As a result, Long concluded: 'We need to seriously re-examine our predictions of future global food production', with production 'likely to be far lower than previously estimated'. Rises in ozone levels are expected in Europe, the US, China, India and the Middle East, and overall these estimates suggest there could be a decline of between 10–15 per cent in world's crop yields by 2050.[19]

This is bad news for everyone, but it is exceptionally bad news for the hundreds of millions of people globally who already do not get enough to eat and who live in places where it is difficult to guarantee that crops will rise from the soil each year to feed them. Lower crop yields overall not only mean less food to go around but also mean higher prices, which hurt the poorest first and most. Africa, in particular, is vulnerable to climate change, as even Prime Minister Tony Blair pointed out:

> The size of its land mass means that in the middle of the continent, overall rises in temperature will be up to double the global rise, with increased risk of extreme droughts, floods and outbreaks of disease.[20]

Such acute awareness of Africa's plight, however, unfortunately failed to stop Britain missing its own greenhouse gas emission reduction targets, or ensuring that two key global funds set up to help poor countries cope with climate change contained more than around one-tenth of the money pledged by the time it was due in 2005.

The consequences are only too real. Severe drought hit the Horn of Africa as well as East Africa in 2005–06, leaving around 8 million people across East Africa with a food crisis even after better rains returned. So many animals died that herders will need years to recover their livestock and livelihoods. When the rains did come back they were 'patchy and erratic' in parts of northern Kenya and Somalia that are still recovering from a four-year long drought.[21] In July 2006 the World Food Programme announced that it was running out of food stocks for millions of people in vulnerable communities in Kenya.

Africa's climate has always been erratic, especially in semi-arid areas, but the continent is warming. Its six warmest years on record have occurred since 1987. Worldwide, 2005 was the hottest year on record. If the science is even remotely right, further warming, changes in rainfall and disruption to farming are inevitable. As mentioned in the previous chapter, the climate modelling from the Hadley Centre predicts that by 2090 half the world's land surface will be prone to some form of drought, and nearly one-third will be prone to extreme drought.

It's not just a problem for places like Africa, which are rightly or wrongly already synonymous in the Western imagination with hunger. A recent report from the UK-based Working Group on Climate Change and development detailed threats to livelihoods across Latin America and the Caribbean. Farming employs around one-third of the working population of Latin America. Studies in Brazil, Chile, Argentina and Uruguay show falls in yields for a number of key crops such as barley, grapes, maize, potatoes, soybeans and wheat, possibly linked to global warming. Climate change could also threaten more damaging impacts from plant and animal diseases and pests.

The IPCC noted:

> Large alterations in Latin American ecosystems resulting from climate change impacts would have the potential to endanger the livelihoods of subsistence farmers and pastoral peoples, who make up a large portion of the rural populations of the Andean plateaus and tropical and subtropical forest areas.

Urban populations that depend on food and other resources from rural areas are also at risk. Asia is home to the world's most populated countries and to 87 per cent of the world's known 400 million small farms. China alone accounts for almost half followed by India with 23 per cent. Indonesia, Bangladesh and Vietnam are also home to millions of small-scale farmers.[22]

There are now at least 815 million chronically malnourished people in the world; 95 per cent of them are in developing countries. Inequitable access to food is a major factor in fuelling world hunger, but global warming is now set to further undermine food security.

For several years we've been aware of the link between food and its impact on the environment, thanks to the concept of 'food miles'. It's a measure that shows the crazy inefficiency of a food system that can use more energy to move food around than might actually be contained in the calorific value in the food itself.

A Tesco advert for sugar snap peas shows a pair of perky peas above some snappy copy highlighting the fact that, although the vegetables had been flown by jet all the way from Guatemala they would have to be delivered to your door in a Tesco van: 'Oh well, you can't have it all', the ad knowingly bemoaned.

It's mid-September. There is a race to get the first citrus fruit of the new season into supermarkets. Oranges, grapefruits and what the industry calls 'easy peelers' – in other words, satsumas and tangerines – are ready for picking and shipping. One supplier airfreights early-ripening red pomelo, a relative of the grapefruit, from Israel into the UK for Tesco.[23] The form of transport is less than climate-friendly. Israeli exporters see opportunities opening up because doubts hang over their US competitors in Florida due to the impact of hurricanes and extreme weather. Why would Tesco, which at this point has publicly protested its environmental credentials, see food flown into its stores when other, more energy-efficient forms of transport are available?

Tara Garnett of the Food Climate Research Network at the University of Surrey observed:

The purpose of airfreighting in this case is not to bring in foods that are so perishable that they would not survive a sea or road journey, since citrus fruits are reasonably robust. Tesco's use of airfreight on this occasion is simply to secure a competitive advantage – for Tesco to be the first and the earliest, if only for 10 days.[24]

The numbers reveal a worsening problem. As a government study showed, the transport of food has a huge and growing range of effects on both the environment and our immediate quality of life. Road congestion, road accidents, climate change, noise and air pollution all increase as the amount and distance travelled by our food goes up. Reduced to a financial cost, the government estimated that the environmental and social costs of food transport come to £9 billion per year. Shopping by car accounts for 40 per cent of that sum, and over half of the total cost was caused by road congestion.[25]

Figures are not easy to find about individual supermarkets, but in 2004, MP Norman Baker, the environment spokesperson for the Liberal Democrat Party, produced a report on the supermarkets' environmental performance. The identity of individual stores was notionally disguised. However, data on the supermarkets' staff, outlets and profits is so distinctive that Tesco stuck out like an elephant hiding behind a curtain.

Baker revealed that Tesco lorries travelled 68 million miles in the course of a year. To put that into perspective, it is the equivalent of roughly 142 round trips to the moon. At a rate of one round trip per two and a half days, it is a bit like interplanetary commuting to work. [26]

The National Consumer Council rated British supermarkets on how green their operations were. They looked at issues of waste, food transport, impacts on nature and promotion of more environmentally friendly farming. In the resulting league table, starting with the best performers, Tesco came behind Waitrose, Marks & Spencer, Sainsbury's, Asda/Wal-Mart and the Co-op.[27]

Not only is more food being flown, shipped and trucked around the world, but because of the growth of out-of-town shopping, we're also driving further to buy it. Exactly how far we are driving to shop depends of whose figures you rely upon. The government's Department for Environment, Food and Rural Affairs (Defra) estimates that we all travel, on average, 136 miles a year by car to shop for food. So-called 'urban food kilometres' increased by an enormous 27 per cent in a single decade between 1992 and 2002. The Department for Transport gives a higher figure, estimating that we drive 209 miles per year to buy food.[28] Defra also calculates that double the amount of food now moves around British roads by heavy lorry compared to three decades ago, and that this form of food transport now accounts for one-quarter of all heavy lorries on the road.

Our supposedly advanced, service-driven, 'weightless' economy seems to just be getting heavier. More stuff is travelling further. In the UK we have 1,580 million tonnes of freight (including food) moving around, up nearly one-quarter in twenty years, and it travels 149 billion tonne-km (a measure of weight and distance travelled), up by two-thirds in two decades.[29] Food freight is also growing significantly faster than the average for all sectors, travelling both further and making a more complex journey along supply lines.

Compared to both government figures, leading academics working on the food industry think we're each driving even further for our food, up to 255 miles a year.[30] Jules Pretty and Tim Lang both analyse what can be done to make how we produce, buy and eat our food more environmentally friendly. They estimate that if we bought more local and organic food and shopped by bus, bike and on foot, leaving the car at home, we could save over £4 billion worth of environmental damages to the British economy.

Although, according to this study we drive an average of 5 miles per week to shop for food and nearly half as much again for other things, car use has become so automatic that it often seems we have forgotten how to walk. At the bottom of the road where I live, there is a large supermarket that dominates the town centre. It is perhaps 200m from my house. Yet as I walk towards it, before veering off to go either to the train station or to my wonderful small, local food shop, I pass people in my street unloading their cars with just one or two bags of shopping that they have driven to and from the supermarket to buy. Being English, I resist the temptation to scream, 'What are you doing – it is *so* much easier to walk!' and just tut quietly to myself instead.

Supermarkets have almost single-handedly created an expectation among consumers that we should be able to eat a wide range of exotic fruit and vegetables at any time of year. They set up complex global supply lines to make sure that they can deliver on the demand they have manufactured.

Defenders of the status quo like to point out that the most environmentally damaging form of freight – flying goods around the world – represents only a small percentage of food transport and an even smaller percentage of total, global greenhouse gas emissions.

It's possible to see the flaw in this argument by considering the analogy of the overflowing bath. If a tap is running only slightly faster than the ability of the overflow pipe to cope, the bath will still flood the house regardless. This is the problem with greenhouse gas emissions: if the tap of the global economy is running faster than the ability of the atmosphere to safely absorb its waste greenhouse gases, we get overflow. Whatever adds to that makes the problem worse. We now know that in climate terms, the tap is running too fast. Without more radical cuts elsewhere (which, for the record, are not happening), the fossil-fuel-intensive transport of food along the supermarket supply chain is unsustainable.

Food has become very important to the airfreight industry. It is the biggest single sector for airfreight, making up about 1 tonne in every 7.5 tonnes of goods flown. In the three years up to

2003, food imports by air went up by nearly half – 47 per cent. Exports by air grew, too. Both are helped by the fact that, in a deliberately negotiated oversight, aviation fuel is neither taxed, nor its greenhouse gas emissions included in global agreements to control climate change. Some suggest that to transport food, planes are simply making the best use of empty luggage space on passenger aircraft. This isn't true. Over half of food, needing special storage arrangements, flies in on dedicated freight planes.[31] The use of specialized airfreighters is also growing faster than the amount of goods carried in the bellies of passenger aircraft.

Airlines refer to passengers as 'self-loading cargo', but the goods the airlines have to load themselves are increasing more quickly in volume, especially to and from markets in Asia, the continent especially targeted for massive supermarket expansion. There are few better examples of the difference between measures of economic and ecological efficiency. You can grow exotic fruit with cheap labour in a poor country and then transport it cheaply because fuel has low or, internationally, no environmental taxes. It's economically efficient according to daftly limited criteria, but ecological nonsense; because of rigged international markets, it frequently makes no difference in terms of raising people out of poverty.

Supermarket Subsidy

Following in the footsteps of the US, long-distance road transport systems are increasingly common in Europe and are subsidized by government. The European Roundtable of Industrialists (ERT) is made up of the chief executives and chairs of around forty-five of Europe's largest companies. Together the roundtable represents a corporate turnover worth €1.5 trillion.[32] The ERT called for $60 billion worth of new motorways and rail projects, and threatened to relocate out of Europe if it didn't get it.

The European Commission largely embraced its demands, and is contributing to the funding of a €400 billion Trans-European Network, the largest transport infrastructure programme in history.[33] A recent priority demanded by the ERT is the expansion of the Trans-European Network into Central and Eastern Europe as part of the EU's enlargement programme. The EU accordingly designated €15 billion to spend on this by 2006.[34] By convenient coincidence (Tesco is not a member of the ERT), Central and Eastern Europe happen to be markets prioritized by Tesco for expansion, and the new roads will make life much easier for its delivery lorries.

In Britain, traffic volumes are predicted to keep rising. Government transport officials see this as a natural corollary of economic growth. According to Paul Hamblin, the head of transport at the Council for the Protection of Rural England:

> Billions are to be spent on new roads which will increase traffic levels, damage the countryside and further erode its tranquillity. And all this to shave a paltry 23 seconds off a 10 km journey in ten years' time.

The House of Commons Select Committee for Transport, Local Government and the Regions commented that, 'The [government's ten-year transport] plan should not be dominated by high-cost infrastructure projects at the expense of smaller but equally effective measures.'[35] The latest ten-year plan for transport focuses on reducing congestion rather than total traffic volume. It neglects the role of urban regeneration and the need for greater 'localization' of food shopping in reducing the need to travel. Instead, it perversely provides benefits to those who travel the most.

Get Rich Quick, Stay Poor Long

Failing to account for the environment means that we end up treating the planet as if it were a business in liquidation, observed the great environmental economist Herman Daly. If you were managing a business, it would be considered grossly negligent to have no idea of what your assets were or the level of your cash flow. Yet this is how we manage our environmental resources. When we deplete oil in the North Sea and then burn it without restraint, causing climate change, or overfish our oceans and push stocks to the edge of collapse, we treat those resources as if they were free income to the economy.

If pushed, we look for easy ways out. Oil companies and airlines give us the opportunity to offset our carbon emissions so that we can keep flying and driving with a clear conscience and not worry about global warming; but these evasions are chimerical. Apart from anything else, they ignore the laws of physics. You can't hide from entropy. Planting trees, though sometimes innately attractive, will not stop climate change. You cannot swap stable storehouses of carbon like coal or oil for unstable ones like forests. This is not carbon offsetting, it is carbon laundering. Woodlands can be 'sinks' of carbon, in other words storing more than they release into the atmosphere, but if they die or burn they become sources. The whole practice of sequestering carbon is unreliable and inefficient. As Dr Kevin Anderson of the Manchester University-based Tyndall Centre points out that to generate a single unit's worth of light energy from a household bulb takes over thirteen units of total energy. That's because so much energy gets lost due to waste during fuel production, energy generation, transmission and final consumption.[36] He believes the approach is both uncertain and ineffective. 'Offsetting is a dangerous delaying technique,' he says, 'because it helps us avoid tackling the task. It helps us sleep well at night when we shouldn't sleep well at night.'[37] Even the *Financial Times* described as 'satisfyingly Machiavellian' the way businesses can 'forestall regulation by behaving with conspicuous virtue'.[38] But as Winston Churchill pointed out during the Second World War, it is not enough that we are 'doing our best, we have got to do what is necessary'. It is an enduring myth that technology will allow us to tackle all environmental problems and excuse us from making serious changes to how we live.

The UK Treasury and the Prime Minister's office commissioned a report on the economics of climate change that became known as the Stern Review, after the civil servant, Sir Nicholas Stern, who oversaw it. At its launch, Prime Minister Tony Blair, Chancellor Gordon Brown and Stern repeated a mantra that there is no clash or barely even a connection between growth and meeting targets on climate change.

The review itself suggested something very different. It said that a global temperature of $2°C$ or more above pre-industrial levels is likely to trigger 'rapid, major, irreversible' impacts from climate change. To have a good chance of staying below that level, it said that greenhouse gas concentration in the atmosphere should not go above a threshold of 450ppmv[39] CO_2 equivalent. At current rates of accumulation in the atmosphere, that leaves less than ten years from 2006 to turn the corner. The world economy depends on fossil fuels for more than 80 per cent of its energy. Even allowing for greater efficiency and use of renewable energy, more global economic growth will burn more carbon.

To hit any given target to stabilize atmospheric greenhouse gases, there will be a level of growth commensurate with it. In other words, there will, yes, be an unavoidable climate-related limit to growth. This might be economic heresy, but it will also be obvious to any schoolchild studying maths, chemistry and physics. When I asked Blair, Brown and Stern what level of global economic growth, even under optimistic low-carbon scenarios, might be compatible with preventing runaway climate change, they could not even compute the question. People in the audience, however, understood it perfectly well as the murmur of acknowledgement attested.

A double whammy is set to hit the world's most vulnerable people, upon whom rests the responsibility to get food into the mouths of hundreds of millions in the global South. As climate change increases the precariousness of livelihoods everywhere from Latin America to China and Africa, small-scale farmers stand to be further marginalized by the centralized logistics and international expansion of the supermarkets. The danger is that if the climate doesn't get them, then the supermarkets will.

Yet it is possible, if far from guaranteed, that we could converge on a global food system capable of working within environmental limits, meeting the needs of vulnerable, hungry people and promoting vibrant, diverse and distinctive local communities. Chapters Ten and Eleven ask in more detail what that system might look like. What would be the role of super-markets in a more equitable and sustainable future?

Colin Tudge's *So Shall We Reap* provides a practical and convincing picture of how better to organize farming globally. He thinks the big chain retailers don't fit, and that the future is much more local. As long as the global food system is designed primarily to profit multinationals by supplying the whims of wealthy consumers, he says, it will be impossible to design a way of farming that is both resilient to climate change and that feeds people in need. Says Tudge:

> [Supermarkets] are playing the international trade game, buying as cheaply as possible, which means that they are buying from the people who are most desperate. If you have an agriculture that is designed to feed people they [super-

markets] have no role, there is nothing they do that could not be done by smaller companies.[40]

Jane Jacobs drew an analogy between the functioning of eco-systems and the way economies work. She asked the question:

Can the way fields and forests maximize their intakes and uses of sunlight teach us something about how economies expand wealth and jobs and can do this in environmentally beneficial ways?[41]

Such a simple question has profound implications for how the world does business. Jacobs criticizes conventional approaches to tackling poverty as being a 'thing theory' of development: 'The Thing Theory supposes that development is the result of possessing things such as factories, dams, schools, tractors . . . things subsumed under the category of infrastructure.' (Hyper-markets could be added to that list.) These, she adds, 'don't mysteriously carry the process along with them. To suppose that things, per se, are sufficient to produce development creates false expectations and futilities. Worse, it evades measures that might actually foster development.'

Jacobs says it is important to understand that economic life predates foreign-aid programmes and the investments of multi-national corporations. These, she says, are 'relatively recent froth on economic life'.[42]

The economy-ecology analogy sees exports as essentially 'discharges of economic energy' like clear-felling and extracting timber from a forest. Successful regeneration, though, is built on maximum economic diversification. At the heart of conven-tional economic models, however, there is a tendency towards specialization based on the flawed assumptions of comparative advantage and international competitiveness. Jacobs writes:

In an ecosystem, the essential contributions made within the [natural] conduit are created by diverse biological activities. In the teeming economy, the essential contributions made within the [social and economic] conduit are created by diverse economic activities.[43]

In both systems, thanks to the diversity with which received energy in the form of either sunlight or, for example, foreign aid is used, fragmented and reused, that incoming energy will leave more or less lasting evidence of its passage through the forest or community. Under this model, supermarket-led centralization and control of the global food chain becomes anathema to meeting human needs or environmental challenges.

Farming in the future will need to be resilient in the face of climate change, productive enough to feed a still-growing population and able to survive on a shrinking diet of fossil fuels. That is an enormous challenge, and there is a growing library of detailed, optimistic accounts of how it might be met in practice.[44] Put simply, though, what is a low-carbon farming system going to look like? Huge amounts of fossil fuels go both to make the pesticides and fertilizers and to power the large-scale mechanized infrastructure relied upon by chemical-intensive commercial farming. For that reason alone (and there are many others), organic farming methods and a wider range of low-input, sustainable agricultural approaches will become increasingly important. The more successful of these have already turned their backs on the mindset embodied by a countryside covered in vast deserts of wheat, and tend to grow a diverse range of crops that are well adapted to the local climate and ecology. Some may balk at the prospect, but more vegetarian-type diets are also much less energy-intensive than dinner tables heaving with pounds of steak. It's incredibly inefficient to use animals to convert plants into meat-fat and protein for us to eat.

Some of the world's most populated regions, like parts of Asia, have cuisines that are essentially vegetarian. The great variety of Indian dishes has given Britain some of its most popular and flavoursome cooking; there's no reason why we can't feast on climate-friendly food. The more we can do to reduce the distance food travels by growing it as close as reasonably possible to the plate it will be eaten off will obviously help too, as will minimizing wasteful packaging.

In years to come, when we reflect with a disbelieving shake of the head on our current profligacy, I believe we may be haunted by a variation of Hannah Arendt's observation on 'the banality of evil'. For our generation it will instead be the banality of conspicuous consumption that ushered in a domino effect of linked economic, social and environmental crises. Climate change, rising fuel prices, the need for hungry people to be able to feed themselves and not to mention a backlash against clone towns, impersonal big business and a new popular desire for real, local food – suddenly supermarkets look very out of place in the modern world.

CHAPTER NINE

Win Back Where You Live

*'I deny that the big shop is the best shop; and I especially deny that
people go there because it is the best shop. And if I be asked why, I
answer at the end with the unanswerable fact with which I began at the
beginning. I know it is not merely a matter of business, for the simple
reason that the business men themselves tell me it is merely a matter of
bluff. It is they who say that nothing succeeds like a mere appearance of
success. It is they who say that publicity influences us without our will
or knowledge. It is they who say that "It Pays to Advertise"; that is, to
tell people in a bullying way that they must "Do It Now", when they
need not do it at all.'*

G. K. Chesterton, *The Outline Of Sanity*, 1927

Curious new acronyms are spontaneously appearing in communities around the country: RATRUN, HASSLE and PINBAT;
SCAMROD, CAASH, CHRISS and Unthank Road. Could this
be the result of a mass escape from Internet-based virtual reality
of the pseudonyms people increasingly hide behind?

It's only when you come across TESCNO that it becomes
apparent what is happening. Even as the giant supermarket
continues to grow, a counter-tide is rising. Across the UK,
communities have begun to organize against the impact of Tesco
and the other big retailers. Sooner or later, news of what they are
doing finds its way to Judith Whately and her overworked and
underpaid (if paid at all) colleagues. Together they help run the
website Tescopoly.[1] The idea for it came from her, together with
food campaigners Vicki Hird, Jacqui Mackay and Josh Gilbert.

Judith doesn't have much time to answer the phone or reply to emails. She's too busy dealing with angry people. They're not angry with her; they're angry with Tesco. Most are determined to do something to stop the company's further expansion. As of late 2006, Tescopoly has uncovered more than 330 different battles over supermarket sites. In the twelve months up to October of that year, there were 175 active local campaigns against supermarkets; 125 were to do with new store developments. Of the total for the year, a staggering 138 were mobilized against Tesco. The next-highest number of campaigns was seventeen, and they were focused on Asda/Wal-Mart.

Whately had been involved in another coalition called Breaking the Armlock, which took its name from Tony Blair's famous observation to suppliers and farmers that supermarkets had them trapped. Of the origins of Tescopoly, she says:

> We hadn't wanted to pick on any one supermarket, but we
> got more and more calls from councillors and local people
> complaining about Tesco. There is a movement. We get more
> and more calls saying, 'We're happy you're there.' We've
> almost become a therapeutic support group for people who
> feel pushed around by Tesco.

Like many other people, Whately has a kind of respect for Tesco, calling it a smart company of slick operators. But she also sees the fallout from the store's arrogance: 'You hear the frustration of the people who encounter them. They [Tesco] always seem to be one step ahead.' However, one community in East Suffolk in a town called Saxmundham has managed, so far at least, to keep one step ahead of Tesco.

Saxmundham Thrives by Saying No to Tesco

That fact that we trip over a Tesco wherever we go can make it hard to imagine what a town would be like without the supermarkets. The company's disingenuous argument is that it is successful because it gives customers what they want. The reality, as we've seen, is a little different: Tesco pushes its way into and around towns and cities by playing the planning game, then indulges in a range of anti-competitive practices to put competitors out of business. High visibility plus the killing of competition presents consumers with a fait accompli: Of course they'll shop at Tesco, it's a self-fulfilling prophecy – there's nowhere else to go. The only waterhole in a drought is bound to have a queue.

Of course, lots of communities don't want a Tesco, and sometimes they're successful in stopping the incursion. In 1998 Saxmundham said 'no' to Tesco. How did they resist Tesco's good neighbourliness, and offer of 'every little helps'? Surely the town suffered by turning its back on Tesco's promised power to regenerate communities, not to mention the daily range of special offers?

In fact, life without Tesco is going alarmingly well. When it first made its planning application, Caroline Cranbrook, a Saxmundham resident and part of the Campaign to Protect Rural England (CPRE), surveyed a number of towns and villages that would have fallen within the supermarket's catchment area. Then she kept a unique record of what happened next.

Tesco's own impact study showed that the proposed store's influence would touch on eighty-one shops in six market towns and nineteen villages. Cranbrook's survey at the time revealed that, out of the eighty-one, only two welcomed Tesco; twelve hoped for their own survival; and sixty-seven believed the superstore would put them out of business. This mattered, because local traders employed over 500 people and bought products from over 200 local producers.

However, supermarkets, as detailed earlier, have a terrible record of sourcing local products, which might make up as little as 1–2 per cent of a store's turnover.[2] So-called 'locality foods', where the area producing them is part of the product's identity (e.g. Wensleydale cheese), also get poor representation.

In the eight years since Cranbrook's first study, the general landscape of British retail had been transformed. Independent stores died off like indigenous plants and animals unable to compete with the exotic, invasive species of supermarkets. In and around Saxmundham, the town that said no to Tesco, things were different. In Cranbrook's 2006 survey, she found vibrant, diverse, strong and independent local economies along with communities that supported them.

The number of local shops hadn't gone down, but remained constant. Market towns had kept their butchers, bakers, fish-mongers and grocers selling fresh vegetables. The number of local and regional food suppliers in the area actually went up, rising from 300 to 370, and they were selling an even wider range of local products. Farm shops and farmers' markets also grew in number. The CPRE concluded that this left the country with 'a stark choice: more superstores . . . or more local food, shops and jobs linking people with the places and landscapes where they live'.

The experience in East Suffolk showed, according to the CPRE, a 'viable alternative to being spoon-fed by the super-markets'. In just a few years, living without Tesco resulted in small shops prospering; more businesses providing more con-sumer choice; more people knowing where their food came from and trusting its origins; increased 'food tourism'; a well-managed local countryside connected to the community; more vibrant towns and villages; and more direct human contact.[3]

Saxmundham's success drew nationwide attention. The suc-cessful Friday Street farm shop on the Aldeburgh Road sent one national newspaper into panegyrics:

Set up by Pauline and Roger Blyth on their farm, this sprawling independent supermarket, with its teashop and its maize maze, stocks produce from 80–100 local suppliers, ranging from organic beef to premium chutney in clay pots handpainted by a local artist. The choice is impressive: you can buy local eggs, quail eggs or duck eggs, and local ice-cream from three different farms.[4]

The CPRE study also revealed some of the more subtly corrosive effects of having supermarkets like Tesco dominate the economy. For example, the small fruit and vegetable shop in Saxmundham's marketplace called Cherries would never have existed. 'If Tesco had been here, we wouldn't have opened,' said Tina Hennessey, who began the shop with her daughter. 'There wouldn't have been any point.' Half the shop's products are locally sourced, and half nationally. In season, its asparagus arrives daily from a farmer three minutes up the road, getting from 'ground to shop in half an hour' – faster than frozen food purveyor Birds Eye's famous 'one hour to frozen' promise on its peas: now, *that's* fresh, not frozen.[5]

Inspired by Cranbrook's work, the local community in Hadleigh, another Suffolk town, formed CAASH – the Campaign Against Another Supermarket in Hadleigh. So far, it has successfully fought off repeated attempts by Tesco to develop a supermarket at the edge of town. CAASH was able to demonstrate, using Cranbrook's work as a model, that over 150 local jobs would be threatened. The local Hadleigh Society showed that 56 per cent of people opposed any supermarket for the town at all, and that 77 per cent opposed the particular application by Tesco. The company is persistent, though, and seemingly incapable of knowing when it is not wanted. After the rejected application in 1999, Tesco reappeared in 2004, and in 2006 residents were bracing themselves for yet another attempt. As for the community, the Hadleigh Society said long ago that it would be perfectly happy for the Ipswich & Norwich Cooperative Society simply to redevelop its food store on the high street.

There will always be resistance to new developments in relatively affluent, pretty, rural areas of Britain, but the striking thing about the backlash against Tesco is that it is happening everywhere. In every direction on the compass, in big cities, towns and villages, in poor neighbourhoods and in wealthy ones, people have started saying 'no' to Tesco.

In the rural town of Hereford, an enterprising group of residents formed HASSLE: Hereford Against Supermarkets Squashing our Local Economy. There are also urban rebels to match the country ones. In Harlow, Essex, local people are setting up a campaign called RATRUN: Residents Against Thundering Rattling Unbearable Noise. Its aim is to expose 'the true cost to Harlow's residents of Tesco's round-the-clock HGV delivery network'.

People in North Berwick, East Lothian, organized against Tesco, took one look at themselves and quite logically formed PINBAT (People In North Berwick Against Tesco). In 2006 they helped to coordinate a raft of objections to East Lothian Council against a planning objection by Tesco. Although the council subsequently approved the application, PINBAT took the fight to the Scottish Executive, which it hopes will 'call in' the application for investigation.

Inverness earned the tag 'Tesco Town' because the company takes over 50 pence of every £1 spent on groceries there. It also has three out of four of the city's supermarkets. But Tesco's insatiable appetite for market share led it to apply for permission to build yet another, bigger store – its fourth. This triggered beleaguered residents and shopkeepers to act. A single resident working with one local shop collected 1,000 signatures opposing Tesco in under a fortnight. It quickly doubled. Elected representatives also oppose it, including a community councillor chairman from the area of the proposed store and the Green Party MSP for the Highlands. They say it threatens existing businesses, is too big for the area, will consolidate a Tesco monopoly and will generate too much traffic. With a sense of comic endurance and self-awareness, the campaign set up a website called www.tescotown.co.uk.

In 2000, local residents in Worcester launched a campaign aimed at the relationship between Tesco and Worcestershire County Council, which was perceived to be too cosy. At the heart of the community sits the Christopher Whitehead High School; its location allows over seven out of ten pupils to walk to school, which is fortunate, because many of the local houses lack garages for cars. But the community discovered that Tesco and the county council had other plans for the site of the school. They wanted it moved to a field outside its existing catchment area, so that a huge new supermarket could be built where it stood.

That's when CHRISS was born, the campaign also known as The Community Has Rights In School Site. Work by CHRISS, with the support of the city council, forced a public inquiry; the plans were rejected in September 2004.

The award for the most straightforward campaign acronym goes to the residents and shopkeepers of Colchester, Essex. Traders enduring the supermarkets' continued new openings followed the example of the people of North Berwick, held a mirror up to themselves and realized that they had formed 'TESCNO'. Their focus in 2006 was opposing a Tesco application to open a store near to Colchester's centre.

Unthank Road, if you were wondering, is the peculiarly appropriate name of an area in Norwich where residents got together to oppose Tesco's bid to develop an Express store.

The Rebels of Ballards Lane

Many councils are cautious about resisting supermarkets, even if they do not want them. The fear of costly, long, drawn-out legal and planning disputes is off-putting. The supermarkets' persistence and the knowledge of Tesco's enormous planning expertise and resources are often enough for them to get their own way. Some councils are growing bolder, though.

One of them is Barnet Borough Council. It created a precedent not simply by rejecting a proposed Tesco Express convenience store, but because of the grounds on which it did so. The development was proposed for the site of a former carpet warehouse at Ballards Lane in Finchley, London, less than a mile from another Tesco store. Barnet said no because it thought the Tesco branch would undermine other shops on the high street, and in doing so would attack both the 'vitality and viability' of the town centre.

The decision came as a present for local shopkeepers just in time for Christmas, on 21 December. Laid out on a planning form under the heading 'Putting the Community First', Barnet's officers refused Tesco's application because it represented, it said, 'a form of retail development' that would have 'a significantly greater harmful impact' than current uses. If there was any doubt about whether the decision was taken lightly, according to the council allowing Tesco to develop the site would have been contrary to (feel free to skip the following passage): 'Policy S1.1 of the Adopted Unitary Development Plan (1991), Policies TCR1 and TCR7 of the Unitary Development Plan Draft Deposit Modifications (28/06/05), Policy 3D.1 of the Mayors London Plan (2004) and Planning Policy Statement 6.' Phew.

Councillor Melvin Cohen, the cabinet member for planning who rejected the application, said:

To have allowed this application to proceed would have set a precedent to other food retailers and could have encouraged the spread of clone towns, which we do not want to see in Barnet.[6]

Once again, Tesco chose not to accept the ruling, and went to appeal.

Of course, not all campaigns are successful. A salutary tale comes from the region of Dumfries and Galloway in Scotland. Until recently, the two towns, sitting roughly 20 miles apart, had very different fates. The town of Dumfries itself, home to a Tesco Extra (the largest type of store), had one of the worst scores in the first UK Clone Town survey. Until recently, the nearby town of Castle Douglas had no Tesco, and was thriving. Castle Douglas promoted itself as Scotland's first 'Food Town'. The aim, inspired by an initiative of the Soil Association, was to link farming, food processing and tourism together with the town's numerous independent shops and food businesses.

The town was hugely proud of the economic benefits that came from focusing on produce from local farmers, which was also processed and sold in the town. The Castle Douglas website describes 'traditional butchers, fishmongers, bakers and delica- tessens offer[ing] a cornucopia of premier quality foods . . . locally produced pickles, preserves and honey' and 'locally- brewed ales from the town's family-run brewery'. Then Tesco came knocking. In February 2004 it applied to build a large store at the edge of Castle Douglas. Shortly afterwards, a campaign called Save Our Stewarty Shops was launched, backed by twenty local businesses and over 1,000 local residents; but campaigners were advised 'off-record' by councillors and council officers, that 'if Tesco wanted to come to Castle Douglas, no one could stop them'. In April 2005, in spite of the glaring contradiction to what Castle Douglas wanted for itself, planning permission was granted to the supermarket. However, three councillors voted against Tesco: they were from the town that already had the supermarket in its back yard – Dumfries. They were convinced that Tesco would damage 'the vitality and viability' of Castle Douglas and other communities in the area.

In the town of Sheringham, Norfolk, locals thought they had won a lasting victory against an unwanted Tesco store, only to be defeated by deal from beyond the planning grave. The Sheringham Campaign Against Major Retail Over-Development (SCAMROD, one of the more inspired acronyms) began in 1996 and ran a highly effective campaign. Other groups joined SCAMROD to oppose Tesco opening in the supermarket-free town; they included the Sheringham Preservation Society, the Chamber of Trade and the CPRE. Sheringham is a town of around only 7,000 people and, according to the campaign, the proposed Tesco store is designed to serve nearer to 40,000.

The usual valid fears were aired. In the town are two bakers, two butchers, two wet fish shops, three greengrocers, two general food stores, two florists, two bookshops, three newsagents, and an ironmonger that sells, among other things, four varieties of mole trap. What chance of survival would they have if Tesco opened, and why would the outcome be different from the aftermath of the arrival of any other major supermarket?

Residents and planners agreed: Tesco wasn't wanted. After being previously unsuccessful, Tesco submitted a planning application in 2003. Following fears from councillors over the potential cost of drawn-out appeals, Tesco initially won approval for its store in January 2004. The meeting, however, was anything but convivial. Councillor B. Cabbell Manners warned that the effect of Tesco stores in nearby Stalham and Hunstanton had been 'disastrous'. Candy Sheriden, a Stalham resident and the former chair of the town business association, was against Tesco coming to where she lived. Running a farmers' market and community shop, she had good reason and, she feels, her fears were justified:

> The site where Tesco built was our car park, marketplace and weekly auction. There were 70 good businesses in the town when they opened but it has become a ghost town. All that made Stalham different is slipping away.[7]

Another councillor lamented that Stalham had seen local shops close or be taken over following Tesco's arrival, and yet another feared the night-time rumble of delivery lorries. Twenty extensive conditions were attached to the approval.[8]

Building was then delayed by haggling over the conditions; also, results from a new study came to light that assessed the fact that there were actually four approved planning applications for supermarkets in the area. It concluded that would be too many big shops for too few people.

When there was another vote in September 2005, councillors voted 20–0 to reject the application. It seemed the campaign had beaten the supermarket. But Tesco wasn't finished: its appeal in February 2006 led to another inquiry, and then something extraordinary happened. In April the same year, North Norfolk District Council performed a U-turn and voted to support Tesco's proposals. What could possibly have overturned a crushing 20–0 vote against? No one outside the tiny group originally involved in striking a deal with Tesco could have guessed the truth.

It emerged that an agreement had been signed in 2003 between the store and the local authority. The action, by a senior officer on behalf of the council, had the effect of 'binding' the local authority to Tesco.[9] More disturbingly, it transpired that the deal was signed 'between one administration leaving office after the 1st May elections in 2003 and the newly elected members taking up their posts'. Somehow, just as the local democracy entered a brief, transitory blind spot, a piece of paper designed to tie the hands of councillors and not even revealed to most councillors and local people until three years later got signed.

After it was revealed, the local government ombudsman called in the agreement with Tesco for investigation. At the time of writing, the final decision on the future of Sheringham's shops is undecided, but many feel the deal and Tesco's resources have tilted the scales. John Sweeney, late leader of the Liberal Democrat-controlled North Norfolk district council, said:

> They [Tesco] are too big and powerful for us. If we try and deny them they will appeal, and we cannot afford to fight a planning appeal and lose. If they got costs it would bankrupt us.

But if a Tesco does get built, Ronald Wright, whose business Blyth and Wright Ironmongers has been going for more than a century, thinks Sheringham will lose more than its independent shops; the town's identity, which makes it attractive to visitors, will be eroded as well:

> This is a wonderful town but Tesco will suck the life out of the greengrocers, butchers, off-licence, and then it is only a matter of time for us too. The personal service is why holidaymakers come to Sheringham, but with a giant Tesco it will be like everywhere else.[10]

These campaigns give just a flavour of the British backlash against Tesco. There are many more. Each year we now have an 'Independents Day' that celebrates small, non-clone shops, and a 'No Shopping Day' to help us kick overconsumption. The 'slow food' movement continues to gain followers in Britain. Websites and blogs targeting Tesco and other supermarkets proliferate: breakingthearmlock.com, tescodeconstruct.blogspot.com and supermarket-sweep-up.com are just a few.

It's not just in Britain that Tesco is running into problems, either. The company seems to find itself in a world of trouble wherever it goes.

The World Not According to Tesco

Tesco moved quickly into Central and Eastern Europe after the breakup of the former Soviet Union. By the mid-1990s it had established itself in Hungary, Slovakia, Poland and the Czech Republic. In 2003 it set up on the geographical bridge between West and East, in Turkey. All these countries are the subject of ambitious Tesco expansion plans. But the backlash against Tesco at the local level is rising to match the scale of its ambition.

Hungary is home to a dynamic environmental movement. It was resistance to a proposed dam on the Danube at Nagymaros in the late 1980s, led by a group called *Duna Kör* (Danube Circle), which gave birth to the pro-democracy movement in that country. Hungary then became one of the first 'dominos' to fall, signalling the end of the Cold War. It's no surprise, then, that campaigners unafraid of the former might of the Soviet Union would also not be afraid to tackle Tesco – and that's exactly what they did.

Dunaújváros is a town of 56,000 people to the south of Budapest. In 2000 it emerged that Tesco wanted to cut down 9 hectares of forest around the town to build a hypermarket. (The supermarket likes to build big in Hungary; the average store size of Tesco developments there is over three times the average for the UK.) A mixture of oak, hornbeam and pine were planted in the 1950s to form a woodland buffer between the town and heavily polluting factories. The proposed development would have seen half the forest cut down.

A petition against the Tesco store was started, and people signed despite actually wanting a supermarket for the town. They knew that the air in other towns unprotected by woods was worse. When the petition wasn't enough, the campaigners discovered that by law inner-city forests could only be cut down under very special circumstances, such as to build a hospital or fire station. The woods were thus saved. Victory was only partial, though. Development went ahead elsewhere, near the brow of a scenic hill overlooking the town.

Gödöllõ is a smaller town to the east of Budapest. Already beset by too much traffic, air and noise pollution, in 2003 local people were disturbed to see plans for a huge Tesco hypermarket. The proposed store would mean the disappearance under tarmac of yet more green space, a stream and two wells. But it wasn't just the environmental impacts that caused concern; town leaders were petitioned with information over the potentially ruinous impact of the hypermarket on local jobs, open-air markets, small producers, smaller shops – overall, on the local commercial fabric.

The campaign by two Hungarian groups, the GATE Green Club Association and the Tölgy Nature Conservation Association, had unexpectedly positive results. First, it forced the local authorities to engage local people more in decision-making. Then, even though the development wasn't halted entirely, the campaign succeeded in reducing the size of the hypermarket from the original proposal for a store of 12,500 sq. m to one of 8,500 sq. m.[11]

Poland is another important market for Tesco, its next largest sphere of operations after South Korea, Thailand and Hungary. Just as in so many other places, soon after the influx of foreign supermarkets to Poland, a now-all-too-familiar litany arose. Small shops, small-scale producers and local food cultures were under threat. Initially, to counteract some immediate dangers,

Poland has enacted its own version of the French Royer law: local authorities were given the power of veto over new shopping centres, and the government was urged to stop predatory pricing targeted against small shops. However, the more sophisticated supermarket operators had anticipated the action, and slipped under the legal barrier by gaining planning permission for new store sites before the law came into force.[12]

That wasn't the end of friction for the foreign supermarket operators in Poland; Tesco was soon to find itself at the centre of a major political controversy. When Teresa Lubinska was on the city council of Szczecin, in northwest Poland, her presence might have annoyed foreign supermarkets, but it wasn't a real threat. She put her energy into trying to 'chase out' hypermarkets because, she believed, they were destroying the city centre and driving out a rich variety of small shops. In doing so, she merely echoed the fears and actions of communities wherever Tesco now sets up shop. The company has become adept at 'handling' local disaffection, moreover. But then Lubinska changed jobs: as Poland's new finance minister, she presented an entirely different prospect for the British retailer.

It seemed her mood had grown no friendlier, and her criticisms had become more sophisticated. Poland wanted foreign investment, she said, but not the kind that Tesco had to offer. Hypermarkets were 'the simplest type of investment' that brought only low-skilled jobs. The challenge for Poland was to produce more for itself but, said Lubinska, 'Hypermarkets like Tesco are no investment. I mean they are not vital for economic growth.'[13]

A striking consensus seemed to be emerging. Aligned with Lubinska's conservative and traditionalist Catholic Law and Justice Party was the populist, left-leaning Self-Defence Party and the nationalist, right-wing League of Polish Families.[14] On reflection, the foreign retailers including Tesco might have concluded that opening on national holidays was a bad idea in a country where ideas of home and family are still central to the social fabric, and where the Church still has a large role in public life. Tales of toiling for long hours and low pay working in the hypermarkets also fuelled a backlash in a country that, after the promise of the end of Cold War, has seen the dark side of the free-market dream. Tesco boasts that having Polish managers in its Polish stores helps it to understand 'the unique needs of local customers and helps the company to think and act locally'. Clearly there was a breakdown of communication: when Tesco bought the French-owned Leader Price chain in Poland in July 2006, no mention was made of its generally unwelcome status.[15]

Going East

From the UK to Central Europe, Tesco spread east around the globe like a latter-day conquering retail army. To itself, though, its self-image is probably more one of a liberating force. It comes to bring the benefits of own-label products and ready meals, where before there was only the mess and inconvenience of crude local fruit and vegetables. Instead of a *Pax Britannica* offering democracy, trade and the rule of law (but only on the terms of the colonial power), we have a *Pax Tescona* offering homogenization, monopoly and Clubcard points.

After arriving in Central Europe Tesco expanded into Asia, following in the footsteps of empire. It first opened shop in Thailand in 1998 after buying the Thai Lotus chain of stores, which Tesco now describes as the local market leader. Thailand became Tesco's third-largest market after the UK and South Korea. There were plans to open over 200 more stores in 2006–07. But like many an occupying force before it, Tesco misread its local popularity.

The company is most proud of its 'Value' stores, described as 'very low cost build hypermarkets'. According to Tesco these proved 'a very popular innovation, allowing us to bring the Tesco offer to low income rural areas'.[16] Events, however, were to judge them differently.

Small shopkeepers across the country began a high-profile campaign in the buildup to an election, putting pressure on the government to stop the spread of international stores that were putting local retailers out of business. In response, Thailand's ministry of commerce announced plans to embargo any further expansion by international retailers until new rules could be introduced to protect small shopkeepers.[17] Both Tesco and Carrefour were asked to sign a voluntary agreement saying that they would halt new store openings until the regulations were in place; both reportedly refused.

Within days of Tesco discovering that its plans to redesign Thailand's shopping landscape were not welcome, circumstances took an even more dramatic turn. On 19 September 2006, news emerged that a military coup had taken place. A ban on protests was quickly introduced, seeming, at least, to buy Tesco and other foreign retailers time.

But the level of discontent against Tesco proved so high that Thailand's small shopkeepers threatened to defy martial law to protest against it. The shopkeepers wanted a five-year breathing space before Tesco could be allowed to build more stores. Unheeding of the consequences, just three weeks after the coup, they took to the streets and marched through the centre of Bangkok waving banners with 'Stop Tesco's Expansion' and 'We don't need Tesco' scrawled across them. Their demands were delivered to the new military-supported Prime Minister Surayud Chulanont at Government House.[18] Protest leader Panthep Suleesatira said:

> If the superstore refuses to cooperate, that means it has no respect for Thailand. If the government does not stop it, the foreign superstores will eventually take over all Thai business.[19]

How would Tesco respond? Its corporate website conveys the secrets of its international success so far. A 'flexible' approach is called for, 'tailored' to 'local customers, local cultures, local supply chains and local regulations'. Where Thailand is concerned, this means customers who are 'used to shopping at traditional wet markets, interacting with vendors and rummaging through piles of produce'.[20]

Tesco's actual response, however, seemed to come from a different manual and a different age. Speaking to the retail press, fresh in the face of the military coup, Tesco announced that it would continue to press for 'unbridled expansion in the Thai retail sector' and the roll-out of its cheaply built hypermarkets, in spite of growing opposition from local shopkeepers. Tesco's approach would be to 'explain the benefits of modern retail in Thailand'.[21] In late 2006, sales from Tesco stores in Hungary dropped, and in Thailand they stagnated.[22]

Malaysia is another of Tesco's overseas markets that has taken a dim view of foreign-owned hypermarkets, of which Carrefour and Tesco between them have nearly half the market share.[23] The government announced a block on the development and construction of any new foreign-owned hypermarkets beginning on 1 January 2004, in the areas of the Klang Valley, which includes Kuala Lumpur, and in the states of Johor and Penang. The ban was initially intended to last until 2008. Tesco, along with other global chains like Carrefour and the Dutch firms Makro and Ahold, operate hypermarkets in Malaysia. Once again, in announcing the new rules, Tan Sri Muhyiddin Yassin, Minister of Domestic Trade and Consumer Affairs said the three regions were already saturated with hypermarkets, and that any more would adversely impact thousands of small businesses.[24]

In addition, a set of guidelines has been in place since 2002 that state that any proposed development must apply two years in advance; not be built within a 3.5 km radius of housing or a city centre; not be part of a complex; pay for a socio-economic impact study to be conducted by local authorities before an application is considered; be limited to 8,000 sq. m in size; and ensure that applications are only to be made for locations where the population is 350,000 or higher.[25] A national group, the Federation of Malaysian Consumers' Associations, campaigned to prevent a threatened early removal of the block on new hypermarkets, to protect 'the livelihoods of thousands of small retailers'.[26]

Fears are understandable. There is nothing to suggest that the retailers behave any better overseas than at home. In yet another of Tesco's important overseas markets, South Korea, its chief international competitor Carrefour was found guilty and fined for similar sorts of unfair business practices that Tesco is known for in the UK. The South Korean Fair Trade Commission found the French supermarket guilty of a range of abusive practices in its treatment of suppliers.[27]

China, yet another important market, is unpredictable and paradoxical. A regulatory race to the bottom is gathering pace in already-industrialized countries, brought on by fear of not being able to compete with China (which defies orthodox trade theory by seeming to have a comparative advantage in everything). The irony is that workers in China could soon, on paper at least, end up with more rights than employees in the UK. A range of proposals under consideration include shortening the maximum working week to below the level of Europe's forty-eight hours – something that itself proved so controversial in the UK that opt-outs were negotiated.

Measures in the new Labour Contract Law could also include greater job security; short-term contracts naturally maturing into open-ended ones if a worker continues beyond the initial contractual period; and better severance terms, including two months' pay for every year of service. These proposals so horrified Western multinationals that the American Chamber of Commerce reportedly wrote a forty-two-page plea to the Chinese government asking it to reconsider.[28]

Perhaps more threatening than the actual measures themselves is how the Chinese proposals stand to remove from Western managers a powerful threat at their disposal when they negotiate pay and conditions with their own domestic workforces. Management's room to play 'hardball' with unions by raising the spectre of jobs lost to China will be severely curtailed if they are simultaneously threatening to cut and run from China due to improved protection of workers *there*.

The Americas are, as yet, untried ground for Tesco. While it is in the process of establishing itself in North America, it is yet to venture south to Latin America, where competitors like Wal-Mart are well established. However, it's already possible to see the kind of reaction Tesco would be likely to receive.

In Cuernavaca, 50 miles south of Mexico City, residents fought against plans by the US retail giant Costco, which wanted to build a new store on a site of historical significance. The location was home to the former Hotel Casino de la Selva, over 900 century-old trees and dozens of murals. Plans for the development were first made public in the summer of 2002, after the city sold the site to Costco for one-sixth of its market value. Local people launched the Civic Front for the Defence of the Casino de la Selva, organizing rallies, gathering signatures for petitions, writing to Costco executives and meeting with national and local officials.

Cuernavaca's climate has earned it the nickname 'the City of Eternal Spring'. The campaigners pointed out that uncontrolled retail sprawl was turning it into 'the City of the Eternal Shopping Mall'. In place of Costco, local people wanted a park. In late August 2002, around 300 protesters blocked roads to prevent construction crews, to whom city officials had given the green light. The police beat and arrested protesters; within hours, 3,000 people converged to demand their release. Things were beginning to snowball, and the protestors were let out. Several days later they organized a rally of more than 15,000 people – but construction went ahead, regardless. Although Costco appeared to have won the battle, it lost the struggle for hearts and minds, and its victory could well have been pyrrhic.

As a result of its behaviour, an international boycott of Costco was called for. It was yet another rumbling that, added to the feelings of other disaffected local communities around the world, could be the beginnings of a bigger backlash against the range of global chains like Tesco, Wal-Mart, Carrefour, Blockbuster and Starbucks. One of the Mexican activists, Flora Guerrero Goff, told the *Dallas Morning News*:

> Investment by multinational companies . . . has reached its limit. They have disrespected Mexicans not only because the megastores bring a lifestyle based on brutal consumption, but they are also destroying our customs, our culture, our traditional food.[29]

Something Weird

Browsing an online bookstore for books about Wal-Mart, I started to count them: I lost track after noting twenty different volumes devoted to the world's biggest shop. Almost all of them were hostile. Wal-Mart may be big, but there is an equally huge reaction against the company in its domestic market. Ferocity of criticism perhaps reaches its peak in the exhaustively substantiated and unremittingly hostile book and film *Wal-Mart: The High Cost of Low Price*. Wal-Mart's reputation and its purchase of the British store Asda meant the film had a ready UK audience.

Importing culture and economic and political ideas from the US has long been popular right across the political spectrum in Britain. Labour and Conservative governments alike carefully nurture our so-called 'special relationship'. Where the rise of clone towns is concerned the relationship feels decidedly abusive, but counselling could also be at hand. A growing number of people in the US have learned how to stand up to the 'big-box' operators and chain stores, and are walking away to build separate lives.

Things in the US have become, well, *weird*. More specifically, residents of Louisville, Kentucky decided that chain stores were in danger of destroying their city's character and launched a 'Keep Louisville Weird' movement. It began with a guerrilla marketing campaign. 'Keep Louisville Weird' started appearing as a slogan on billboards, T-shirts and postcards. Support gathered among independent local businesses worried about the 'spreading homogenization' of the town. They were also inspired by a study in Austin, Texas that showed spending in independent local stores was worth substantially more to the local economy.[30] Independently, they discovered the same thing as researchers in the UK. The campaign won the support of local TV stations and led to copycat initiatives in other cities. Local development agencies like Montana's Associated Technology Roundtables also became involved, setting an example for the extensive network of regional agencies in the UK.

In particular, the New Rules Project, set up by the Institute for Local Self-Reliance, catalogues the many inventive ways that municipalities have found to choose their own local economic development path and to prevent being rolled over by the 'big-box' retailers.

A number of communities now require a comprehensive review of economic and community impacts before approving any new retail construction. A review is typically triggered when any development exceeds a certain size or is likely to generate, for example, more than 500 vehicle trips per day. New York, declared by Wal-Mart a 'new frontier' in January 2005, is investigating legislation that would require any 'big-box' retailer above 85,000 sq. ft – virtually all hypermarkets would fall into this category – to specify its economic impact on the community. Power would also be given to the Commissioner of Consumer Affairs to withhold a licence if the company had been 'involved in excessive employment related claims'.[31]

Often, the effects of the big retailers are felt in neighbouring towns as well. To solve that problem, in some areas neighbouring communities have worked together to assess very large developments that would have impacts beyond the borders of their host town. In 2004, the National Trust for Historic Preservation named the entire state of Vermont as one of its eleven endangered historic places because of the onslaught of 'big-box' stores – the state is now considering introducing legislation that could lead to a ban on 'big-box' stores statewide.

Some communities have concluded that, regardless of their size, 'formula' businesses are rarely if at all acceptable due to their impacts on community character and the local economy. A formula business is defined as one that adopts standardized services, methods of operation, decor, uniforms, architecture or other features virtually identical to businesses elsewhere. About a dozen towns have decided to break the formula and banned or limited the number of formula restaurants or retail stores allowed within their borders.

In the UK, the government's commitment to reinvigorating town centres can, perversely, accelerate the process of town-centre 'cloning'. After the growth of the mall and the out-of-town shopping centre, the recolonization of the high street by chain stores is happening in both the US and UK.

According to the New Rules Project:

. . . chain drugstores, fast-food outlets, clothing retailers like The Gap and Banana Republic, and even Wal-Mart and Home Depot, which recently unveiled urban prototype stores, increasingly seek locations in town centres and urban neighbourhoods.

As a result, the use of local 'ordinances' to control formula businesses is gathering interest. Writes Stacy Mitchell of the New Rules Project:

San Francisco, for example, is considering a measure that would ban formula businesses entirely from certain areas and require neighbourhood notification and a public hearing for those proposed.[32]

Another urgent cautionary note to the UK's planners and local authorities is the long-term experience that the US, home of the shopping mall, has had with large retail developments. Like the failed high-rise housing developments of the 1960s, what once looked good in an architect's drawing loses its lustre once age and economic realities kick in. In the US, people are arguing that:

. . . one of the most compelling reasons to establish limits and standards for retail development is to avoid the epidemic of vacancy and shopping center blight that is now sweeping the country.[33]

Strip malls stand shuttered and idle. According to the New Rules Project:

. . . one-third of all enclosed malls are in serious financial distress; hundreds have already closed . . . even the big boxes are going dark as companies like Wal-Mart and Home Depot abandon existing outlets to build ever larger stores. Wal-Mart alone was found to have more than 350 empty stores nation-wide.[34]

Limiting the size of stores is an approach used widely in Europe (e.g. in France), but it is beginning to be applied in quite sophisticated ways in the US. Beyond a certain point in any given area, more new retailers causes existing businesses to close, so zoning rules are used to block stores over a certain size. This helps, according to US experts on the local economy, 'to sustain the vitality of small-scale, pedestrian-oriented business districts, which in turn nurture local business development'. Limits on store size also prevent problems like increased traffic congestion, too much pressure on public infrastructure and, essentially, on local distinctiveness. Working out 'how big is too big' depends on several factors like the size of the town, the scale of its existing buildings and the community's long-term goals.

Belfast, Maine, banned stores above 75,000 sq. ft in size. Others chose limits of 36,000 sq. ft. Restrictions can apply to an entire city or a single neighbourhood. A ban on new stores larger than 4,000 sq. ft in certain neighbourhoods applies in San Francisco. In Maryland, Wal-Mart tried to dodge the limit on store size simply by building more, smaller stores adjacent to each other. The answer was for planners to treat multiple buildings as 'single use'.[35]

Another idea being resurrected is the use of dedicated taxes on chain stores, mentioned in Chapter Two, which were common in the US in the first half of the last century. In the 1920s and 1930s, monopolies and any concentration of economic power were seen as threats to democracy. Attempts to revive the idea, even with the enormous power of the 'big-box' stores, only narrowly failed – further evidence that in the US as in the UK, public sentiment once again seems to be turning against insensitive and unaccountable big business.

In April 2003, the Montana legislature narrowly defeated a bill to levy a tax on the revenue of 'big-box' retailers. Supporters said the measure was needed because these retailers use state services, pay low wages and siphon money out of Montana. 'This bill protects Main Street Montana,' said then-Senator Ken Toole.[36]

How do you tell when something reaches a tipping point? How do you spot that indefinable moment when it becomes no longer acceptable to drink and drive, blow smoke in someone else's face, send children up chimneys to clean them or have them working in factories to make cheap clothes?

For me, that moment came in a single edition of the comic strip *The Beano*. One of the comic's most long-established characters is Minnie the Minx. In one story, Minnie desperately needs to go to the toilet, but can't find one on Beanotown High Street because all the shops have closed, bankrupted by an out-of-town shopping centre. An emergency meeting of small shopkeepers is held, and then Minnie stomps off to a shop called 'Toscos' (in the world of comics, disguises are usually this thin). Then, intentionally or not, she terrifies customers who think she is a ghost after getting covered in flour. Toscos customers are driven away, and Beanotown High Street is revived as a result. One newspaper described Minnie as a 'terrifying new recruit' to campaigners against Tesco. Something is happening when ideas penetrate this deeply into the popular imagination.[37]

These examples from the UK and around the world show the depth and breadth of opposition to Tesco. So, what real hope is there? The next chapter looks at a whole range of ways to turn the battle of Tescopoly into a more even fight. The final one looks at more ways in which people are already finding alternatives for themselves.

CHAPTER TEN

Freshening the Dragon's Breath: Corporate Responsibility and the Role of Regulators

'Tesco will now be removed from our approved list.'
Review by Henderson Global Investors, Sustainable
and Responsible Investment (SRI) funds, 2005.

The letter from Head Office at the Christian overseas development agency informed its regional staff that they were to start marketing fairly traded cigarettes and red wine from Augusto Pinochet's Chile. It was 1 April, and it was a spoof, but that didn't stop most recipients believing it was true and reacting with outrage. My friend, who was responsible, received a light reprimand and advice that he should assess his colleagues' sense of humour before repeating the exercise.

But irony died (once again) when the weapons manufacturer BAE Systems really did launch a range of 'environmentally friendly' munitions as part of its 'Corporate Responsibility' initiative.[1] These immortal words appeared on BAE's website: 'Lead used in ammunition can harm the environment and pose a risk to people.'[2] So the company developed 'lead-free ammunition' as well as 'new explosives that are significantly less likely to explode in an accident', which leaves you wondering about what it used before. Unlike Wal-Mart in the US, which sells a wide range of guns alongside the more usual groceries, Tesco is not a purveyor of firearms – not yet, at least. Along with nearly all other large companies, the company has enthusiastically embraced the notion of corporate social responsibility.

Shouldn't a combination of public pressure, the need to protect its reputation and a sophisticated logistical ability to manage its global and UK supply chains be enough to create a responsible, even 'ethical' business?

Not long ago, Tesco experienced a conversion and began actively promoting 'ethical business'. It's too soon to meaningfully predict long-term outcomes, but recent history drops several hints. Other major global companies are, however, further down the line, and we can begin to answer the question by holding up an ethical corporate mirror to them. The fate of Tesco's business model, for example, is deeply linked to another eminent British company that has won huge praise by reinventing itself as a socially responsible corporation: the oil company British Petroleum (BP).

Supermarkets as we see them today would probably never have existed without the discovery of oil and the internal combustion engine. Fleets of lorries and delivery vehicles that service their centralized logistics run on fossil fuels and wouldn't exist without a heavily subsidized road transport infrastructure. Tesco's growing focus on out-of-town hypermarkets assumes most customers will get to them by private car. Tesco will also, of course, fill your tank with petrol in one of its own store-based stations.

It's only possible for Tesco to sell much of its food at the prices it does because the fossil-fuel cost to the environment of producing it doesn't get paid. The modern supermarket is both a cause and a consequence of our carbon addiction.

In 2006, a 'think tank' called Tomorrow's Company, comprising some of the largest global multinationals, launched an inquiry into corporate responsibility called 'Tomorrow's Global Company'. The reason given for the inquiry by one of the group's co-chairs, John Manzoni, the head of refining and marketing at BP (an interesting combination in its own right), was that, 'We seem to be among the least-trusted institutions.' The biggest challenge, he explained, was for multinationals to overcome public mistrust about their core activities.[3] Stronger than any concern for global problems themselves, it seems, was the deep-seated fear that companies might lose what has been called the 'social licence to operate'. In other words, if public disapproval of you gets too great, it can get in the way of making a big enough profit. By coincidence, the same day that the oil giant helped launch the inquiry, it reported record profits of £1.4 million per hour in July 2006 (£6.14 billion over six months) off the back of high oil prices.[4]

This is the same company that, since 2000, has aggressively rebranded itself, reinterpreting the initials BP in its marketing to change their meaning from 'British Petroleum' to 'Beyond Petroleum'. Others suggested a more appropriate meaning might be 'Beyond Propaganda'.[5] In 2005, BP reportedly doubled its advertising budget to £85 million.[6] Brightly coloured advertisements in newspapers, magazines and on television focus mostly on the company's environmental credentials. Coupled with the company's award-winning 'Beyond Petroleum' rebranding, they might easily lead a casual observer to conclude that BP's primary concern and main business activity is environmentally friendly renewable energy.

It might be surprising for some, then, to learn that what lies 'beyond petroleum' for BP is, in fact, more petroleum. Search its website for information of interest to investors and you soon discover that, rather than taking steps beyond petroleum, it is wading into a deep pool of the stuff, right up to its neck. In the summer of 2006 the company declared, on its website:

> Our main activities are the exploration and production of crude oil and natural gas; refining, marketing, supply and transportation; and the manufacture and marketing of petrochemicals.[7]

Even more to the point, its pattern of investments in research and development shows that this is exactly how things will stay. In 2005, in spite of all the advertising emphasizing BP's commitment to renewable energy, only around one-twentieth of its investment went into what it termed 'alternative energy' (a definition in which BP includes some fossil-fuel and gas-powered generation). On the other hand, over 70 per cent of its capital investment went towards finding even more oil and gas. The oil firm Shell, which also likes to boast about its clean, green credentials in its advertisements, was even worse. Just 1 per cent of its investment went towards renewable energy and 69 per cent to explore for more oil and gas.[8]

BP has set the standard for repositioning itself as a responsible company. It was lauded in public for setting itself aside from the rest of the oil industry. Audiences sat in awed silence to hear BP's chief executive Lord Browne acknowledge the reality of global warming. Yet all this was achieved without any fundamental shift of direction in BP's core business. Without missing a beat, it continued to mine, burn and sell fossil fuels, by far the biggest contributor to catastrophic climate change.

The case of BP shows that it is entirely possible to promote, demonstrate and be applauded for your stance on corporate social responsibility and 'positively engage' with your critics while all along your core business is on a steady, unerring path towards killing the planet. BP's most recent ruse is to offer motorists the chance to become 'carbon neutral' by offsetting their emissions from driving. But, as we have seen, climate science gives little credibility to the whole idea of offsetting. In terms of the clash between corporate ethical rebranding and the real world of climate change, oil scarcity and the challenge of human development, BP and Tesco are romantically entangled. The problem is that their relationship is destructive. The romance is a love of cheap oil and the unmanaged market. It's a codependent relationship, and it is drawing them and us inexorably, into an unplanned suicide pact. But by holding on to our presence of mind, we still have the right to say no, as in all relationships.

Tesco's own flirtation with ethical business got off to a rather shaky start. It was a proud founder member of the Ethical Trading Initiative (ETI) in 1998 and still regularly mentions it in reports on the company's social responsibility. What Tesco's materials fail to mention is that it was making suppliers pay for the costs incurred by Tesco to live up to the ETI. A letter published in the weekly retailer's bible *The Grocer* claimed that Tesco had demanded payments of £278 each year from all its primary suppliers to cover the cost of complying with the ETI codes of conduct. Tesco wanted to be seen as ethical – it just wanted someone else to pay for it, and in this case it happened to be precisely the suppliers to whom it was supposed to be giving better treatment.

The ETI has been thoroughly criticized for reducing complex political questions to simple issues of ethical sourcing, also as becoming something of an ethical 'fig-leaf'.[9] The supermarkets' increasing role as gatekeepers of the global food system, pe-versely, 'creates a mechanism for companies to pass responsi-bility on to other, often less powerful, actors'.[10] The responsibility for compliance with the ETI basically lay with suppliers.

Following the campaign on supermarkets by the development agency Christian Aid, and after the ETI, another initiative came along. This one, called Race to the Top (RTTT), tried to engage positively with the supermarkets. The idea was that following the desire of firms to be socially responsible, the project could trigger an upward spiral of best practice in which everyone would follow and try to match the market leader with the highest standards. It aimed to develop 'comparable and credible benchmarks for measuring progress towards greater sustainability'.

Once again, Tesco's approach was, erm, *interesting*. It refused to take part. In doing so, it effectively killed the project. A review concluded, 'The other retailers cannot afford to be outside certain initiatives once Tesco and/or Asda commit to taking part – and the opposite is also true.'[11]

In a fairly kind assessment by the project managers on why years' worth of their effort came to nothing due to the disinterest of Tesco, they commented, 'Two of the smallest and therefore comparatively most thinly resourced retailers – the Cooperative Group and Somerfield – were able to compile and report on RTTT data, while the largest retailer Tesco was not.' Their conclusion was that Tesco simply didn't see the issue as a priority. Interestingly, its lack of enthusiasm may have been counterproductive even on Tesco's own terms. It 'hardened' the attitude of other groups, leading them to the conclusion that, 'Only command-and-control regulation can tame the supermarket sector, marking an end to a period of openness to work through voluntary, collaborative initiatives.'[12]

Within stores themselves, fair trade, despite certain key weaknesses, has a responsibility role to play. But fair trade products make up only a minuscule share of all the things sold by Tesco. On top of that, some believe that the store is exploiting the goodwill of customers seeking fairly traded products. John McCabe, an expert in retail pricing with the firm Connect Global, alleged that Tesco, in common with Asda/Wal-Mart and Sainsbury's, were adding an excessive markup in addition to the price premium paid as part of the fair trade arrangement. He said, 'The supermarkets know that people do not go for the cheapest product when buying fair trade because they think the extra money is helping someone in the developing world.'[13]

On the domestic front, huge concern has focused on how easy, or difficult it is to buy healthy food in supermarkets. The official Food Standards Agency came up with a labelling scheme to make it easier to choose healthy food. It proposed a system of 'traffic light' symbols: green for eat away, amber for approach with caution, and red for eat occasionally in small doses.

Which? (formerly known as The Consumers' Association) found that this was the best system, and easiest to understand. Ninety-seven per cent of shoppers followed it and were able to easily compare one product with another. Asda/Wal-Mart, The Co-operative Group, Sainsbury's, Waitrose and Marks & Spencer agreed to use the system. Tesco, however, did not. It chose to go with its own system, described by *Which?* as 'more of a hindrance than a help'. The Tesco scheme proved to be 'the weakest system for understanding – particularly with lower income groups – with just 37 per cent of consumers being able to correctly interpret the meaning of the Tesco colour scheme'.[14]

As mentioned earlier, when the National Consumer Council rated British supermarkets on their comprehensive environmental record, Tesco came behind Waitrose, Marks & Spencer, Sainsbury's, Asda/Wal-Mart and the Co-op.[15]

The City firm Henderson Global Investors operates one of the world's largest investment funds focused on sustainable and responsible investment. It puts money into what it considers 'best practice companies'. Reviewing its options for who to invest in across the food retail sector in December 2005, it noted, 'In spite of its market position, Tesco showed a disappointing performance' and concluded, 'Tesco will now be removed from our approved list.'[16] In January 2007 news leaked of Tesco's intention to launch jointly with the world's other three largest supermarket chains, Wal-Mart, Carrefour and Metro, a new code of standards for supply chains called the 'global social compliance programme.' Time will tell if this represents an improvement on other initiatives. But, judged on adherence to enlightened process, it too got off to a shaky start when advocates for labour rights pointed out that they were excluded from both the code's development and direct involvement in its governing board.[17]

In the context of all of this, and as clamour for action by the regulators against the supermarkets grew, Tesco launched its bid for corporate redemption: its 'good neighbour' policy, or 'community plan'.

Tesco's Plan

To big fanfare in May 2006, Tesco announced a plan to promote a more friendly face. It covered a range of social and environmental issues and had ten points (it's odd how often such plans do).

First, it pledged to invest in environmental technology, in particular more efficient energy supplies for its stores and more renewable energy. Its aim was to 'halve by 2010 the average energy use in all our buildings against a baseline of 2000'. There are two things that can be said about this: with a world facing oil shortages and rocketing energy prices, it simply makes good business sense, regardless of whether or not it is the 'right' thing to do; also, the proposal comes against the background of a company whose basic business model is, and will become more so, designed around people jumping in their cars to drive to superstores and to out-of-town hypermarkets. Detailed questions about the sincerity of the Tesco pledge were also asked and left unanswered.[18]

The Tesco plan's second point was to promise to double the amount of waste recycling customers returned to stores. But how much waste *do* customers return for recycling in the first place, and wouldn't it be more effective to tackle the problem at the source and radically reduce the amount of unnecessary packaging on products? Third, Tesco aimed to cut the number of plastic bags given out by one-quarter – which is fine, but the bustling city of New Delhi in India banned all plastic bags years ago, and in Bangladesh, former Permanent Secretary at the Environment Ministry, Sabihuddin Ahmed, banned plastic bags entirely. The supermarket also promised to make its bags degradable, another technology that has been available for decades.

Fourth, Tesco promised to roll out 'on all 7000 Tesco own-brand products' the food health labelling scheme that *Which?* had condemned. Fifth, it pledged to sponsor some school materials on good eating; sixth, to sponsor some sports events; and seventh, to design some less offensive shopfronts.

Some of these promises build on existing Tesco initiatives to provide schools with computers and sports equipment. Both win the store publicity and praise, and help to develop an 'emotional bond' with the consumer. At a low cost to Tesco, this is exactly what they are designed to do. It is known in the trade as 'cause-related marketing', and even has its own award scheme. In 1998, Tesco Computers for Schools won the 'Cause Related Marketing Award for Excellence and Example of Best Practice', bestowed by an outfit called Business in the Community. The scheme was commended for its impact on increased sales, enhancing Tesco's profile in the local community, positioning Tesco as the number-one retailer locally for customers, reinforcing Tesco's brand values, and improving customer loyalty and creating recognition as an innovative retailer (and, of course, it gave some computers to schools).[19]

The problem, as this award makes rather clear, is that the emphasis is more on the marketing than the cause. Not immediately obvious is how much money you have to spend at Tesco to benefit from the scheme. Vouchers to exchange for equipment are available at limited times during the year (although for running the scheme Tesco gets the publicity benefit all year round). In order to get one of the mid-rank computers on offer, you have to spend around £250,000. Similarly astonishing figures apply to Tesco's scheme supplying sports equipment to schools. To get a pack of three tennis balls, available from any average online retailer at around just £1.25, you would have to spend £1,140 at a Tesco supermarket. A pair of plastic inflatable armbands for swimming would set you back £840; a football, £2,200; a hockey stick, £2,360; and to get a trampoline for your school, you would have to buy just under £1 million worth of Tesco groceries. That is one expensive bounce.

Next on the plan came a more interesting promise:

> Our eighth change is that we will improve the way we consult local communities before building new stores so that we can be sure that we have understood local issues and concerns.

(As mentioned in Chapter Four, though, this is the point at which Terry Leahy said Tesco would seek out a favourable silent majority in favour of a store if a community did reject Tesco's plans to build one.)

Ninth, the store promised to increase its sourcing of local goods, which could be a good or bad thing depending on how it treats suppliers (the track record, of course, being very shaky). More local sourcing means, potentially, that supermarkets could increase a beneficial multiplier effect in the local economy. Retail research suggests that there is still huge unmet demand for more local goods. One poll showed that 44 per cent of shoppers wanted to buy more. According to Asda/Wal-Mart, the market for local food is worth £160 million.[20]

However, greater local sourcing by supermarkets is a double-edged sword. Powerful international food manufacturers can find themselves out-manoeuvred in negotiations by supermarkets, so what chance do small operators have in getting fair contracts? If the supermarkets made typical requests for exclusivity, coupled with the fact that they can change their minds on a whim, the danger is that small producers would become trapped in highly unequal commercial relationships in which they become dependent on single large contracts. Their profit margins would then be squeezed to subsistence levels to meet the supermarkets' price requirements.

Finally, as the tenth point in the plan, Tesco promised to promote regional British foods in-store – which, of course, presents the same concern as previously, with local sourcing. So far, then, there's not much to get excited about.

In early 2007, following in the footsteps of smaller retailer Marks & Spencer, Tesco took their environmental plans further. New targets announced to reduce energy use and green house gas emissions, if realized, would constitute noticeable improvements for the supermarket. But two doubts remained. First the promises cut across Tesco's core business model, based on expanding massive, drive-to hypermarkets and, simply, selling ever more stuff (even if energy use per square metre of store, for example, went down, an overall doubling of floor space would likely drown-out any efficiency gains). Secondly, without clear, independent monitoring and verification, it will be hard to know when, and if, targets are ever met.

An Alternative Plan

What would a plan for Tesco's behaviour look like if it were to match the rhetoric on responsibility? Nick Robins, Head of SRI Funds for Henderson Global Investors, made a range of suggestions designed to apply to Tesco at home and abroad, and to be achieved over a five-year period. Paraphrased here, adapted and added to, they also cover ten broad points – but these are rather different ones than Tesco's.

1. *On power.* The first problem is market power, so being a responsible retailer, under this alternative plan Tesco would voluntarily implement a Fair, Open Markets Plan, restraining its share of the grocery market to no more than 10 per cent in each of the markets where it is present. In fact, as the Competition Commission noted in its 2000 investigation, a mere 8 per cent of market share delivers enough power to abuse the supply chain – so maybe we should lower the 10 to 8 per cent.

2. *On going local.* Tesco would set itself the target of sourcing three-quarters of seasonal food in-country, and set 90 per cent as a goal.[21]

3. *On sharing the benefits.* Tesco has one of the most expensive company boards in the FTSE 100 list of biggest corporations, costing £19.7 million in 2006. It also has one of the lowest average salaries for its workers, at just £11,594, a figure that shrank from the previous year and includes overseas staff.[22] This figure is probably understated to a degree, because Tesco has many part-time workers, but even if this figure were higher by a few thousand pounds it wouldn't even come close to Chief Executive Terry Leahy's pay, which rose by 25 per cent in 2006 to nearly £4 million, including bonuses of £2.8 million.[23]

Someone earning the average Tesco salary would have to work for 345 years to catch up with Leahy. Robins suggests that Tesco introduce a maximum ratio between top and bottom pay of fifteen times. Interestingly, more than 100 years ago, that giant of the business world J. P. Morgan said, that in order to effectively motivate staff, no company needs to have a differential between highest- and lowest-paid greater than ten. Historically, the Royal Navy had a de facto differential of eight. For the sake of argument, let's settle on a ratio of ten as a target for Tesco.

4. *On healthy living.* As part of a meaningful commitment to public health, Tesco would launch a Health Action Plan, linked to international initiatives like the WHO's Global Strategy on Diet, Physical Activity and Health. Tesco would commit to removing from its shelves products with poor health profiles, an approach similar to one used to phase out electrical goods that use energy inefficiently that has been referred to as 'choice editing'. For example, in support of government targets to reduce smoking, Tesco would cut its cigarette sales by one-quarter in five years and halve them in ten.[24]

5. *On fair trade.* All of Tesco's own-brand products sourced from overseas would be bought according to proper fair trade guidelines.

6. *On global warming.* The shift to more efficient and sustainable energy use was a big part of Tesco's rebranding as a 'responsible' company. It was welcomed, but left a lot out. Perhaps the biggest weakness is that Tesco focused mainly on its own infrastructure, and ignored the fact that its whole business model encourages the wasteful use of private transport. To change that, Robins proposes a target in line with government aims to reduce greenhouse gas emissions by 60 per cent by the year 2050. The target would apply to all of Tesco's own energy use including fuel for vehicles, the emissions that stem from all the stores supporting logistics and, vitally, emissions from the transport its customers use to shop at Tesco stores.

This aim would be a start, and is good as far as it goes, but environmental realities might mean we need to turn the screw a little tighter. The latest science of climate change suggests that the target for 2050 may need to be higher and reached much sooner to prevent catastrophic, runaway global warming. So we might need to change the year from 2050 to 2030, and the 60 per cent to around 80 per cent or higher.

7. *On sustainable farming, fishing and forestry.* After climate change, depletion and inefficient use of the world's fresh-water supplies is the next major environmental threat. To improve its record on sustainability, Tesco would extend current commitments on farm management, fish, palm oil, and timber to all of its global operations, and would launch a plan called Every Little Drop Helps, to measure and report on the water used in the production of its products, and would set targets to cut water use.

8. *On waste.* Tesco would set out to reduce carrier bag use by 90 per cent, introducing a charge for their use with the proceeds going to appropriate charities (e.g. Bag Relief). In the Republic of Ireland, a tax on plastic carrier bags has achieved exactly this result and raised large amounts of money. An alternative would be to follow the New Delhi or Bangladesh example, and simply ban them. It is remarkable how quickly people adapt.

9. *On community investment.* Robins suggests that Tesco shift from its current commitment to donate the equivalent of 1 per cent of pre-tax profits to 5 per cent of post-tax profits, matching the practice of the major US retailer Whole Food Markets.

10. *On decision-making.* Tesco's approach to communities that don't like their decisions (remember those active campaigns, 138 at last count) is like when the government gets into trouble with a deeply unpopular policy and doesn't admit that the policy is wrong, but merely suggests that it has failed to communicate the policy well enough.

Sir Terry Leahy's 'good neighbour' policy says: 'We will improve the way we consult local communities before building new stores.' In other words, Tesco will not simply walk away if a community does not want a new store. The new approach seems designed to make it easier for Tesco to get its own way in the end.

Stronger local democracy is the only real answer. For example, proposed new legislation like the Sustainable Communities Bill[25] seeks to establish in law the principle that decisions should be taken at the lowest appropriate and practicable level and be financially supported by central government funds available for local development. In late 2006 the bill had won the support of over half the House of Commons and was picked by the MP who came top in the lottery for private members' bills, pushing it to the front of the queue of non-government proposed legislation. Under the new scenario Tesco would support the terms of this bill, or similar.

What Should We Do with the Corporation?

So far, these are techno-fixes. Some are admittedly ambitious, but they do not address deeper systemic problems. There are a number of levels at which we can try to do that. On one hand, our expectation of what the global economy can or should provide for us has become boundless. On the other, the legal privileges given to corporations and, in particular, the owners of finance, have strayed a very long way from their original purpose.

Although trade relationships are as old as human civilization, most basic needs have been met locally for much of human history. Trade was for luxuries like spices and silk, and for special items not obtainable at home. When large-scale trade did build the wealth of the first industrialized nations it was often one-sided, exploitative, backed by gunboats and to the cost of countries in Asia, Africa and Latin America. Of the history of free trade, it is tempting, if not entirely accurate, to adapt Gandhi's famous reply when asked what he thought of Western civilization: 'It would be a good idea.' Where large imbalances of power exist, there can be no such thing as free trade. The nearest you get is compulsory trade on the terms of the most powerful player.

Economic historian Robert Heilbroner pours the cold water of history on to the overenthusiastic advocates of the benefits to be gained from competitive international trade. For much of the last millennia, he observes, the 'notion that a general struggle for gain might actually bind together a community would have been held as little short of madness'.[26] It would thus help to remember the historical purpose of trade and to recalibrate our expectations of its role in the wider scheme of things to something more modest.

In terms of our expectations of corporations, the degree to which corporations can change is constrained by the laws within which they operate. At one extreme the legal obligation – 'fiduciary duty' – on company directors is to maximize the return to shareholders. This means that of all the things and people connected to a company, like the community in which it is located, its workers, its customers and the environment, the law demands that the interests of the investor come first. At another extreme, modern corporations enjoy a form of legal protection in 'limited liability' that was never designed for its current purpose. A little history is needed.

Where Does the Corporation Come From?[27]

When Henry VIII broke away from papal authority, he needed revenue and used his new nation-state to give royal trading rights to merchants in the City of London. In this way grew the Levant Company, the Baltic Company and others. The Levant

Company would ultimately evolve into the British East India Company and help found the Empire. Under Elizabeth I, out-and-out pirates operating in the Caribbean were legitimized by the Crown so that the state could earn income from their international 'trading'.

Adventurers and pirates like John Hawkins and Francis Drake were knighted to pillage the Spanish Armada, colonize overseas territories and bring back gold and plunder.[28] This 'reformed piracy' evolved into mercantilism. In the seventeenth century, the first political economists like William Petty developed national accounting systems to put the tracking of world trade on a more scientific basis. Their other concern was how to issue charters most efficiently to bring in maximum income for the Crown.

The earliest form of corporatism under mercantilism, there-fore, linked up big business and the nation-state – much as it does still today with, for example, the revolving door between supermarkets and the government. Monopoly rights in trade within empires came under Adam Smith's successful intellectual assaults even though his deep antipathy towards large corpora-tions is conveniently forgotten today. Clearly, for maximizing profit, monopoly wins out against competition all the time. That is why the British monarchs preferred royal charters, as taxation was a percentage cut of corporate profits. Smith, though, was the mouthpiece of industrialists, not the earlier mercantile capital-ists in the City of London. Smith's manufacturers were fru-strated by the global trade barons. They could not 'get on' without breaking down the special interests in trade.

Prior to Smith, the only corporations were those with royal charters, each of which required its own act of Parliament to create. These ranged from the famous ones like the Hudson Bay Company and the East India Company to domestic ones such as cities whose charters governed taxation and especially the means of domestic transport from turnpikes, canals and, later, rail.

Partly in response to the investment crash of the South Sea Bubble, a 1720 Parliamentary Act introduced into law the idea of limited liability, but only in a very restricted sense. Today, the privilege and the protection it provides is taken for granted. Company law, however, is based on the notion that legal benefits are given in return for obligations. In this case it was to restore investors' confidence so that they would put money into the growth of the railways.

The 1844 Companies Act enabled businesses to be incorporated without having to seek a royal charter and legal statute. Broader access to limited liability came later. Legislators were deeply worried it would be abused, fearing fraud and 'moral hazard'. It was not conceded to more widely until 1862, allowing them to take commercial risks without risking personal ruin as well, but it was only intended for enterprises specifically to benefit the public through major public works. In 1852 a Mercantile Law Commission supported limited liability for two purposes:

(a) for those 'many useful enterprises calculated to produce benefit to the public and profit to those who engage in them' that are 'of such magnitude that no private partnership can be expected to provide the funds necessary . . . of which docks, railways and extensive shipping companies may be taken as examples'.

(b) 'there are others of a more limited character, from which benefit to the humbler classes of society may be expected to accrue . . . such as baths and wash-houses, lodging houses and reading rooms, to the establishment of which by large capitalists there is little inducement.'[29]

Today corporations still enjoy limited liability but their obligations to investors come before contributing to the good of the general public. Tesco is a public limited company, though modern global financial structures also allow it to minimize the amount it contributes to the public purse through clever tax-avoidance strategies. Tesco, for example, sells CDs, DVDs and computer games from a special branch of the company in the tax haven of Jersey.

To tackle such legal obstacles, a wide range of concerned groups got together to push for three key principles to be introduced into company law. Known as the CORE campaign, they called for:

1. Companies to be legally required to report on their social and environmental impacts.
2. Directors to be legally obliged to minimize any damage their company does to local communities and the environment.
3. People overseas who are harmed by the activities of a UK company to be able to take action against it in a UK court.

After winning the support of several hundred MPs, the campaign made progress when some changes it sought were included in a complex new reporting requirement for companies, called the Operating and Financial Review. To get to this point took years of assiduous lobbying. What happened next opens a disturbing window on how politics actually works: following just two conversations had by Treasury officials with a City investment firm and a business trade association, Chancellor Gordon Brown summarily dropped the new obligations. Friends of the Earth challenged the decision in court, and the government lost. Negotiations began again.

By the time the new Companies Act became law in November 2006, campaigners for greater corporate accountability scored a tactical victory. A late amendment was introduced to the bill, unnoticed by corporate lobbyists, that meant company directors were given a duty to 'have regard' to their social and environmental impacts, including the effect they have on communities. Although weak-sounding and yet to be tested in law, it set a precedent by acknowledging a wider 'duty of care' beyond just that owed to shareholders. Also, publicly listed companies now have to report not only on their social and environmental impacts, but on what happens along the supply chain. 'The longer-term vision would be to move to full stakeholder accountability,' said Deborah Doane, one of the campaigners, 'so that companies are truly run in the interests of the wider community.'

Whatever the law says, no corporation will ever be entirely reliable. Problems emerge when imperfections are magnified by size, one of the reasons why no single private enterprise should be allowed to dominate its market. It's a lesson from history that we could have learned from a multinational ancestor of Tesco, the British East India Company. One modern account of the colonial company puts it like this:

> When it was small, the damage that the Company could inflict was relatively limited. When it grew in size to dominate whole markets and territories, its potential for harm grew correspondingly large.[30]

As it was then, so it is today.

The Trouble with Regulators

The mere fact of size conveys unfair advantage – granting unequal access to finance, policymakers, marketing, consumers and control of supply chains. As a result, one of the greatest challenges for the contemporary regulator is how to limit the size of dominant retailers like Tesco in order to keep the market open and prevent the abuse of power. Although timid to date, several courses of action are open to the Competition Commission and OFT. The question will be whether they can escape what the great economist John Kenneth Galbraith described, in the aftermath of the 1929 Wall Street Crash, as the short, debilitating lifespan of the regulator:

> In youth they are vigorous, aggressive, evangelistic, and even intolerant. Later they mellow, and in old age – after a matter of ten or fifteen years – they become, with some exceptions, either an arm of the industry they are regulating or senile.[31]

Even though Galbraith's words refer to another time and another market – the market for money, one of the purest and perhaps most honest forms of capitalism, undiluted by the muddy business of making and selling actual things – his insight remains acute and more relevant than ever. Galbraith identified a vital tendency of weakly regulated markets to devour both themselves and any bystanders caught in the feeding frenzy.

In 1929, Galbraith saw how the inability of the world of finance to express self-criticism blinded the sector to how its own behaviour was destroying the foundations on which it stood. It was the proverbial case of a man in a tree sawing off the branch he is sitting on because he needs the wood. 'The sense of responsibility in the financial community for the community as a whole is not small,' Galbraith wrote, 'It is nearly nil.' The same is true of the self-undermining nature of the supermarkets' low-price model. It may not be in their longer-term interests, but that certainly doesn't stop them doing it.

With these thoughts in mind, I went to the OFT to drink tea from a paper cup with a senior official from the 'Markets and Policy Initiatives Division'. I was curious to find out which of Galbraith's regulators the OFT had become. My notes from that meeting, which were later to find themselves at the centre of a national media story because of a telling and almost certainly unintentional admission by the official, drop big clues about where on the scale from youthful vigour to senility the OFT sat.[32] Its comments seemed to combine a certain dogged adherence to a set point of view combined with an element of confusion.

The OFT reviews its 'mechanisms' every five years. Since the previous supermarket review it witnessed 'the emergence of the big four and especially the big one', yet thought, 'Thus far, they [Tesco] are not dominant.' It would be possible to use a definition of 'dominance' to defend this remark; but with Tesco dominant in 81 out of 121 UK postcode areas and the number-two retailer in another twenty-four, it would be hard to find one that didn't reduce people to incredulity or laughter. However, in the eyes of the OFT, 'Tesco's have achieved a virtuous circle.' (Unless, that is, you happen to be a community that doesn't want one of its stores, a shop put out of business by its anti-competitive practices or a supplier on the rack.)

The generally favourable attitude of the OFT towards Tesco explains why, following the previous major investigation, it said, 'We took the view that there couldn't be a prescriptive code [of conduct governing relationships with suppliers].' But now it was keen to show no complacency, promising to be more 'proactive' and 'persuasive' and to 'raise the profile' of the monitoring and evaluation of its non-prescriptive code for supermarkets. The code would be revisited, said Bob MacDowell of the OFT, if consumers got a raw deal, or a lot of complaints were received.

This was a very strange comment for the regulator to make, and I will explain why. We were meeting more than a year and half after an internal OFT review had concluded that the code was a complete failure. Over eight out of ten of those consulted from among supermarkets, their suppliers and trade associations said the voluntary code 'failed to bring about any change in

the supermarkets' behaviour'.[33] Why? Three-quarters attributed
the failure of the code to fear among suppliers about complaining. No one wanted to use the system. The code was introduced
in March 2003 and by the time the review was published in
February 2004, not a single case had gone to 'mediation'.

MacDowell would have known this, and known that suppliers
fearing for their already-precarious livelihoods were unlikely to
risk the wrath of Tesco. The situation between supermarkets and
their suppliers is a one-sided deadlock. Imagine a Mafia god-
father sitting at the head of a table around which sit his 'business
associates'. 'Any complaints?' he asks. Is it surprising when no
hands go up? What's more, it's clear that there are plenty of
things that the regulator could do if it wanted to shake off that
aforementioned sobriquet 'Office in Favour of Tesco'; Mac-
Dowell admitted as much in our meeting.

I reminded him that 8 per cent of market share was the size at
which the Competition Commission had concluded that retailers attain potentially abusive power to control the supply chain,
and asked if that threshold could, technically, be introduced. 'It's
not impossible in law,' he replied, 'theoretically possible, [it]
would be a big structural remedy, the biggest since the cap was
introduced on brewers.'[34] MacDowell added that, as a result,
'Small brewers are now in rude health.' So, from the horse's
mouth, we learn that breaking up the big boys is both possible
and effective. Let's proceed from there. What else is possible?

More than one expert in anti-monopoly law thinks that the
regulators have been asleep on the job. Regardless of the actions
of any individual supermarket, Michael Hutchings, a leading
light of the British Institute of International and Comparative
Law, points out that the regulator has to deal with the problem
of 'collective dominance'.[35] This is when competition overall is
limited, and common policies are followed by the dominant
market players. 'The fact that the large supermarkets never

compete on adjacent sites demonstrates the former,' Hutchings writes, 'and the fact that they all engage in similar anti-competitive practices illustrates the latter.' None of this should surprise a regulator. The tendency of corporations to escape the insecurities of real competition is hardly news. The economist James K. Galbraith (son of John Kenneth) writes:

> Corporations exist to control markets, and often to replace them. Business leaders reduce uncertainty not through clairvoyance, nor by confident exploitation of probability. They do it forming organizations large enough to forge the future for themselves.[36]

Legally, according to Hutchings and others, a huge range of remedies is possible.[37] The following table gives a selection.

Figure 10: A few things regulators can do . . .

Problem	Solution
Supermarkets are too big	Require supermarkets to sell off part of their businesses
Supermarkets take over new markets such as pharmacies, news agencies, legal and financial services	Introduce licensing to prevent domination
Supermarkets get even bigger through merging with and buying other stores	Refer all proposals to the regulator and introduce a new, lower cap on market share Prohibit supermarkets from buying more convenience stores and require them to sell off those already controlled
Supermarkets have too much control of the supply chain	Require supermarkets to sell off their wholesale divisions
Supermarkets use the threat of de-listing to control suppliers	Introduce a mandatory, enforceable Code of Conduct

Supermarkets make random demands on suppliers not included in their contracts (if they ever received any)	As above
Supermarkets hoard land for their own expansion and to block competitors	Require supermarkets to sell off the land (with its future use respecting both the community and local council's wishes)[38]
In collusion with local planners, supermarkets create local monopolies	Give new guidance to planners to not allow local monopolies
Supermarkets sell products at 'below cost' to put other shops out of business	Ban below-cost selling
Supermarkets sell identical products for higher prices in places where they can get away with it (and the competition has been removed) – so called 'price flexing'	Ban price flexing
Supermarkets engage in practices that harm suppliers at home in the UK and abroad	Introduce a mandatory, enforceable Code of Conduct
Local councils fear standing up to supermarkets because of the cost of potential legal disputes	Government indemnifies councils against legal costs of 'vexatious' supermarket planning disputes or 'protective cost orders' are used more to the same effect

Other countries can manage it. In France, for example, local authorities were given the right to veto the construction of supermarkets over 1,000 sq. m back in 1973. Between 1993 and 1996, all authorizations for large supermarkets were suspended. In 1996, a law was introduced which requires a public inquiry for the construction of any outlet over 6,000 sq. m, in order to protect 'the social and economic cohesion and the fabric of society'.

Why do our regulators appear so impotent, given that there are so many things that they could be doing? Partly it's because they see their role only on a national, rather than a local, scale. They appear to have neither the capacity nor interest to look into the monopolies that already exist in UK towns like Inverness and others where Tesco takes over 50 pence in every £1 spent on groceries. I was told by the OFT that it was 'very unlikely' to investigate a local monopoly unless something was 'so bad . . .' (At which point the official's voice trailed off wistfully and, I imagine, through his head ran images of houses burned, villages looted, the sort of atrocities necessary to trigger an OFT investigation.) Following intense pressure on this issue, early in 2007 the Competition Commission began to display new glimmers of interest in addressing the emergence of local monopolies.

Another problem is the way that 'consumer' or 'public' interest is understood. In the eyes of the regulator it has to do with price alone. Low prices to the consumer means everything is OK; no action is required. The frequently 'high cost of low prices' fails to show on the regulatory radar screen.

Compared to the hidden costs of cheap goods, the price of a product at the point of sale is easy to measure. Partly because of that, it has come to matter disproportionately. The wide range of other impacts that supermarkets have on us and on our neighbourhoods go largely unrecorded, but just because they are harder to measure (though far from impossible), it makes them no less important. The tragedy is that where policymakers are concerned, it is only the shallow conventional measures that matter. One fundamental flaw of the regulators' approach, therefore, is that they rely on prices that do not reveal true costs. Their other mistake is that many things other than price drive our behaviour as consumers or, more properly, as people. Being defined primarily by the act of consumption is symptomatic of the problem.

Regulators apply flawed economic theory when they reduce people to 'rational' actors who respond neatly and robotically to price 'signals', and who are out in the marketplace to maximize their personal 'utility'. (Please excuse the language, but this is how economists actually talk, and it can get much worse.)

The conclusion of this review of options is in fact quite simple. Firstly, in light of all the problems the big supermarkets need to be broken up to nurture a healthy, open market. Secondly, all the warm promises rising like steam from the body of corporate social responsibility need turning into reality by becoming mandatory and being backed with the force of law.

In the next and final chapter, we'll take a more nuanced look at what pleasantly complex beings we are. Even on a simple trip to the shops, people are far too awkward to speak the lines written for them by the playwrights of the economy. If companies can't be relied on to regulate themselves, and the regulators can't be relied on to manage the system either, perhaps we need to ask some deeper questions.

CHAPTER ELEVEN

The Birth of Something Better

'Like capitalism . . . he provided good things and bad things. He didn't think about consequences. He was anti-social and unpatriotic. In fact, he was the forerunner of the multinational corporation and the global economy.'

Author Joseph Heller on his war profiteer character Milo Minderbinder in *Catch-22*.[1]

Under the Mango Tree

Stan sits under a mango tree in the Nilgiri hills in southern India. He marvels at the generosity of the relatively poor local tribal people of Gudalur. Every time they spit when brushing their teeth with imported toothpaste, he tells them, they're making money for rich American investors – people they've never met, who live thousands of miles away. Stan spends a lot of time thinking about the world. He wonders how to change things so that they work a little better.

For most of us, however, it's hard to imagine a world much different from the one we see around ourselves. We go to work, shop and watch TV. Routine and familiarity are the backing tracks to our lives. When we see bad things on the news, we take comfort in the continuity that recognizable personalities and established brands provide. Familiarity makes us feel secure, and it works even if we are anything but. When celebrities, actors, musicians or sport stars endorse something (it could be a political party or a big supermarket), the message is, 'You can trust us, because this

famous person you know is prepared to be seen in public with us.'
But familiarity is often a mask, behind which change and upheaval
can be ushered in more easily.

That's why, under the cover of folksy tales of being a green-
grocer's daughter and leading a party that was meant to stand for
Olde England, former Conservative Prime Minister Margaret
Thatcher was able to push an economic revolution that betrayed
its provenance. With perfect irony, it sounded the death knell
for thousands of small, independent greengrocers and turned
the villages and towns that represented Olde England into ghost
or clone towns. Now the result of that revolution is with us, can
we imagine anything else? The battle cry of the neoliberals was,
'There is no alternative.' It even had its own acronym that
entered the language – TINA. Even if it was never true, it was an
effective strategy. You still hear it coming from mouth of the
Prime Minister or Chancellor of the Exchequer as they talk
about removing checks and balances, although one-sidedly, on
the movement by multinationals of money, goods and services
around the world. If you put a proposal on the table and then say
'there is no alternative', it doesn't leave much choice and you're
quite likely to get your way.

But ask Stan if there's no alternative to business-as-usual, and
he will laugh. He'll find it funny because he knows there are not
just a few, but hundreds of alternatives. He knows, because he is
living in the middle of one of the boldest, most radical and
creative experiments to challenge the power of big business and
make the global food system work for those who need it most.

Stan Thekaekara is laughing when I meet him, not because
anyone has told him a joke, but because we are so far away from
his usual surroundings and he is just about to give a lecture high
up in the shining glass and steel surroundings of London's
Living Room at the new City Hall, home to the mayor's office.
Instead of the usual Nilgiri tea plantations, if he looks over his

shoulder today he can gaze down on the ancient and modern jumble of the City of London, behind whose doors and tinted windows move billions of pounds of investments every hour. I've invited him to give the Alternative Mansion House Speech, an annual opportunity to present a worldview different to what gets heard each year when the Chancellor addresses the City.

For thirty years Stan has worked with some of the poorest people in India, the indigenous *adivasi* communities. He protests that he's not an economist. Neither, however, was the real Chancellor, and the Treasury rarely has one at the helm. But Stan has more experience than most in trying to solve what J. M. Keynes called 'the economic problem' – the daily struggle for subsistence, to meet basic needs, not wants. While the Chancellor 'tries to balance a nation's budget', says Stan, the people he works with 'struggle to scrape together enough money to buy enough rice to ensure that their children don't go to bed hungry'.

I'd met up with Stan because his work in India, despite the economic and cultural differences, had startling similarities with what my colleagues and I at nef were trying to achieve. We were asking the same question: why do poor communities and poor people tend to stay that way, while rich people get richer?

One answer was that the economy is designed like a leaky bucket, in which money seems to flow from the poor to the rich. The latest evidence suggests that in spite of international campaigns to tackle poverty, this trend is getting worse. That's why Stan found himself talking about toothpaste. How do you explain the working of the global economy to people who may never even have been to school? Stan elaborates:

> We asked people to bring from their houses what they use to clean their teeth in the morning. We had one of the older people in the village bringing a twig of *neem*, which he breaks every morning from the tree to clean his teeth, and we had the

young people bringing a tube of Colgate toothpaste. And I said to the young people – just imagine! Every morning each time you spit, when brushing your teeth, somebody in America makes money. The thought that in a small remote tribal village, lost in the mountains of South India, that a tribe every morning can be contributing to the creation of wealth for somebody in America or wherever, is really mind-boggling.

It's possible that the reason some members of his audience weren't aware they were making rich people richer is because they themselves had a very different idea of wealth. Stan asked them, and all the other 167 villages he worked with, what wealth meant to them. By way of reply, they all said the same things: 'Our children, our forests, our culture, our language, our unity, our sharing.' This is what excited Stan so much: the possibility of 'the common good or common well-being being the prime purpose of economic activity'.

To him, the moment you refocus in this way, 'the key factor that determines the success of the economy becomes well-being and the efficient distribution of wealth'. Rather than just think about it, over many years Stan set about making it happen.

It began in the Nilgiri hills with a campaign. Many of the *adivasis* had lost their land. Bitterly, they often ended up working it for others or, worse, found themselves in virtual slavery as bonded labourers. A huge Tribal Land Rights Campaign successfully won them back their land, but to keep it they had to work it; so they turned to growing tea. This might seem simple, but it was revolutionary. 'The thought of an agricultural, unskilled, low-paid *adivasi* labourer being a tea planter was not only economically but also socially and politically considered impossible,' says Stan. (Until then, only wealthy landowners planted tea.) It was a victory, but only partial. They soon realized that merely moving from lowly local labouring to selling cash crops on the global markets made them even more vulnerable. At least in the local employment market, the people could group together and demand better pay by collaring the employer.

To begin with, they tackled the problem in their own communities. From the toothpaste example they learned a lesson, independently – the same one the Marsh Farm community in Luton had learned when they tried to rebuild their neighbourhoods after the urban riots. By plugging and plumbing the leaks in your local economy by buying and providing more of the things you need locally, cutting out the wealthier middlemen, less money will leak out of the system. The *adivasis* developed Village Consumer Societies, a bit like British cooperatives. They traded their tea directly with a cooperative of women weavers in Tamil Nadu. Today there are 10,000 families involved in the system, with 35,000 more waiting to join.

There was still a problem with selling tea internationally. 'When tea prices crash, as they have done in the last few years, whose collar do you grab?' asks Stan. So they turned to fair trade for a while, which disappointed in different ways. Fair trade seemed like little more than another type of charity. The *adivasis* were also uncomfortable charging a premium price to buyers whom they thought of as friends because they were buying tea in solidarity with them.

But it wasn't even just that; for Stan, the problem with fair trade was deeper:

> Marginally increasing the price the producer gets for her labour is not going to significantly change her economy, it will not by itself address or correct the fundamental flaws and injustice of our current global market economy. The challenge for us today is to create a radically new structure, which will directly link consumer and producer communities . . . in a manner that is different from the global marketplace.

That, to cut a very long story short, is exactly what he and the *adivasis* did, and they did it by teaming up with, among others, the underprivileged estates of Marsh Farm. A community-to-community tea trade was born, which they called 'One Sugar Bruv'. Tea is sold at prices comparable to the mainstream brands, and any financial surplus doesn't leak away but is kept in the trade loop of the two relatively cash-poor communities. It's much more than worthy. In a blind, independent taste test conducted by the local BBC radio station, Just Change tea (the name of the enterprise) beat rivals PG Tips, Tetley's, Twinings and Morrisons. Just Change is branching out into other products such as rice and coconut oil, which has numerous uses.

The scale of Just Change is clearly limited at the moment, but the model it is working to has enormous implications. It has managed to set up a parallel international trading system, one that works for local economies at both ends of the trade. It dodges rigged global markets, and there is not a multinational corporation or supermarket in sight. That, if it needs spelling out, is the moral of the story.

Other lessons can be drawn from Just Change's practical experience. One of the biggest questions that stalks the debate about reducing poverty around the world and about the costs and benefits of economic globalization is, 'What should be the role of international trade?' The issue divides anti-poverty campaigners, aid donors, economists and international financial institutions. In 1999, when the WTO's efforts in Seattle to promote (compulsory) free trade collapsed, *The Economist* put on its cover an emotive image of hungry African children with the title: 'The real losers in Seattle.' Should poorer countries grow food for export to fill our supermarkets and earn money to pay for their development? Or should they turn their backs on the global markets and concentrate on their own needs?

Stan's answer is disarmingly simple and based firmly in

commonsense, as a logical way for this part of southern India to trade with the UK. There are basic ground rules:

> We must have a robust domestic market first. The export market is for us the icing on the cake. If a product is produced in the UK, and not by a multinational, we will not compete with it. So tea I'd sell, but not Himachel apples.

With a smile of reconciliation and a hint of irony that alludes to how Britain stole all sorts of Asia's intellectual property and manufacturing techniques in the early days of colonialism, Stan adds, 'Or, for example, with pottery, we might export with the idea of transferring the skills and techniques to the UK, to help grassroots enterprises take off.'

Food Sovereignty

There is a growing global movement that presents a fundamental challenge to the way Tesco does business, gathering around the idea of 'food sovereignty'. To understand the approach of food sovereignty means first seeing the complex question to which it is addressed. Then it becomes clear why the presence of a company like Tesco is either irrelevant to solving the problem or, worse, directly obstructive.

Patrick Mulvany is Senior Policy Advisor for the group Practical Action (formerly known for decades as the Intermediate Technology Development Group), and one of the most respected voices internationally on how to make rural development work in favour of the poorest people. He starts with the world as it is. Too often, we depend on the abstract economic models of a free-market fantasy. Mulvany writes:

Most food in the world is grown, collected and harvested by more than a billion small-scale farmers, pastoralists and artisanal fisherfolk. This food is mainly sold, processed, resold and consumed locally, thereby providing the foundation of people's nutrition, incomes and economies across the world.

Today, the international community is committed to halving world poverty by the year 2015 and eradicating hunger. But things are not going well; according to the UN's special organization on food and farming, limited advances on reducing the number of people going hungry in the early 1990s have been reversed. In the decades from 1995–2005, the number of chronically hungry people in developing countries increased by nearly 5 million per year, rising from 800 million to 852 million.[2]

Now we can add to that the challenges brought by climate change and dwindling water supplies and the creeping marginalization of the poorest people in terms of access to productive land, the cash to work it and the markets in which to sell their products. The problem seems to be getting bigger. How are we responding?

Given the foundations of the world's food systems, Mulvany sees us heading 180 degrees in the wrong direction:

Reinforcing the diversity and vibrancy of local food systems should be at the forefront of the international policy agenda. Yet the rules that govern food and agriculture at all levels – local, national and international – are designed a priori to facilitate not local, but international trade. This reduces diversity and concentrates the wealth of the world's food economies in the hands of ever fewer multinational corporations, while the majority of the world's small-scale food producers, processors, local traders and consumers including, crucially, the poor and malnourished, are marginalized.[3]

This is where the idea of food sovereignty comes in; but what is it? Here is an increasingly recognized definition. It is, in many ways, simply a longer-winded version of Stan's conclusion that people must be allowed to meet their own needs first, before international trade becomes 'the icing on the cake':

Food Sovereignty is the right of peoples to define their own food and agriculture; to protect and regulate domestic agricultural production and trade in order to achieve sustainable development objectives; to determine the extent to which they want to be self-reliant; to restrict the dumping of products in their markets; and to provide local fisheries-based communities the priority in managing the use of and the rights to aquatic resources. Food Sovereignty does not negate trade, but rather it promotes the formulation of trade policies and practices that serve the rights of peoples to food and to safe, healthy and ecologically sustainable production.[4]

Food sovereignty has four key elements:

1. *The Right to Food.* Making such a right meaningful and real has major practical implications. It means that people need physical access to land, water and the seeds to grow the food that's right for them. It means they must also be able to afford to buy what they need or cannot grow. This, in turns, means tackling the power of those who set prices and control land, water and seeds.
2. *Getting Access to Resources.* Linked to the above, there must be a programme of reform that gives smallholder farmers, pastoralists and fisherfolk the means to exercise their right to food. It's here that clashes with powerful vested interests occur. Landless people and farm workers, in particular women, will need to own and control the land they work.

More indigenous peoples will need land returned to them. It will also mean a major relaxation of restrictive rules at the international level that control the intellectual property on seeds, breeds of livestock and other types of biodiversity.

Techniques such as the infamous 'terminator technology' – a way of genetically modifying seeds so that plants become infertile – are anathema in this context.[5] Farmers traditionally collect seeds from a crop to plant in the next season, but this technique forces them to return to the seed company each year, fostering economic dependence on the multinationals that increasingly own and control all aspects of the food chain. There are more general ways that the integrity of plant and animal genetic resources will be compromised, and power shifts even further from the poor with the spread of genetic modification.

3. *Taking Positive Ecological Approaches to Farming.* Environmentally friendly approaches to farming that grow a wider range of crops are, over time and a wide range of conditions and climates, more friendly to small-scale farmers, less vulnerable to external shocks, more resilient and productive. This is called 'agroecology', described as the 'holistic study of agroecosystems, including all environmental and human elements' – and it works. A study published by the FAO in 2002 showed that the approach produced increases in crop yields that averaged 94 per cent. In the best cases, yields went up by an astonishing 600 per cent.[6]

4. *Escaping the Trade Trap.* The last of these four pillars concerns improving international trade policies. Instead of just assuming that any increase in international trade will benefit people in need, this suggests that new policies are needed that 'enable communities and countries vulnerable to hunger and malnutrition to produce sufficient

quantities of safe and secure food supplies'. At the same time, rules are needed to stop 'the negative effects of subsidized exports, food dumping [and] artificially low prices' that mark the current model of agricultural trade.

These points put into context something obvious about Tesco, which needs saying nevertheless. The company is not growing and spreading around the world, along with others of its kind like Carrefour and Wal-Mart, because it is on a mission to feed the world. Of course not; it is a business whose primary purpose is to make a profit. It grows to please already-wealthy City investors who want to get even richer, and to take a bigger slice of the global economic pie. To achieve that, they demand constant growth from Tesco and a high and continuing return on their shareholdings. In this limited sense, the company is successful, but in several other ways it fails, such as in promoting vibrant, distinctive neighbourhoods with the right to say 'no' to the big retailers, or efficiently and fairly distributing benefits from the global economy and enabling us to live within our environmental means.

As we've seen, people working internationally in the field or factory to supply Tesco in the UK get a pitifully small share of the final selling price of the things they grow or make. When stores like Tesco expand abroad, the re-engineering of rural economies to please the supermarkets excludes the poor. Given that we have an overarching, internationally agreed aim of halving poverty, this is a lose–lose situation.

It is hard for people living in countries like Britain to relate easily to such acute challenges and trends. The share of Britain's population actually working the land has shrunk to around 1 per cent, and we buy most of our food neatly wrapped from supermarkets. The upmarket reinvention of the TV dinner by supermarkets as the 'ready meal' coupled with overloaded descriptions of overprocessed food creates an illusion of sophistication. Because the growing, harvesting and preparation of food has already been done for us, we can roll in, load up and roll out of the supermarket car park in our 4x4s; this allows us to feel oddly superior. Meanwhile, out there, the world's majority scrabbles to grow and prepare most of its own food.

Here is an irony. Much of this book suggests that we have been sleepwalking into a fantasy of cost-free shopping convenience, and only now are we waking up to the high price of 'cheap' supermarket food. Yet rather than seeing the status quo as unrealistic, allegations of middle-class indulgence stalk any attempts to change it. Local food, farmers' markets and simple, organic food unthinkingly get derided as impractical luxury and niche markets.

This is where Colin Tudge thinks people are making a big mistake, largely due to ignorance. He believes that to meet the challenge of feeding a hungry world, the future will entail more local production for local consumption, and that we will be the better for it. He says:

People who say it's a middle class fantasy are entirely ignorant. The standard position is that when people around the world, especially the poor, are left to themselves, they eat very well; the best food in the world is based on peasant cooking. Except when people are being wrecked by outside forces, like the Irish under the English, people live very well . . . [This approach is] intrinsically attractive – food produced to feed people is the most attractive food – but it is presented as austere. Serious farming and good nutrition and great gastronomy go hand in hand. Go into a village in India and, unless it's already been Tesco'd, people eat very well. Good food for the poor is cheap. It's the rubbish fast food and junk sold in supermarkets that is expensive and bad. Where people are in charge of their own destiny, they eat very well.[7]

Logical Behaviour?

A summary of the copious and growing research on behavioural economics quickly dismisses the impoverished view that having people as stooges of ignorant price signals is the best way to maximize well-being. For example, who is to say that the 'consumer interest' is better embodied in a four-pack of baked beans that costs less than £1 rather than by having a small, independent shopkeeper who saves you from depression by smiling, remembering your name and having the time to chat each morning and evening?

As shoppers, just as in every other aspect of our lives, we are much more complex than economic theory allows. Far from merely responding to prices, people are powerfully motivated by copying the behaviour of others and by feeling approved of. Habits, too, are powerful, and once developed, are hard to change.

Contrary to the popular media's vision of reality, people are usually steered by morality, and want their actions to be in line with their values. Money can actually 'de-motivate', especially if it undermines your intrinsic motivation. As has been written, 'You would quickly stop inviting friends to dinner if they insisted on paying you.'[8] Fascinating evidence of this flaw in market economics was revealed when researchers compared the different approaches of health services in the UK and the US with regard to blood donation.

In the UK, people give freely. In the US, they are paid to do so. Conventional economics predicts that the financial incentive should leave the US service better off. In reality, the opposite has happened. The financial element has lowered people's intrinsic motivation to donate for the common good. Instead, it has attracted those more desperate for cash. That meant the donors were drawn from people with a higher incidence of drug addiction and health problems. As a result, the blood was of poorer quality, and the whole service ended up being more expensive and less efficient.

A final flaw, and perhaps most important in this case, is that people are very bad at adding up. It's true. Regardless of our qualifications, we are heavily influenced by how information is presented. This leaves us susceptible to the ingratiating deceits of advertisers. When we make choices, we do so between available options. Because of their scale, big, high-profile retailers with large marketing budgets are able to present us with more options. Whether good or bad, we are more likely to choose them because they are under our nose. Add to that a couple of tempting loss-leaders, our inherently bad maths, and the fact that it doesn't say on the supermarket label that by shopping here you will turn your neighbourhood into a tedious clone town, and it's not surprising that the supermarkets are taking over.

Once a retailer crosses a certain size threshold, because of these various flaws and regardless of economic theory, its dominance becomes a self-fulfilling prophecy. When we make decisions, the research shows that we are very bad at assessing risks and what might seem to be far-off events. We are much more likely to be swayed by the immediate fact that we can park by the supermarket, because planners and the law give cheap parking to supermarkets and 'big-box' retailers as a de facto subsidy.

Behavioural economics reveals people as complex and contrary. We are moral, but get dragged down by habits that stifle our ability to change our actions. We are motivated by much more than price, but are swayed by the crowd, and by what we find under our noses. And, again, we're bad at adding up. How many people would be aware, as we've seen, that it only takes some people to shift some of their weekly shopping to an out-of-town retail centre to change the economics of the high street so much that it kills it for everyone but the clones?

Altogether, it is easy to see how the big supermarkets are able to exploit our contradictions. Without effective regulation, supermarket domination quickly becomes self-reinforcing. Yet, more promisingly, if people feel involved and effective, change becomes likely.

Slowly and cautiously, the concept of 'consumer detriment' is creeping into discussions. Awareness is growing that 'it is absolutely necessary' to consider not just prices when managing the market, but 'overall benefits' and people's welfare.[9] That means looking to see if Tescopoly leaves us all better or worse off.

Beyond this legislative and theoretical trench warfare is a huge debate and much experimentation on new, old and different ways to do business. In the US there are town-centre, community-run department stores replacing the 'big-box' retailers. These keep more money and life in the heart of communities. There is Stan and Marsh Farm's One Sugar Bruv, providing a hot-beverage economic backbone to local economies in India and Luton.

There are farmer's markets, organic box delivery schemes, cooperatives, public interest companies, stakeholder and mutual initiatives and networks like Food Links that hook up otherwise-isolated small producers for mutual benefit and to help them compete. There are still many straightforward independent, local retailers hanging on in spite of everything. Now, new local loyalty schemes designed to help small shops compete with similar supermarket cards are beginning to spread. The Wedge Card launched by John Bird, the founder of *The Big Issue* magazine, is just one. There are community land trusts and community-supported farming schemes. There are countless invitations to go local, go organic, go fair trade, go further, and to 'eat the view'.[10] Log on to a website like bigbarn.co.uk, and you'll be shown every local producer with an address and contact number within a certain radius of your home. If, after reading this, you want to change how you shop, I don't need to tell you how. The information is increasingly easy to find. Most important is that we have the desire for things to be different.

There is no single alternative to Tescopoly, but many. That's the point. Yet the alternatives need support to get up and running. They need it at least to the same degree that supermarkets have been subsidized by a favourable planning regime and massive public investments in the transport infrastructure they depend on. The many alternatives also need an open market in which to set up business. That means a cap on the further concentration of power and market share among and by the major retailers, and a breakup of the current monopolistic situation. Supermarkets are unlikely to do this voluntarily, so the regulators will have to act.

Oddly, given much of the evidence in this book, I am optimistic. I believe the mood is changing. The reductive economic logic upon which the supermarkets have risen to power is crumbling. It reveals poverty at its heart, in both the old-fashioned economic sense and in a much broader one. There is the poverty of our 'cloned' commercial surroundings, the poverty of knowing the hardship of the people who fill the supermarket shelves with produce, workers in the fields and packhouses and suppliers, the poverty of the independent retailers ruined by anti-competitive supermarket sleights of hand, the poverty of the natural environment denuded by overexploitation and homogenization, and there is the hassled, frustrating, anxious and overwhelming poverty of actually getting to and shopping in a big supermarket. Who wants to be poor?

The mood *is* changing. A new way of understanding the purpose of the economy and its absolute dependence on the natural environment is emerging. Both points call into question the way we currently do business.

Alain de Botton is a prolific writer on philosophy whose books outrage academia by trying to apply the lessons of the great thinkers to everyday life. His overriding concern is answering how it is possible to be happy, given that we live in a complicated, difficult world, and that we seem to have a predilection for emotional self-sabotage. In one book he investigated the relationship between happiness and the built environment. Because nobody builds as much or as quickly as Tesco, I asked him what he thought about the supermarket's effect on our well-being. This was his eloquent reply:

There's a view that the free market always delivers what is best, because commercial success accurately reflects 'what people really want'. Therefore, if Tesco succeeds commercially, this must be proof that what it is doing is right. However, this is to ignore an unfortunate truth about human beings that operates right across the range of our behaviour, namely that we don't always want what is best. We want love and kindness and beauty sometimes, of course, but we also want war, death to our enemies, cruelty, junk food and hard drugs. One can't dispute Tesco's success, but one can surely dispute whether commercial success must be seen as an a priori good. Only if humans were utterly rational and wise would the shops that 'succeeded' always be good.

So what's wrong with Tesco? Its success is based on all kinds of flaws in our nature. For example, it feeds off our selfish disregard for the suffering of other humans whom we can't see and know (the growers, the pickers, the stackers . . .). It feeds off our appetite for food that is instantly satisfying but not necessarily good for us in the long term. It feeds off our neglect for beauty, as its stores pay no attention to architectural merit and are almost wilfully ugly (as though to experience beauty while shopping for lemons was inherently incompatible).

What should be done about Tesco? Many critics want the place banned and hemmed in by regulation. These are the same people who want to close down McDonald's. But ultimately the real trick is not to ban such places, but to create different desires in consumers, to reach a situation where people are sufficiently sensitized to the drawbacks of Tesco or McDonald's that they won't want to shop there, or these institutions will have to change.

In other words, education is needed, education about the drawbacks of a place that could initially seem like an unambiguous good, but which – on closer reflection – reflects some of the most unfortunate sides of our flawed nature.

What's It All For?

Let's make a wild assumption that a good purpose of the economy is to give people long and happy lives, while working within the fuzzy limits of the Earth's natural resources. Some say we have no choice but to work with the grain of how things are. If so, we have to trust in finding a benign management system, able to better distribute economic benefits and guarantee environmental sustainability. None is in sight. Many environmentalists who prefer 'positive engagement' with big business as opposed to campaigning and promoting alternatives tend to underestimate the voracious life force of capitalism. They close their eyes and ears to its beating heart of capital accumulation, which in turn depends on the cycle of commodification, monetization and spiralling consumption.

Those who do so are partly excused by the seductive simplicity of the assumptions underlying orthodox economics. If people are always rational and know what will increase their personal happiness and well-being, then all economic growth must be good, because it is a sign of people pursuing those ends. In economics it is called 'utility'. This is the satisfaction derived from consuming goods and using services, or the pleasure taken from owning so-called 'positional goods' – things in strictly limited supply such as rare, original artworks or houses in beautiful, exclusive locations. Economists find utility itself hard to define. It is wrapped in complex and often contradictory human emotions. So to make sure it is maximized, they simply trust in how it is expressed through our choices to purchase things.

Growth indicates rising consumption, increased utility and hence rising welfare, so when it goes up it must, by conventional definition, be a good thing. It has become the ultimate proxy indicator of positive human outcomes from economic activity. However, there is one small problem. It doesn't work. For example, in the UK, over more than the last three decades, as economic growth steadily rose, our life satisfaction flatlined.[11] Awareness of people's responses to buying rare luxuries, generic 'positional goods', helped reveal an important flaw in the theory. No matter how wealthy people become, their appetite to possess more – a certain 'material frustration' – doesn't appear to lessen. The 'goods', it seems, don't deliver the goods.

The relationship between growth and human welfare only lasts up to the point that our basic needs for food, clothing, shelter and health care are met. Even then, it is variable. Growth can happen that only benefits a wealthy national minority, or that fails to generate or even destroys employment. Also, all growth tends to increase our collective environmental burden. Even where technology improves efficiency, the so-called Jevons' Paradox means that the unintended consequence is that we end up consuming more.[12] In short, economists have not allowed for the fact that there can be uneconomic as well as economic growth. In policy terms, if growth is your chosen destination, it is the town where you are likely to arrive. What you won't know until you get there is whether it will be a pleasant place to live, or a town full of crime, poverty and pollution. If, however, you want human well-being and a healthy environment, then that needs to be your primary goal; otherwise, finding it will be left to chance.

To get to a better place, we need a different map and compass. Leaving behind old-fashioned economic indicators altogether, nef came up with one. We took life expectancy as a good general measure of several aspects of human development like health, and multiplied it by how satisfied people felt about their lives. Although the latter is a subjective indicator, it correlates closely with hard data on things such as suicide rates and depression. In other words, people do know, generally, how happy they are. Finally, we divided the result by the size of ecological footprint. The result gave an indication of the ecological efficiency with which different societies delivered long and happy lives.

Conventionally rich nations like Britain did badly because of their large ecological footprints. Conventionally very poor countries did badly because of low life expectancy. Middle-income countries in Central and South America did well, along with many small island nations. They managed to create relatively long and happy lives, with only moderate environmental burdens. We called it the Happy Planet Index. It's possible to go into immense depth explaining how to get a good score on the index. But there are also a few simple observations to be made. To improve life expectancy in poor countries, we need a global economy better at sharing out wealth. Tescopoly is not part of that solution. A huge literature is growing up around well-being, which reminds us that we are social animals with fairly basic material needs, who like to feel secure and to have some control over our lives. To increase well-being, we need to get off the economic treadmill that steals our time, clones our towns, dissolves the bonds of community life, makes us miserable and offers only the compensation of material consumption and supermarket 'convenience'. To use a dietary analogy, consumerism is like a junk food diet in which a quick hit of satisfaction is soon followed by disaffection – a kind of psychological nausea. A well-being approach to life, on the other hand, can be seen more like a GI diet (in which food with a low glycemic index leaves you feeling fuller for longer, evening out the blood sugar highs and lows of a diet built on junk). To promote well-being there are simple things we can do that don't involve shopping such as exercising, volunteering, developing a creative past-time, walking in parks, gardens and the countryside, and carving-out more hours in the day for friends and family. To tackle problems like climate change, we have to set a natural resource budget and learn to live within our environmental means.

The Paradox of Economic Freedom

One of the biggest struggles in economics is over the idea of freedom. It raises questions about what it means to be free, how freedom can flourish, what can destroy it, and about freedom's paradoxes. The economic globalization of the last forty years marched beneath a flag of 'free markets'. Who could be against freedom? By definition, it liberates. Its appeal as a concept explains why a creeping international coalition of think tanks, committed to an extreme version of market economics, groups itself under the banner of the 'economic freedom network'. Just in case they hadn't milked the attraction of freedom enough, the network's website address is freetheworld.com. Sadly, the ideas they promote produce the very opposite of freedom. This is something that more enlightened conservative thinkers have long pointed out.

In *The Open Society and its Enemies*, published in 1962 when neoliberal economics was beginning to mount its challenge for power, conservative philosopher Karl Popper observed:

Unqualified freedom . . . is not only self-destructive but bound to produce its opposite – for if all restraints were removed there would be nothing whatever to stop the strong enslaving the weak. So complete freedom would bring about the end of freedom, and therefore proponents of complete freedom are in actuality, whatever their intentions, enemies of freedom.[13]

He applied this insight quite specifically to the economic domain. In the light of the huge growth of the size and power of multinational corporations since, its importance is even greater. 'The paradox of economic freedom,' Popper wrote, 'which makes possible the unrestrained exploitation of the poor by the rich . . . results in the almost complete loss of economic freedom by the poor.'

There is a logical conclusion for Tescopoly. Just as you need to garden to prevent favourite plants being suffocated by invasive weeds, so economies need checks and balances to prevent suffocation by invasive corporations. Yet the thrust of most economic policy is towards a teenage fantasy of a rule-free global economic playground, forgetting that playgrounds without rules become the fiefdoms of bullies.

John Kenneth Galbraith saw that a weakly regulated system, in which the powerful are free to pursue their interests, might be capable of accumulating wealth (as well as destroying it), but was very bad at distributing or 'irrigating' it among the whole population. He also prefigured the growing field of research into the economics of well-being by observing, as long ago as the 1950s, that a society based primarily on maximizing people's material consumption was not a happy society.

Jane Jacobs, on the other hand, writing in the 1960s, implicitly understood that diversity and highly specialized local adaptation created the most vibrant, productive and satisfying environments.

To her, the urban planners' slash-and-burn approach to regeneration coupled with the march of the remotely owned modern chain store was anathema. They had the same impact on communities that chemical-intensive, industrialized agriculture was having on the land. The result was a lot of pain with only short-term and questionable gain. Real solutions, she wrote, grew out of thousands of tiny human interactions.

In society as in nature, diversity also has innate value. 'Animals and plants give us pleasure and so they matter,' says Tudge. 'That is the aesthetic, moral point.' The same could be said for local distinctiveness. More than that, there is a 'meddle at your peril' lesson about destroying diversity. From years as a writer for the *New Scientist* magazine, Tudge witnessed the self-belief (he called it 'stupidity') that you can exploit nature with impunity because you understand what you are doing. 'But we can't,' he says, 'because of emergent consequences. When you try to interact with any natural system you cannot know what will happen.'

In spite of all we can learn from nature about complex systems and invasive species, across the political spectrum people are suspicious of nature. A kind of unbridled modernism that seeks, bizarrely, to free itself from nature embraces people from the far left to those at the heart of designing social democratic projects for government. Whether former Marxists who today sit comfortably with neoconservatives in their approval of multinational corporations, or prominent professors with access to a prime minister's ear, there's a denial about our inescapable connection to the biosphere that smells like self-loathing. They yearn after technocratic answers and for magic bullets that come dressed in laboratory coats. Effective solutions are more often human, though, and drawn from a science and an economics more embedded in place and people.

Alternatives don't come more locally rooted or better-designed to dispel the myth that all supermarket critics are Golden Age rural fantasists than the urban social enterprise Growing Communities. Based in the otherwise run-down inner-city London borough of Hackney, it puts the 'culture' back into agriculture and represents a comprehensively different approach to food. Anyone despairing that another world is impossible should look at what has pushed its way up through the pavements of Hackney.

Salad crops ranging from mizuna to basil, oakleaf and cos lettuces are grown at one of its urban market gardens at Springfield Park in Upper Clapton, in spite of the fact that the road nearby linking Upper and Lower Clapton is known as 'Murder Mile' and is notorious for crime. Growing Communities chose salad crops because of their perishability and the related fact that imported salad is more likely to be airfreighted to the UK. Its gardens are certified as organic. In 2003, a new greenhouse allowed it to experiment with growing figs and grapes. Their organic vegetable box scheme supplies fresh, seasonal produce to over 300 local households on a weekly basis. It works through a network of collection points around the area, has a waiting list to join in some parts and is growing. Everyone who participates can have a say in how the business is run.

The same enterprise is also behind the UK's first all-organic weekly farmers' market in Stoke Newington, also in Hackney. It draws its produce from farmers within a 100-mile radius, but only those who follow environmentally sustainable practices. Growing Communities goes even further still. It encourages the local community to 'make, bake, grow or pick good food throughout the year', helping them to evolve from passive consumers into active producers in their own right. Each year in October, coinciding with the ageless celebration of the harvest, it holds the Good Food Swap. It's cash-free and allows people to exchange recipes, good food and to get to know others in their community.

If you live in a more rural area, closer contact with growing food makes it a little easier to lose the supermarket glaze and reconnect to the real world of natural resources. Whether it's bread, beef or biscuits you want, lucky residents in the southwest of England have the services of Somerset Local Food Direct to rely upon. This community business is typical of new collaborations among local producers that are springing up to meet a demand for quality food, and for those who have had enough of the supermarkets.

Darlington, in the northeast of England, literally said 'no' to Tesco, becoming another refusenik town like Torrington in Devon. Both considered, then rejected the supermarket following local campaigns. Torrington said no to protect the town's 'vitality and viability'. An embarrassingly lame online petition in favour of Tesco gathered 150 names over four months; most of these, however, went by the name of 'anonymous' or 'bb', signed on the same day and left no other details. One other Tesco supporter was apparently christened 'uosadzvpr jbcr'.[14]

In Darlington, the company proposed a development in which its store would virtually have become the town centre. A superstore and car park were to replace the existing town hall and bus depot. Under Tesco's scheme, around 115,000 sq. ft of land next to an ancient parish church and the market square would be covered with shelving loaded with a wide range of food, drink, clothes, household and electrical goods. To its credit, the council said that the plan would only be approved with the support of local people. After the community supported a 'Say No To Tesco' campaign organized by local businesses, the proposal was rejected. Earlier, a report commissioned by the council from a firm of London-based consultants, Colliers CRE, had 'welcomed' the proposed Tesco development. It later emerged that the consultants had previously worked for Tesco, and that the council 'had no idea' of this fact. CRE rejected any criticism, pointing out that prohibiting any consultants who'd worked for a supermarket would exclude a large number of the top consultancy firms. The issue of such conflicts of interest is now a cause for political concern.[15]

The official statement from the council was headlined simply 'Tesco Scheme Rejected – Now Council Looks To The Future'. An independent poll found that over three-quarters of residents opposed the scheme. Darlington Council leader John Williams said that no 'large supermarket or superstore-led development' should ever set up in the town centre or at its edge. In a statement that might stand as testimony to the beginning of a long-term shift in attitudes toward supermarkets, he said at the time of the decision:

> I am delighted that the Tesco scheme has been formally rejected. We listened carefully to the views of the people of Darlington and took the decision in accordance with their wishes. We must work together to ensure that Darlington has the vibrant and thriving town centre everyone wants to see.[16]

And Then . . .

On a bright autumn afternoon I set out to visit my nearest Tesco Extra hypermarket. I wanted to see the planned future of shopping at first hand. I don't drive, so I went on to the Transport for London website to see how to get there by bus, tube or train. The nearest store was in south London, about a mile from any train station. There were two options. One involved two trains and a bus, but there were engineering works on the line. The other option required a tube journey in the dimness and thick air of the Northern Line followed by a bus. I went for the tube. The destination was outside the zones covered by my season ticket, so I had to queue for a supplement. It was an extra £4.30, off-peak. I took a coffee bought from friendly Amy at my local independent coffee and food shop, Trinity Stores.

It quickly became obvious that there was going to be a long delay, so I found a bench to sit down and wait. Eventually the train came, and I settled into a grubby carriage with takeaway food wrappers littering the floor. The word 'ominous' kept recurring. My mood darkened as the train passed through a station, the memory of which is inextricably linked in my mind with an old and particularly disastrous relationship.

Getting out at Morden, the end of the line, I wandered around until I found the right bus stop. Tesco Extra was between Raynes Park Junction Tavern and West Barnes Crossing. Extraordinarily, it had its very own bus stop – Shannon Corner Tesco.

Then I noticed it was Saturday. There was only one bus every hour, and I had just missed it. There's no bus at all on Sunday. This was south London, so the soft option of getting a taxi wasn't going to happen. (The folklore is true. Just try getting a taxi more than a mile or two south of the river in London, especially at the weekend.) The man at the minicab office just looked at me and shrugged.

With time to kill, for three-quarters of an hour I walked around the high street. There's a big Sainsbury's, so the rest of the shops had been reduced mostly to fast-food outlets, charity shops and the minicab office with no minicabs.

Finally the bus came, and we swerved through estates of nondescript suburban housing. The stop reserved for Tesco Extra is on a multi-lane bypass. I hopped off and slipped into Tescoville through a side entrance, finding myself in the middle of a vast car park. The store is on one side, and there's a petrol station on the other. From several positions, your whole world is Tesco; you can see nothing else. The whole place looks like a cross between a medieval town and an industrial estate. Once again, the first thing you see on entering the shop is a strategically positioned security guard operating a CCTV monitoring desk.

I walked up the first aisle, one of about three dozen, and flirted with the idea of buying a Halloween costume for my daughter. Then I was put off by the the warning to 'Keep your child away from naked flames' as fireworks night was approaching, and moved on to toys and electricals. I hadn't been inside the store for more than five minutes when, suddenly, I got a splitting headache. For relief I went to sit down at the in-store cafe. Walking past rows of rapidly dehydrating trays of hot food – unidentifiable varieties of pie and mush – I went to buy a cup of tea for 59 pence. But the checkout was abandoned. In fact, although the store was full of people, the whole place felt abandoned, and bleak. I sat down anyway, deciding to pay when someone showed up. Staring at my tray I realized it was encrusted with what looked like someone's day-old pasta and tomato sauce.

The cafe was on a mezzanine level, so you could see across all the aisles. Along them were countless signs hanging like old Roman standards. Instead of announcing military allegiances, though, they repeated, over and over again: 'Tesco Finest/SALE SALE SALE/Buy 1 get 1 free.' There was a picture, too, of a pound sign being cut in half.

It was getting late now. The sky was darkening outside. I started to think about the store closing. Then I remembered that, like many other Tesco Extras, this one stayed open twenty-four hours a day. I decided to leave. Later, on the bus going home, all I could think about was Stan sitting beneath his mango tree, thinking about a better world and making it happen.

Useful contacts and further information

www.tescopoly.org

The Tescopoly website was launched in June 2005 to raise public awareness about the consequences of the supermarkets' domination of shopping, and to be a resource for community groups concerned about their local areas. It highlights and challenges the negative impacts of Tesco's behaviour both at home in the UK and internationally. The website is backed by a broad alliance of organizations ranging from large international poverty-relief agencies to unions and small campaign groups that are calling for new curbs on the power of all the major British supermarkets, including:

- A block on any new takeovers by major supermarkets.
- Stronger planning policies to protect local shops and high streets.
- A legally binding supermarket code of practice to ensure that all farmers at home and overseas are treated fairly.
- An independent watchdog with teeth to protect the interests of consumers, farmers and small retailers.
- Rules to protect people's rights in the workplace at home and overseas.

To contact the Tescopoly alliance, please email info@tescopoly.org.uk

BigBarn

www.bigbarn.co.uk
BigBarn is a website that enables people to find good food from their nearest local sources.

Common Ground

www.commonground.org.uk
Gold Hill House, 21 High Street, Shaftesbury, Dorset SP7 8JE
+44 (0)1747 850820
Common Ground plays a unique role linking the arts and environmental fields with a focus on celebrating nature and culture.

The Fairtrade Foundation

www.fairtrade.org.uk
Room 204, 16 Baldwin's Gardens, London EC1N 7RJ
+44 (0)20 7405 5942
The Foundation promotes certified, fairly traded products and is the UK member of Fairtrade Labelling Organisations International (FLO), which unites twenty national initiatives across Europe, Japan, North America, Mexico and Australia/New Zealand.

Food Climate Research Network

www.fcrn.org.uk
The Food Climate Research Network is an interdisciplinary, intersectoral initiative to research and promote ways of achieving absolute reductions in greenhouse gas emissions from the whole UK food chain.

The Food Ethics Council

www.foodethicscouncil.org
The Food Ethics Council is an independent champion for better food and farming.

Friends of the Earth

www.foe.co.uk
26–28 Underwood Street, London N1 7JQ +44 (0)20 7490 1555
The largest international network of environmental groups in the world, represented in 58 countries.

GRAIN

www.grain.org
GRAIN is an international non-governmental organization (NGO) which promotes the sustainable management and use of agricultural biodiversity based on people's control over genetic resources and local knowledge.

Growing Communities

www.btinternet.com/~grow.communities
The Old Fire Station, 61 Leswin Road, London N16 7NY
+44 (0)20 7502 7588
Growing Communities is a model local food project based in north London. Run as a social enterprise by local people, it works to make the food system more sustainable by supplying good food in a way which benefits the environment and the community.

Henry Doubleday Research Association (HDRA)

www.hdra.org.uk
Garden Organic, Ryton Organic Gardens, Coventry CV8 3LG
+44 (0)24 7630 3517
Europe's largest organic organization, specializing in organic gardening and food in the UK, and small-scale agriculture in developing countries.

The Institute for Agriculture and Trade Policy

www.iatp.org
The Institute for Agriculture and Trade Policy promotes resilient family farms, rural communities and ecosystems around the world through research and education, science and technology, and advocacy.

Local Food Works

www.localfoodworks.org
Local Food Works exists to foster sustainable local food systems through the development of local food networks.

National Consumer Council

www.ncc.org.uk
20 Grosvenor Gardens, London SW1W 0DH +44 (0)20 7730 3469
The NCC works in the UK with public service providers, businesses and regulators, and the Department of Trade and Industry – its main funder – to protect the interests of consumers.

The National Farmers' Markets Association

www.farmersmarkets.net
P.O. Box 575, Southampton, Hampshire SO15 7BZ
+44 (0)845 45 88 420

nef (the new economics foundation)

www.neweconomics.org
3 Jonathan Street, London SE11 5NH +44 (0)20 7820 6300
nef is one of the leading UK organizations working on local
economic regeneration. It is an independent 'think and do' tank
that promotes well-being, social justice, sustainability and economics as if people and the planet mattered.

Practical Action

www.practicalaction.org
Practical Action was founded in 1966, as ITDG (the Intermediate
Technology Development Group), by the radical economist Dr E.
F. Schumacher to prove that his philosophy of 'Small is Beautiful'
could bring real and sustainable improvements to people's lives.

rivercottage.net

www.rivercottage.net
+44 (0)1297 630300
A website about food, where it comes from, and why that
matters. Set up by the cook Hugh Fearnley-Whittingstall.

Soil Association

www.soilassociation.org
Bristol House, 40–56 Victoria Street, Bristol BS1 6BY
+44 (0)117 929 0661

The UK's leading campaigning and certification body for organic food and farming. They develop and provide practical and sustainable solutions which combine food production and environmental protection and human health.

Sustain

www.sustainweb.org
94 White Lion Street, London N1 9PF +44 (0)20 7837 1228
Sustain advocates food and agriculture policies and practices that enhance the health and welfare of people and animals, improve the working and living environment, promote equity and enrich society and culture. They represent around 100 national public interest organizations working at international, national, regional and local level.

The UK Food Group

www.ukfg.org.uk
PO Box 100, London SE1 7RT +44 (0)20 7523 2369
The UK Food Group (UKFG) is a UK network for non-governmental organizations (NGOs) working on global food and agriculture issues.

The Women's Institute (WI)

www.womens-institute.org.uk
104 New Kings Road, London, SW6 4LY +44 (0)20 7371 9300
The WI has campaigned for better food and farming since its inception in 1915. It calls on people who are 'concerned about the power the major supermarkets are having over small independent businesses and farmers both at home and abroad' to 'take action'.

Notes

Introduction: Every Little Helps

1 'Directory Inquiries – From 192 to 118: Report by the Comptroller and Auditor General, HC 211 2004–2005', 2005, National Audit Office.
2 Paul Ormerod, *Butterfly Economics*, 1998, Faber and Faber, London.
3 'Short-changed on health? How supermarkets can affect your chances of a healthy diet', report, 2006, National Consumer Council, London.
4 'Family Spending: A report on the 2004–05 Expenditure and Food Survey', 2006, Office of National Statistics, London.
5 'How shoppers feel about the multiples', *The Grocer*, 25 March 2006.
6 Carlos Grande, 'Tesco Customer Loyalty On Wane', *Financial Times*, 19 December 2006.

1   Identity Theft

1 G. K. Chesterton, *The Outline Of Sanity*, 1927, Dodd, Mead & Company, New York.
2 'Controversial Tesco to finally get the nod', *Balham & Tooting Guardian*, 9 November 2006; 'Checkouts, but no check-in at Tesco's SW4 scheme', *Evening Standard Homes & Property*, 1 November 2006.
3 Richard Layard, *Happiness: Lessons from a New Science*, 2005, Penguin, London.
4 The Nobel laureate Muhammad Yunus, founder of Bangladesh's incredibly successful micro-credit institution The Grameen Bank once asked the same question of banks.
5 Emma Dawnay and Hetan Shah, 'Behavioural economics: seven principles for policy-makers', *Theoretical New Economics* no. 1, 2005, new economics foundation, London.
6 'How shoppers feel about the multiples', *The Grocer*, 25 March 2006.
7 'Britain's love-hate-spend supermarket habit', Clerical Medical, research reported on www.myfinance.co.uk, 11 May 2006.
8 See Charles Mackay, *Extraordinary Popular Delusions & the Madness of Crowds*, 1841, Richard Bentley, London.
9 Anti-Apathy, a campaigning social enterprise set up by the new economics foundation, carried out this social experiment in January 2004. See http://antiapathy.phpwebhosting.com.

10 'The MT Interview: Sir Terry Leahy, interviewed by Chris Blackhurst', *Management Today*, 1 February 2004.

11 'CACI research reveals geography of local market share leadership', *IGD Retail Analysis*, 10 October 2006. See www.igd.com/analysis/news/news_detail.asp?articleid=3227; 'Tesco resident in two thirds of postcodes', *Fresh Produce Journal*, 10 October 2006; see www.freshinfo.com.

12 'UK Non-food in Grocers 2006', Verdict Research, Datamonitor Group, August 2006, London.

13 See '*Lates niloticus*', Global Invasive Species Database, World Conservation Union (IUCN); www.issg.org.

14 The term 'Homogocene' was coined by the ecologist Dr Gordon Orians in 1994.

15 Invasive Species Specialist Group, The World Conservation Union (IUCN); see www.issg.org.

16 Ibid.

17 See '*Lates niloticus*', Global Invasive Species Database, World Conservation Union (IUCN); www.issg.org.

18 Ibid.

19 Ibid.

20 The correct term is actually 'monopsony', but this is an awkward word. The meaning is clear without requiring its use.

21 Andrew Clark, 'Starbucks blames setback on Frappuccino queues', *Guardian*, 4 August 2006.

22 Starbucks' annual report in 1995 said, 'As part of its expansion strategy of clustering stores in existing markets, Starbucks has experienced a certain level of cannibalization of existing stores by new stores.' Quoted in Joanna Blythman, 'Spilling the Beans', *Guardian*, 4 August 2001.

23 'Oxfam calls on Starbucks to stop bullying poor people: Starbucks must respect Ethiopia's right to choose its own path to development', Oxfam, press release, 3 November 2006; 'Oxfam responds to National Coffee Association and Starbucks', Oxfam, press release, 27 October 2006; 'Starbucks opposes Ethiopia's plan to trademark speciality coffee names', Oxfam, press release, 26 October 2006. See www.oxfam.org.uk.

24 'McDonald's to close 25 UK outlets', *BBC News Online*, 28 February 2006.

25 Greg Palast, 'Big Macs, small horizons', *Observer*, 1 January 2000.

26 See www.slowfoodfoundation.com.

27 *Small Wonder*, Barbara Kingsolver, (2002), HarperCollins.

28 Interview with the author.

29 James Robinson, 'Can we stomach Tesco's taste for censorship?', *Observer*, 28 November 2004.

30 George Monbiot, 'Bad news from Tesco', *Guardian*, 17 May 2005.

31 Jonathan Glancey, 'Coming to a high street near you . . .', *Guardian*, 22 November 2004.

32 *Multinational Monitor*, vol. 18, no. 4, April 1998.

33 Adam Webb, 'A musical tail of hits and misses', *Guardian* (*Technology Guardian*), 17 August 2006.

34 Neil Hickey, 'Unshackling big media', *Columbia Journalism Review*, May/June 2001.

:

35 Letter from print media buyer McCann-Erickson on behalf of Coca-Cola, dated 6 March 1998.
36 As the critic Judith Williamson once pointed out, nature is the primary reference point for a culture.
37 Quoted in Mark Abley, *Spoken Here: Travels Among Threatened Languages*, 2005, Arrow, London.

2 Welcome to the Dead Zone: The Rise of the Giant Retailers

1 For those interested, see: www.napoleon.org/en/fun_stuff/dico/index.asp.
2 Stacy Mitchell, *The Home Town Advantage*, 2000, Institute for Local Self-Reliance, Washington, DC.
3 Frank Farrington, *Meeting Chain Store Competition*, 1922, quoted in Robert Spector, *Category Killers: The Retail Revolution and Its Impact on Consumer Culture*, 2005, Harvard Business School Press, Boston.
4 Ibid.
5 Mitchell, *The Home Town Advantage*.
6 Spector, *Category Killers*.
7 Ibid.
8 Michael Hutchings, 'Buyer power and retailer consolidation: The implications of vertical integration on competition', mimeo, 6 October 2005; and personal correspondence.
9 Nelson Lichtenstein, *Wal-Mart: The Face of Twenty-First-Century Capitalism*, 2006, The New Press, New York.
10 Andrew Rowell, 'The Wal-Martians Have Landed', in *The Case Against the Global Economy and For a Turn Toward the Local*, Edward Goldsmith and Jerry Mander, eds, 2001, Earthscan, London; *USA Today*, 13 August 2001; Ayn Rand Institute, 17 February 2004.
11 Stacy Mitchell, 'Will Wal-Mart eat Britain? And what can we learn from US communities fighting back?', economics foundation Alternative Mansion House Speech, Thursday 26 May 2005, Foreign Press Association, London.
12 Andrew Seth and Geoffrey Randall, *The Grocers: The Rise and Rise of the Supermarket Chains*, 1999, Kogan Page, London.
13 Ibid.
14 Ibid.
15 Spector, *Category Killers*.
16 Patricia Callahan and Ann Zimmerman, 'Wal-Mart tops grocery list with its super-center format', *Wall Street Journal*, 27 May 2003, quoted in Bill Vorley, 'Food Inc.: Corporate Concentration from Farm to Consumer', report, UK Food Group, 2003.
17 'The Super 50', table, *Progressive Grocer*, 1 May 2006.
18 Richard Fletcher and John Harlow, 'Tesco's Leahy is wild about the West,' the *Sunday Times*, 3 September 2006.

19 Jonathan Birchall, 'Tesco job ads follow non-union line', *Financial Times*, 26 May 2006.

20 Kris Hudson and Kris Maher, 'Wal-Mart adjusts attendance policy', *Wall Street Journal*, 14 October 2006.

21 Barrie Clement, 'Asda staff plan walk-out over union recognition', *Independent*, 23 June 2006; Julia Finch, 'Asda seeks injunction to block depot strike', *Guardian*, 28 June 2006.

22 Nelson Lichtenstein, *Wal-Mart: The Face of Twenty-First-Century Capitalism*, 2006, The New Press, New York.

23 'UK: Asda strengthens hold on number two spot', www.just-food.com, report quoting TNS Worldpanel research data, 19 October 2006.

24 Fletcher and Harlow, 'Tesco's Leahy is wild about the West'.

25 Nick Robins, *The Corporation that Changed the World*, 2006, Pluto Press, London.

26 A version of this account first appeared in Andrew Simms et al., 'Ghost Town Britain', 2002, the new economics foundation, London.

27 Dan Keech, *The Common Ground Book of Orchards: Conservation, Culture and Community*, 2000, Common Ground, London.

28 Seth and Randall, *The Grocers*.

29 Matthew Hilton, 'The duties of citizens, the rights of consumers', *Consumer Policy Review*, vol. 15, no. 1, January–February 2005.

30 *The Grocer*, 31 March 2001.

31 'Investment in rural services can pay dividends: Rural Services in 2000 (CA 48)', report, 6 November 2001, Countryside Agency. See www.countryside.gov.uk/rural services.

32 Ibid.

33 'Grocery market: Proposed decision to make a market investigation reference', OFT 838, report, 2006, Office of Fair Trading, London.

34 'The Impact of Large Foodstores on Market Towns and District Centres', report, 1998, Department for the Environment, Transport and the Regions, HMSO.

35 Hugh Barton, Marcus Grant and Richard Guise, *Shaping Neighbourhoods: A Guide for Health, Sustainability and Vitality*, 2002, Spon Press, London.

36 Research by analysts AC Nielsen, cited in 'Grocery Retailing 2000: The Market Review', p. 268, report, 2000, Institute of Grocery Distribution.

37 Lords Hansard text, col. 1174, 30 March 2004.

38 Hansard Written Answers, 13 January 2006: Schedule of meetings and stakeholder events of the Office of the Deputy Prime Minister discussing draft Planning Policy Statement 6, disclosed to Friends of the Earth under the Freedom of Information Act, 3 February 2005.

39 'Publications on Retail Planning in 2004', study, May 2005, Institute for Retail Studies, University of Stirling.

40 'The grocery market: The OFT's reasons for making a reference to the Competition Commission', OFT 845, report, 2006, Office of Fair Trading, London.

41 Ibid.

42 Office of Fair Trading, OFT 838.

43 Simms et al., 'Ghost Town Britain'. This figure counts only those registered for VAT.

44 Ibid.

45 V. W. Mitchell & S. Kyris, 'Trends on Small Retail Outlets', study, 1999, Manchester School of Management.

46 The Institute of Grocery Distribution, quoted in an issues paper by the Association of Convenience Stores prepared for the Competition Commission – Grocery Market Investigation, 6 June 2006.

47 'Business Start-Ups and Closures: VAT Registrations and De-registrations: 1994–2002', 2003, Department for Trade and Industry.

48 John Vidal, 'Supermarkets "shun" British apples', *Guardian*, 19 November 2003.

49 'Orchard Fruit Survey 2004', Department for Environmental, Food and Rural Affairs (Defra); agricultural census, 1930.

50 'The Post Office Network: A consultation document', December 2006, Department of Trade and Industry, London; Guy Rubin, Polly Raymond, John Taylor, 'The last post: the social and economic impact of changes to the postal service in Manchester', 2006, new economics foundation, London.

51 Molly Conisbee, 'Ghost Town Britain: A Lethal Prescription', 2003, new economics foundation, London.

52 'United Kingdom: Retail Food Sector Report', 1999, US Department of Agriculture.

53 ASA Ruling viewed at: www.asa.org.uk/asa/adjudications/Public/TF_ADJ_41722.htm.

3 Any Shop You Like, As Long As It's Tesco: How One Store Came Out on Top

1 'The MT Interview: Sir Terry Leahy, interviewed by Chris Blackhurst'.

2 Seth and Randall, *The Grocers*.

3 Ibid.

4 Ibid.

5 Ibid.

6 AC Nielsen Homescan figures for share of total grocery spending, quoted in *The Grocer*, 19 November 2005; *McKinsey Quarterly*, 'Tesco in 2003'.

7 Richard Fletcher, 'Focus: Tesco Tactics', the *Sunday Times*, 18 September 2005.

8 Lords Hansard text, col. 135 WH, 30 Jun 2004.

9 Tesco Annual Review and Summary Financial Statement, 2006.

10 See http://siteresources.worldbank.org/DATASTATISTICS/Resources/GDP.pdf.

11 See www.ft.com, Markets Data; viewed 11 October 2006.

12 Elizabeth Rigby and Lucy Killgren, 'Tesco towers above rivals as sales soar', *Financial Times*, 4 October 2006.

13 Tesco Plc. Interim results 2006/7, viewed at http://www.tescocorporate.com/ images/pr_interims06final_0.pdf; Nick Mathiasson, 'Is there a limit to Tesco's horizons?' 14 January 2007, *Observer*.

14 All Party Parliamentary Small Shops Group investigation into High Street Britain 2015, interview of Lucy Neville-Rolfe, Tesco Group Corporate Affairs Director, oral evidence session, House of Commons, 3 November 2005.

15 See www.tescocorporate.com/page.aspx?pointerid=3DB554FCAE344BD88E EEEFA63D71B831.

16 'Every Little Helps: The Clubcard Story', Tesco presentation, 2003, at the Dunnhumby Acadamy of Consumer Research, University of Kent.

17 'All ready for RFID roll-out', *The Grocer*, 25 March 2006.

18 'Tesco Trial Tag Technology', *Checkout*, Jan/Feb 2003; see www.checkout.ie/ WorldReport.asp?ID=15.

19 Gaby Hinsliff, 'Brown plans major ID card expansion', *Observer*, 6 August 2006.

20 'Every Little Helps: The Clubcard Story', Tesco presentation, 2003, at the Dunnhumby Acadamy of Consumer Research, University of Kent.

21 *Grumpy Old Women*, 9 June 2006, BBC 2.

22 From an unpublished presentation.

23 Sarah Boseley, 'Doctors oppose surgeries in supermarkets', *Guardian*, 28 June 2006.

24 Lords Hansard text, col. 196, 5 February 2003.

25 Dr Jacky Davis, 'As doctors, we see the cancer that eats away at the NHS', *Guardian*, 27 June 2005.

26 *Tesco Magazine*, May/June 2005, p. 43.

27 'MHRA intervenes over Tesco "two for one" offer for medicines', press release, 4 October 2006, MHRA, Department of Health, London.

28 'Conflicting views expressed over Parliamentary responses to OFT report', *The Pharmaceutical Journal*, vol. 270, no. 7243, p. 462, 5 April 2003.

29 'Relaxed Pharmacy Rules for UK', *Checkout*, Jan/Feb 2003; see www.check-out.ie/WorldReport.asp?ID=15.

30 Conisbee, 'Ghost Town Britain: A Lethal Prescription'.

31 The Index is prepared by the Department for Communities and Local Government.

32 Author interview.

33 'Government crisis of confidence on pharmacy rules will hasten Ghost Town Britain', 20 August 2003, new economics foundation, London.

34 'Ref: 12191, Appeals against PCT decision to grant Tesco Stores ltd's application for inclusion in the pharmaceutical list at Tesco Superstore, Kingston Road, Dereham', Sarah Breach, Panel Chairman, oral hearing report, April 2006. See www.nhsla.com/NR/rdonlyres/20968F25-EF11-4785-AB5C-C41245FEDCE7/0/12191ohPharmaceuticalDecisions2005.pdf.

35 'Doing it by the book', *The Grocer*, 25 March 2006.

36 Michael Peel, 'MPs and Lords attack "Tesco law" bill', *Financial Times*, 25 July 2006.

37 Bob Sherwood, 'Falconer aims for "Tesco law"', *Financial Times*, 25 July 2003.

38 The service became available at www.tescolegalstore.com on 25 July 2006.
39 Colin Finch, 'Should supermarkets be allowed to control press distribution?', discussion, Labour Party Conference fringe event, 25 September 2006, Manchester.
40 Alan Kemp of Haymarket Publishers and the Periodical Publishers Association, 'Should supermarkets be allowed to control press distribution?', 25 September 2006, discussion, Labour Party Conference fringe event, Manchester.
41 Toby Hicks, PPA briefing, undated.

4 Land, Money, Goods – and How to Get Them

1 Sir Terry Leahy speech to The Work Foundation, www.tescocorporate.com/page.aspx?pointerid=65AB8D49E95F4996ADBC0326A8ED2B7C.
2 Christopher Hope, 'Tesco adopts hard sell for planners', *Daily Telegraph*, 7 November 2005.
3 Seth and Randall, *The Grocers*.
4 'The grocery market: The OFT's reasons for making a reference to the Competition Commission', OFT 845, report, 2006, Office of Fair Trading, London.
5 Ibid., quoting 'Supermarkets, Competition Commission 2003', paragraph 2.172, Office of Fair Trading, London.
6 Ibid.
7 'Calling the shots: How supermarkets get their way in planning decisions', report, January 2006, Friends of the Earth, London.
8 John Waite, presenter, *Face the Facts: Tesco*, BBC Radio 4, programme broadcast Friday 18 August 2006, 1230-1300.
9 All Party Parliamentary Small Shops Group investigation into High Street Britain 2015, interview of Lucy Neville-Rolfe, Tesco Group Corporate Affairs Director, oral evidence session, House of Commons, 3 November 2005.
10 'Calling the shots: How supermarkets get their way in planning decisions', report, January 2006, Friends of the Earth, London.
11 Ibid.
12 Waite, *Face the Facts: Tesco*.
13 John Plender, Martin Simons and Henry Tricks, 'Cash benefit: how big supermarkets fund expansion by using suppliers as bankers; Tesco and Asda fund growth via credit ploy', *Financial Times*, 7 December 2005.
14 'Supermarkets: A report on the supply of groceries from multiple stores in the United Kingdom, Volume 1: Summary and Conclusions', 2000, Competition Commission, presented to Parliament by the Secretary of State for Trade and Industry.
15 Ibid.
16 'The grocery market: The OFT's reasons for making a reference to the Competition Commission', OFT 845, 2006, Office of Fair Trading, London.
17 Brendan Barber, General Secretary of the Trades Union Congress, evidence to the Competition Commission, 6 June 2006.
18 National Farmers' Union, evidence to the Competition Commission, June 2006.

19 'Small suppliers hit by retailers' 'shocking' late payment record: Super-markets' late payment record in 2006 is dramatically worse than the previous year', Kevin Reed, *Accountancy Age*, 31 Aug 2006.

20 Association of Convenience Stores and Federation of Wholesale Distributors, evidence to the Competition Commission, 2006.

21 The Forum for Private Business, evidence to the Competition Commission, 2006.

22 'Labour Behind the Label', 2006, joint letter to the Competition Commission, co-signed by Steve Tibbett, Director of Policy and Campaigns, ActionAid; Alistair Smith, Director, Banana Link; George Gelber, Head of Public Policy, CAFOD; Charles Abugre, Head of Policy, Christian Aid; Bill Vorley, Head, Sustainable Markets Group, International Institute for Environment and Development; Maggie Burns, Chair, Labour Behind the Label; Phil Bloomer, Director of Campaigns and Policy, Oxfam; James Lloyd, Head of Campaigns, People and Planet; Paul Chitnis, Chief Executive, SCIAF; Michael Gidney, Director of Policy, Traidcraft Exchange; John Hilary, Director of Campaigns and Policy, War on Want; Camille Warren, Acting Director, Women Working Worldwide.

23 'Comments and Evidence relating to OFT 783, "Supermarkets: The code of practice and other competition issues" ', March 2005, Banana Link.

24 Bestway (Holdings) Ltd, incorporating Bestway Cash and Carry and Euro-impex Ltd, evidence to the Competition Commission, May 2006.

25 *Face the Facts: Tesco*, BBC Radio 4, programme broadcast Friday 18 August 2006, 1230-1300.

26 Richard Fletcher, 'Probe into supermarket sites', the *Sunday Times*, 28 May 2006.

27 Clover, 'Beckett tells supermarkets to stop squeezing farmers'.

28 *Supermarket code of practice conclusion is a whitewash says Grant Thornton,* 3 August 2005; *Number of food/drink and tobacco retailers halves as insolvencies increase,* 16 July 2006, both at www.grant-thornton.co.uk; *Rise in retail insolvencies adds to high street fears,* 29 October 2006, *Financial Times*.

29 Ibid.

30 Ibid.

31 'Proposed Closure Of Trafford Park Bakery', press statement, 24 August 2006, Northern Foods; William Hall, 'Northern Closure Recipe', *The North West Inquirer* ('Inside Edge'), 31 August 2006.

5   Parasitic Retail:
Why Too Many Chain Stores Kill Communities

1 Jonathan Raban, *Passage to Juneau: A Sea and Its Meaning*, 2000, Picador.

2 'The call for choice, balance and diversity', April 2005, Opinion Matters, FWD Research 2005.

3 Nationally representative survey of more than 1,100 local retailers across nine regions, May 2006, Opinion Matters, FWD Research 2006.

4 Professor Ian Clarke, Fellow, Advanced Institute of Management Research and Chair in Marketing, Lancaster University Management School, introduction to Opinion Matters, FWD Research 2005, 25 April 2005.

5 'Tesco to face ban on booze', Claire Truscott, *The Argus*, Brighton, 4 January 2007.

6 'The world on a plate: Queen's Market: The economic and social value of London's most ethnically diverse street market', 2006, new economics foundation, London.

7 See www.newham.gov.uk/Services/RegenerationProjects/AboutUs/queensmkt qtnsgeneral.htm?

8 'The world on a plate: Queen's Market: The economic and social value of London's most ethnically diverse street market', 2006, new economics foundation, London.

9 'Supermarket savings', *Which?* report, 1 November 2006, reported in Hilary Osborne, 'Supermarket loans "bad value"', *Guardian*, 3 November 2006.

10 Michael Haralambos and Martin Holborn, *Sociology: Themes and Perspectives*, 1995, HarperCollins.

11 'The world on a plate: Queen's Market: The economic and social value of London's most ethnically diverse street market', 2006, new economics foundation, London.

12 See Newham Council's website explanation at: http://www.newham.gov.uk/Services/RegenerationProjects/AboutUs/queensmktqtnsgeneral.htm.

13 Smith's seminal book *An Enquiry into the Nature and Causes of the Wealth of Nations* (1776) argues that an increase in the standard of living would result from adopting practices to increase worker productivity. He posited a pin factory that could greatly improve its output by having each worker perform a specific task instead of making whole pins from start to finish. This concept of the division of labour has remained a cornerstone of industrial thought right down to our own era.

14 'Voices from the edge', 1 May 1999; see www.childrens-express.org.

15 'Plugging the Leaks: Making the most of every pound that enters your local economy', 2002, the new economics foundation, the Esmée Fairbairn Foundation and the Neighbourhood Renewal Unit, London.

16 Ibid.

17 'The Money Trail: Measuring your impact on the local economy using LM3', 2002, the new economics foundation and The Countryside Agency, London.

18 'Local food better for rural economy than supermarket shopping', survey results, 7 August 2001, new economics foundation, London.

19 'Buying local worth 400 per cent more', press release, 7 March 2005, new economics foundation, London.

20 'LABGI: Local Authority Business Growth Incentive - Does it do what it says on the can?', review, November 2006, Hewdon Consulting.

21 All Party Parliamentary Small Shops Group investigation into High Street Britain 2015, 2005, House of Commons.

22 *The Grocer*, 15 May 2004; Tesco, Annual Review and Summary Financial Statement, 2005.

23 Andrew Simms et al. 'Ghost Town Britain: The threat from economic

globalisation to livelihoods, liberty and local economic freedom', new economics foundation, 2002, London.

24 S. Porter and P. Raistrick, 'The impact of out-of-centre stores on local retail employment', 1998, National Retail Planning Forum.

25 On this occasion two subsequent research papers, also from the National Retail Planning Forum, interrogated the earlier research. The first (D. Fell, 'The impact of out-of-centre food superstores on local retail employment', Occasional Paper 3, 1999), criticized the use of 'full-time equivalent employment' to assess impacts. The implication is that more people in actual employment, even if part-time and casualized in nature, compensates for the overall loss. But another subsequent paper, again published by the National Retail Planning Forum (D. Thorpe, 'Superstores and employment in retailing', Occasional Paper 4, 1999) supported the evidence and analysis of Porter and Raistrick and disagreed with Fell. By including the effect of store openings also on self-employment, which declined significantly, it found an overall decline in retail jobs. This paper also criticizes the previous contrary research for not accounting for jobs lost in nearby affected centres.

26 David Neumark, Junfu Zhang and Stephen Ciccarella, *The Effects of Wal-Mart on Local Labor Markets*, April 2006, Public Policy Institute of California.

27 'Barker Review of Land Use Planning: Final Report – Recommendations', HM Treasury, 2006, HMSO Norwich; Catherine Early, *Planning*, 8 December 2006.

28 Royal Town Planning Institute, Press Release: No 'Quick-And-Dirty Permits' Says Planning Body Pr2006/62, 15 December 2006.

29 Barton, Grant and Guise, *Shaping Neighbourhoods*.

30 *The Grower*, 20 May 2004.

31 'Supermarkets urged to intervene to end modern day slavery', 14 July 2006, Transport and General Workers' Union; see www.tgwu.org.uk; 'S&A dismisses allegations of mistreatment', *Fresh Produce Journal*, 21 July 2006; see www.freshinfo.com; 'The abuse of our migrant workers', *Independent*, 15 July 2006.

32 'First English strawberries arrive 10 days early despite the cold snap', Tesco, 20 April 2005; see www.tescocorporate.com/page.aspx?printpage=1&pointerid=F8FB059E0AF247B7A3DA61D3C4881A7C.

33 Lucy Mangan, 'Why have strawberries lost their taste?', *Guardian*, 3 July 2006.

34 Interview with the author.

35 'Severed Fingers Spark Mass Meeting – GMB To Force Katsouris Fresh Foods To Improve Dangerous Workplace', 8 September 2006, GMB; see www.gmb.org.uk/Templates/Internal.asp?NodeID=94403; Felicity Lawrence, 'Food firm defends safety record as staff lose fingertips', *Guardian*, 25 November 2006.

36 Bill Vorley, 'Food Inc.'; Race to the Top briefing on producers; see www.racetothetop.org/indicators/module2/.

37 This section is based on an article of mine written for the *New Statesman* magazine in February 2004, at the height of the pre-election party political exploitation of refugee and migration issues.

38 See updates on key cases at www.contingentlaw.com: 'Federal Court Ap-

proves Class Action Status in Janitors' Co-employment Class Action Lawsuit against Walmart charging Violations of FLSA and RICO' (*Zavala et.al. v. Walmart Stores, Inc.* , U.S. D.Ct. D. N.J.) December 29, 2004; 'Walmart Agrees to $11 Million Settlement in Illegal Foreign Janitors' Class Action Lawsuit Charging Walmart with Violations of FLSA and RICO' (*Zavala et.al. v. Walmart Stores, Inc.* , U.S. D.Ct. D. N.J.) settled March 18, 2005). Wal-Mart settled without admitting liability.

39 House of Commons Environment, Food and Rural Affairs Committee, 'Gangmasters', Fourteenth Report of Session 2002–2003, 10 September 2003.

40 Felicity Lawrence, *Guardian Unlimited* (*Comment is free*), 25 April 2006; see http://commentisfree.guardian.co.uk/felicity_lawrence/2006/04/tesco_profits.html.

41 Felicity Lawrence, 'The precarious existence of the thousands in Britain's underclass', *Guardian*, 10 January 2005.

42 Andrew Simms et al., Ghost Town Britain.

43 www.cato.org.

44 Julian Oram, Andrew Simms and Molly Conisbee, 'Ghost Town Britain II: Death on the High Street', 2003, new economics foundation, London.

45 Jane Jacobs, *The Death and Life of Great American Cities: The Failure of Town Planning*, 1961, first published in the UK in 1962 by Jonathan Cape, London.

46 Robert Spector, *Category Killers: The Retail Revolution and Its Impact on Consumer Culture*, 2005, Harvard Business School Press, Boston.

6 A Global Plan: Why Scale Matters

1 www.tescocorporate.com/page.aspx?printpage=1&pointerid=3-B3A4B25C27741408604630168DAE624.

2 Vorley, 'Food, Inc.'.

3 Julia Finch, 'Tesco pays £72m for chain of convenience stores in Poland', *Guardian*, 16 July 2006.

4 *US Food Link* (published in association with *Progressive Grocer*), vol. 1, no. 4, April/May 2005.

5 'Wal-Mart Leader in Global Retail, Tesco Closing Gap', press release, 10 May 2006, Planet Retail, *Progressive Grocer*, 11 May 2006; *The State of Agricultural Commodity Markets 2004*, 2005, Food and Agriculture Organization (FAO [United Nations]), Rome.

6 Myriam Vander Stichele, 'The challenge of the role of supermarkets for sustainable agriculture and trade-related issues', report, 2005, The Centre for Research on Multinational Corporations (SOMO), Amsterdam; see www.somo.nl.

7 Ibid.

8 Thomas Reardon, Peter Timmer and Julio Berdegué, 'The Rapid Rise of Supermarkets in Developing Countries: Induced Organizational, Institutional, and Technological Change in Agrifood Systems', *e JADE, electronic Journal of Agricultural and Development economics*, vol. 1, no. 2, pp. 168–83, 2004, Agricultural and Development Economics Division (ESA), FAO [United Nations], Rome; available online at www.fao.org/es/esa/eJADE.

9 'Private capital flows to developing countries: the road to financial integration', 1997, Policy Research Department, World Bank, Washington, DC, quoted in David Woodward, *Direct and Equity Investment in Developing Countries*, 2001, Zed Books, London.

10 Vorley, 'Food, Inc.'.

11 Andrew Simms, Dan Moran and Peter Chowla 'The UK Interdependence Report: How the world sustains the nation's lifestyles and the price it pays', 2006, new economics foundation and The Open University, London.

12 Reardon et al., 'The Rapid Rise of Supermarkets in Developing Countries'.

13 Vorley, 'Food, Inc.'.

14 Ibid.

15 Reardon et al., 'The Rapid Rise of Supermarkets in Developing Countries'.

16 F. Gale, Francis Tuan, Bryan Lohmar, Hsu Hsin-Hui and Brad Gilmour, *China's Food and Agriculture: Issues for the 21st Century*, 2002, Economic Research Service, USDA.

17 Ibid.

18 Reardon et al., 'The Rapid Rise of Supermarkets in Developing Countries'.

19 Vorley, 'Food, Inc.'.

20 Dan Roberts, 'Tesco prepares to take sunbelt suburbs by storm', *Financial Times*, 18 May 2006.

21 James Howard Kunstler, author of *The Long Emergency*, quoted in ' "Dead zone" threat to US suburban dream', *Observer*, 6 August 2006.

22 Andrew Clark, 'Past times', *Guardian (Education Guardian)*, 21 October 2002.

23 'Dare to Lead: public health and company wealth', briefing paper on GlaxoSmithKline, Oxfam, February 2001.

24 'Branding the Cure', Consumers International, 2006; Sarah Boseley, 'Kickbacks, cartels and chatrooms: how unscrupulous drug firms woo the public', *Guardian*, 26 June 2006.

25 Kate Burgess, 'Splits and small shareholders: Sykes outburst widely deplored', *Financial Times*, 15 February 2003.

26 Donald MacLeod, 'UCL and Imperial merger "too big to manage"', *Guardian*, 15 October 2002.

27 *Fortune Magazine*, 2 October 2006.

28 John Kenneth Galbraith, *Money: Whence It Came, Where It Went*, Houghton Mifflin, Boston, 1975.

29 Quadragesimo Anno, encyclical on the 'reconstruction of social order,' following the Great Depression, issued by Pope Pius XI, 15 May 1931.

30 Leopold Kohr, *The Breakdown of Nations*, 1957 Routledge and Kegan Paul.

31 Alex MacGillivray, 'What's Trust Worth?', briefing paper, new economics foundation, 2002, London.

7 Profiting from Poverty: Shelves Full of Global Plunder

1 'Meeting the MDG Drinking Water and Sanitation Target: The Urban and Rural Challenge', WHO and UNICEF, 2006; see www.who.int/water_sanitation_health/monitoring/jmpfinal.pdf.

2 C. J. Vorosmarty, E. M. Douglas, P. A. Green, C. Revenga, 'Geospatial indicators of emerging water stress: an application to Africa', *Ambio*, May 2005; 34(3):230–6; see www.ncbi.nlm.nih.gov/entrez/query.fcgi?cmd=Retrieve&db=PubMed&list_uids=16042282&dopt=Abstract.

3 Eleanor J. Burke, Simon J. Brown and Nikolaos Christidis, 'Modelling the recent evolution of global drought and projections for the twenty-first century with the Hadley Centre climate model', 2006, Hadley Centre for Climate Prediction and Research, Meteorological Office.

4 Mike Davis, *Late Victorian Holocausts: El Niño Famine Cycles and the Making of the Third World*, 2005, Verso Books, London.

5 'Tesco profits at expense of poor', 2006, ActionAid; see www.actionaid.org.uk/1578/tesco_profits_at_expense_of_poor.html.

6 Grant Ringshaw, 'Tesco hit by child labour row', the *Sunday Times*, 8 October 2006.

7 'Child Labour Making Tesco Clothes', 10 October 2006, special report by Faisal Islam for Channel 4.

8 Randeep Ramesh, 'An 80-hour week for 5p an hour: the real price of high street fashion', *Guardian*, 8 December 2006.

9 'Fashion Victims: The true cost of cheap clothes at Primark, Asda and Tesco', report, 2006, War on Want, London.

10 'UK firms "exploiting Bangladesh"', 8 December 2006, BBC News.

11 Clive Humby, Terry Hunt, and Tim Phillips, *Scoring Points: How Tesco is Winning Customer Loyalty*, 2003, Kogan Page, London.

12 *The State of Agricultural Commodity Markets 2004*, FAO [United Nations].

13 'Fairtrade Bananas – Looking Behind the Price Tag', 2002, The Fairtrade Foundation, London.

14 *The State of Agricultural Commodity Markets 2004*, FAO [United Nations].

15 'Comments and Evidence relating to OFT 783', Banana Link.

16 'Bottom bananas: Naboa, Del Monte, Wal-Mart, Tesco', undated, Banana Link; see www.bananalink.org.uk/tuforum/botbans.html.

17 Banana Link-coordinated GMB London/TGWU/MANDATE trade union delegation to Costa Rica, 24 March–1 April 2004, hosted by the Plantation and Agricultural Workers' Union (SITRAP).

18 Ibid.

19 Ibid.

20 Edwin Laurent, speaking at the conference 'Understanding Globalisation', Tuesday 28 November, *Guardian* newsroom, London.

21 *The State of Agricultural Commodity Markets 2004*, FAO [United Nations].

22 Néstor Osorio, Executive Director of International Coffee Organization in 2002, quoted in Duncan Green, 'Conspiracy of silence: old and new directions on commodities', Oxfam paper presented at the International Centre for Trade and Sustainable Development conference 'Strategic Dialogue on Commodities, Trade, Poverty and Sustainable Development', Faculty of Law, Barcelona 13–15 June 2005.

23 *The State of Agricultural Commodity Markets 2004*, FAO [United Nations].

24 Green, 'Conspiracy of silence: old and new directions on commodities'.

25 Vander Stichele, 'The challenge of the role of supermarkets'.

26 Oksana Nagayets, 'Small Farms: Current Status and Key Trends', brief prepared for the International Food Policy Research Institute's Future of Small Farms Research Workshop, Wye College (UK), 26–29 June 2005.

27 Nagayets, 'Small Farms: Current Status and Key Trends'.

28 'World Investment Report 1999: Foreign Direct Investment and the Challenge of Development', 1999, UNCTAD, Geneva.

29 Vander Stichele, 'The challenge of the role of supermarkets'.

30 Ibid.

31 Thomas Reardon, Julio A. Berdegué, Peter Timmer, Thomas Cabot, Denise Mainville, Luis Flores, Ricardo Hernandez, David Neven and Fernando Balsevich, 'Links among Supermarkets, Wholesalers, and Small Farmers in Developing Countries: Conceptualization and Emerging Evidence', paper presented at the International Food Policy Research Institute's Future of Small Farms Research Workshop, Wye College (UK), 26–29 June 2005.

32 Reardon et al., 'The Rapid Rise of Supermarkets in Developing Countries'.

33 David Woodward and Andrew Simms, 'Growth Isn't Working: the Unbalanced Distribution of Benefits and Costs from Economic Growth', 2006, new economics foundation, London.

34 Green, 'Conspiracy of silence: old and new directions on commodities'.

8   How Much is Enough?

1 Dr Martin Luther King, Jr, 'A Christmas Sermon on Peace', 24 December 1967, Ebenezer Baptist Church.

2 Measured by GDP, the UK has the world's fourth-largest economy after the US, Japan and Germany. Figures are GDP (2004) from World Bank statistical tables; see www.worldbank.org/data.

3 Simms, Moran and Chowla, 'The UK Interdependence Report'.

4 Erik Stokstad, 'Global Loss of Biodiversity Harming Ocean Bounty', *Science*, vol. 314, no. 5800, 3 November 2006.

5 See Tesco statement on palm oil: www.tescocorporate.com/page.aspx?pointerid=734528817B954766A6C7298026D9D161.

6 See the Roundtable on Sustainable Palm Oil: www.sustainable-palmoil.org.

7 'The oil for ape scandal: How palm oil is threatening the orang-utan', September 2005, Friends of the Earth; 'Orang-utans go ape in Tesco', press release, 29 October 2005, Friends of the Earth.

8 'Exports and imports of goods and services', 2005, Office of National Statistics, London; see www.statistics.gov.uk/STATBASE/tsdataset.asp?vlnk=219.

9 Jeremy Leggett, *Half Gone: Oil, Gas, Hot Air and the Global Energy Crisis*, 2006, Portobello Books, London.

10 Ben Webster, 'Home-grown crops accelerate drive towards biofuels', *The Times*, 23 August 2006.

11 *Agriculture in the United Kingdom* 2004, 2005, Defra, HMSO Norwich; see http://statistics.defra.gov.uk/esg/index/list.asp?i_id=054.

12 Ibid.

13 'Supermarket prices soar', *Evening Standard*, 23 August 2006.

14 Neil Merrett, 'Poland sweats as heatwave threatens harvest'; www.CEE-foodinsdustry.com, 27 August 2006; see www.cee-foodindustry.com/news/ng.asp?n=69445&m=2CEE728&c=cfreofvjcseajlx.
15 Robert Verkaik, 'Price of bread on the rise after UK's summer heatwave', *Independent*, 14 August 2006.
16 Jenny Wiggins and Jamie Chisholm, 'Food prices jump after heatwave hits harvest', *Financial Times*, 23 August 2006.
17 Roger Harrabin, 'Top scientist's fears for climate', www.bbc.co.uk, 31 August 2006.
18 'Impact of climate change on crops worse than previously thought', The Royal Society, press release, 26 April 2005; see www.royalsoc.ac.uk/news.-asp?year=&id=3084.
19 'Climate Change warning over food production', *New Scientist*, 26 April 2005.
20 Tony Blair, *The Economist*, 1 January 2005.
21 'Africa – Up in Smoke', November 2006, The Working Group on Climate Change and Development, London.
22 Nagayets, 'Small Farms: Current Status and Key Trends'.
23 'Tesco pomelos take flight', *Fresh Produce Journal*, 17 September 2006; see www.freshinfo.com.
24 From Author's correspondence.
25 'The Validity of Food Miles as an Indicator of Sustainable Development', 2005, Defra, London.
26 Norman Baker MP, Liberal Democrat Shadow Environment Secretary, 'How green is your supermarket? A Guide for Best Practice', March 2004. The report elaborates: 'Seven of the supermarkets gave their annual lorry mileage. This totalled 408 million miles per year, which is the equivalent of driving round the M25 about 3 million times, or to the moon and back 854 times - two return trips per day. These journeys were running between 60 and 92% full. The most efficient distribution systems would ensure back-hauling of recycling and waste once produce had been delivered. Extra-polating for the missing survey results (based on turnover) the total lorry mileage from all nine supermarkets is likely to be around 670 million miles.'
27 'Greening supermarkets: how supermarkets can help make greener shopping easier', 2006, National Consumer Council, London.
28 'Travel to the Shops in GB: Personal Travel fact Sheet 6', 2003, Department for Transport and National Statistics.
29 Jules Pretty and Tim Lang, 'Farm costs and food miles: an assessment of the full cost of the UK weekly food basket', *Food Policy*, vol. 30, no. 1, 2005, Elsevier.
30 Calculation based on ibid.
31 Tara Garnett, 'Wise Moves: Exploring the relationship between food, transport and CO2', 2003, Transport 2000 Trust, London.
32 See www.ert.be/home.htm.
33 'The Energy Review: A Performance and Innovation Unit Report', February 2002, Cabinet Office, London.

34 Belen Balanya et al., *Europe Inc.*, 2000, Pluto Press, London; 'Small is Beautiful, Big is Subsidised', October 1998, International Society for Ecology and Culture.

35 '10 Year Plan for Transport', The Eighth Report of the Select Committee on Transport, Local Government and the Regions Select Committee, 2002, House of Commons.

36 Dr Kevin Anderson, Research Director, 'Time to get real: Avoiding dangerous climate change ... what does this mean for the UK?', Energy and Climate Change programme, Tyndall Centre, The University of Manchester, at a Conservative Party Conference, 2006.

37 David Adam, 'Can planting trees really give you a clear carbon conscience?' *Guardian*, 7 October 2006.

38 Jonathan Guthrie, 'Ethics, enterprise and expediency', *Financial Times*, 15 June, 2006.

39 ppmv means the atmospheric concentration of all greenhouse gases measured according to the warming effect that carbon dioxide has once released into the atmosphere, expressed as parts per million by volume.

40 Interview with author.

41 Jane Jacobs, *The Nature of Economies*, 2000, The Modern Library, New York.

42 Ibid.

43 Ibid.

44 See, for example, Colin Tudge, *So Shall We Reap: What's Gone Wrong with the World's Food, and How to Fix It*, 2003, Penguin, London.

9　Win Back Where You Live

1 See www.tescopoly.org.

2 Caroline Cranbrook and CPRE, 'The Real Choice: how local foods can survive the supermarket onslaught', 2006, The Campaign to Protect Rural England, London.

3 Ibid.

4 Patrick Barkham, 'The town that said no to Tesco', *Guardian*, 28 June 2006.

5 Ibid.

6 'Tesco to contest store refusal', *Edgware and Mill Hill Times*, 11 February 2006.

7 Paul Brown, 'Secret deals with Tesco cast shadow over town', *Guardian*, 22 January 2004.

8 Minutes of a joint meeting of the Development Control Committees (East & West) held in the Council Chamber, Council Offices, Holt Road, Cromer, 22 January 2004; see https://www.northnorfolk.org/committee/joint%20development%20control%20committee/22%20jan%202004/minutes%20-%2022%20january%202004.pdf.

9 Nic Rigby, 'Officer signed secret Tesco pact', BBC Online, 6 June 2006; see http://news.bbc.co.uk/1/hi/england/norfolk/5053240.stm.

10 Brown, 'Secret deals with Tesco cast shadow over town'.

11 Ákos Malatinszky, chairman of the GATE Green Club Association, mimeo, www.tescopoly.org.

12 Hillary Shaw, 'Small Shops', 2003, www.fooddeserts.org.

13 Jan Cienski and Stefan Wagstyl, 'Polish finance minister seeks more social spending', *Financial Times*, 5 November 2005; see Ministry of Finance, Poland, www.mf.gov.pl/dokument.php?dzial=16&id=49829.

14 Daniel McLaughlin, 'Polish "moral revolution" targets Tesco', *Observer*, 13 November 2005.

15 'Tesco acquires Leader Price stores in Poland', 18 July 2006; see www.tescocorporate.com/page.aspx?pointerid=1F0974D726FC4-C2E8E4A0A3B63519F34.

16 See www.tescocorporate.com/asiadetailed.htm.

17 'Thailand halts Tesco expansion', *Daily Telegraph*, 15 September 2006.

18 'Thai retailers march to protest Tesco, other major hypermarkets expansion', AFX News Limited update, 17 October 2006; see www.forbes.com/business/feeds/afx/2006/10/17/afx3096337.html; 'Retailers threaten protest against Tesco expansion', www.just-food.com, 16 October 2006.

19 'Retailers protest hypermart expansion', *Bangkok Post*, 17 October 2006; see www.bangkokpost.com/breaking_news/breakingnews.php?id=113628.

20 www.tescocorporate.com.

21 'Tesco expansion continues despite local protest', www.just-food.com, 18 October 2006.

22 Sarah Butler, 'Tesco steps up its plans to expand in Asia and the US', *The Times*, 4 October 2006.

23 Fatimah Mohd Arshad, 'Comment: Biotech thrust for agriculture', *The New Straits Times*, 8 October 2005.

24 'Malaysia Freezes Hypermarket Construction', 1 November 2003, *The Hometown Advantage* bulletin; see www.newrules.org/retail/news_archive.php?browseby=slug&slugid=210.

25 PriceWaterhouseCoopers, *2004/2005 Global Retail & Consumer Study from Beijing to Budapest: Malaysia*, 2005; see www.pwc.com/gx/eng/about/ind/retail/growth/malaysia.pdf.

26 Indrani Thuraisingham for the Federation of Malaysian Consumers' Associations, 'Threat to local retailers', *The New Straits Times*, 20 July 2006.

27 'Carrefour fined for unfair practices in S. Korea', AFX News Limited, 7 April 2006; see www.forbes.com/home/feeds/afx/2006/07/04/afx2856883.html.

28 Chris Gill, 'Come the revolution', *Guardian*, 24 June 2006.

29 'Mexican Communities Fight Costco and McDonald's', *The Hometown Advantage* bulletin, 1 November 2002; see www.newrules.org/retail/news_archive.php?browseby=slug&slugid=141.

30 See www.keeplouisvilleweird.com/index2.html.

31 'Wal-Mart and the Big Apple: Not in my aisle, buddy', *The Economist*, 2 April 2005.

32 According to the New Rules Project: 'Several cities have prohibited formula restaurants, but not other types of formula businesses (including Bainbridge Island, Carmel, Pacific Grove, Sanibel, Solvang, and York). Others (including Bristol, Calistoga, Coronado, and San Francisco) have placed restrictions on formula retail stores as well.'

33 'Commercial Blight', *Main Street News*, no. 204, February 2004; see www. newrules.org/retail/0204msn.pdf.

34 Ibid.

35 'Wal-Mart Tries to Skirt Maryland Size Cap Law', *The Hometown Advantage* bulletin, 9 March 2005; see www.newrules.org/retail/news_slug.php?slug-id=289.

36 'Superstore Tax Narrowly Fails in Montana', *The Hometown Advantage* bulletin, 1 July 2003; see www.newrules.org/retail/news_archive.php?brow-seby=slug&slugid=181.

37 David Derbyshire, 'Minnie the Minx puts Tescos to flight', *Daily Telegraph*, 9 September 2006.

10 Freshening the Dragon's Breath:
Corporate Responsibility and the Role of Regulators

1 See www.baesystems.com/corporateresponsibility/environment/index.htm [accessed 2 December 2006].

2 See www.baesystems.com/corporateresponsibility/environment/stewardship. htm [accessed 2 December 2006].

3 Alison Maitland, 'Four questions for tomorrow's leviathans', *Financial Times*, 25 July 2006.

4 'BP profits rise to £1.4m an hour', The Press Association, 25 July 2006.

5 Kenny Bruno, 'BP: Beyond Petroleum or Beyond Preposterous?', 14 December 2000, Corporate Watch; see www.corpwatch.org.

6 'Advertising: BP doubles corporate ad budget in $150m bid for greener image', *The Times*, 24 December 2005.

7 See www.bp.com/sectiongenericarticle.do?categoryId=14&contentId=2002063.

8 'Shell vs. BP: Who is performing worst on climate change?', press release, 27 July 2006, Friends of the Earth. http://www.foe.co.uk/resource/press_re-leases/shell_vs_bp_who_is_perform_27072006.html

9 Vorley, 'Food, Inc.'

10 Tom Fox and Bill Vorley, 'Stakeholder accountability in the UK supermarket sector: Final report of the "Race to the Top" project', 2004, Race to the Top/ International Institute for Environment and Development, London.

11 Ibid.

12 Ibid.

13 'The Tesco Takeover: Briefing', June 2005, Friends of the Earth, London.

14 'Food package labelling', *Which?*, 10 July 2006.

15 'Greening supermarkets: how supermarkets can help make greener shopping easier', National Consumer Council.

16 Henderson Global Investors, Sustainable and Responsible Investment division (SRI), *SRI Investment News*, December 2005; see www.henderson.com/ home/sri/document_library/newsletters.asp#nov.

17 'Big Retailers join forces in an effort to fight labour abuses', Jonathan Birchall & Elizabeth Rigby, 11 January 2007, *Financial Times*.

18 An Open Letter to Tesco's Chief Executive from George Monbiot, posted on turnuptheheat.org, 1 September 2006, www.turnuptheheat.org/?page_id=17

19 See www.bitc.org.uk/resources/case_studies/crmtescocfs.html.

20 'Doing the local motion', research conducted by the Institute for Grocery Distribution, *The Grocer*, 25 March 2006; 'The Wider Benefits Of Backing A Good Cause', Sue Adkins, *Marketing*, September 2, 1999.

21 The National Consumer Council's 2006 'Greening Supermarkets' report measured the proportion of seasonal produce sourced from the UK: Tesco sourced 61 per cent, behind Asda/Wal-Mart, which sourced 69 per cent of its vegetables.

22 Figures are based on Tesco's 2005–06 financial statement, quoted in Ashley Seager and Mark Milner, 'Gap between the richest and poorest workers widens', *Guardian*, 3 October 2006.

23 'Tesco boss sees pay rise by 25%', *BBC Online*, 28 May 2006.

24 The UK government has set a target of cutting adult smoking rates from 26 per cent in 2002 to 21 per cent or lower by 2010.

25 See www.localworks.org.

26 Robert Heilbroner, *The Worldly Philosophers: The Lives, Times and Ideas of the Great Economic Thinkers*, 7th edn, 2000, Penguin Books, London.

27 Parts of this section draw on conversations with Pat Conaty and my own report for the new economics foundation, 'Five Brothers: The rise and nemesis of the big bean counters', 2002, new economics foundation, London.

28 Galbraith, *Money: Whence It Came, Where it Went*.

29 A. H. Manchester, *A Modern Legal History of England and Wales 1750–1950*, ch. 9, pp. 356–7, 1980, Butterworths, London.

30 Robins, *The Corporation That Changed the World*.

31 John Kenneth Galbraith, *The Great Crash: 1929*, 1954, Mariner, New York (1997 edn cited).

32 Andrew Simms, memo, meeting with Bob MacDowell, 10 October 2005, Office of Fair Trading, Blackfriars, London.

33 'OFT publishes supermarkets code review: OFT to conduct compliance audit with supermarkets', press release, 20 February 2004, Office of Fair Trading, London; see www.oft.gov.uk/News/Press+releases/2004/28-04.htm.

34 This is a reference to controls placed on the big brewers with regard to both the number of pubs they are able to own and the range of beers sold in pubs. As Michael Hutchings notes: 'In brewing, the report of the Monopolies and Mergers Commission in 1989 resulted in the Beer Orders which required the big five brewers to sell off half of any pubs they owned in excess of 2,000; further, they were required to allow their tied houses to sell a "guest" beer.'

35 Hutchings, 'Buyer power and retailer consolidation', and personal correspondence.

36 James K. Galbraith, 'Mission Control', *Mother Jones*, November/December 2006.

37 Michael Hutchings, 'Competition Commission Grocery Market Inquiry: Possible remedies', mimeo, 2006.

38 Author's own insertion in parentheses.

11   The Birth of Something Better

1 Joseph Heller in an interview with the *Financial Times*.
2 FAO [United Nations], quoted in Michael Windfuhr and Jennie Jonsén, 'Food Sovereignty: Towards democracy in localized food systems', 2005, ITDG and FIAN-International.
3 Michael Windfuhr and Jennie Jonsén , 'Food Sovereignty: Towards democracy in localized food systems', 2005, ITDG and FIAN-International.
4 People's Food Sovereignty Network, 2002, quoted in ibid.
5 Andrew Simms, 'Selling suicide – farming, false promises and genetic engineering in developing countries', 1999, Christian Aid, London.
6 FAO [United Nations] and Jules Pretty and Parviz Koohafkan, 2002, quoted in Windfuhr and Jonsén, 'Food Sovereignty'.
7 Andrew Simms, mimeo, personal interview with Colin Tudge.
8 Dawnay and Shah, 'Behavioural economics: seven principles for policy-makers'.
9 Philip Lowe, speech at the British Institute of International and Comparative Law, 10 May 2005, in *Current Competition Law*, vol. V, BIICL, 2005; quoted in Philip Marsden and Peter Whelan, '"Consumer Detriment" and its application in EC and UK Competition Law', 2006, BIICL, London.
10 Eat the View is a campaign by the government's Countryside Agency promoting local produce.
11 Professor Tim Jackson, 'Chasing Progress: Beyond measuring economic growth', 2004, new economics foundation, London.
12 William Stanley Jevons was a nineteenth-century British economist who observed that the consumption of coal greatly increased after James Watt introduced his much more efficient version of the steam engine, displacing the design of Thomas Newcommen.
13 Karl Popper, *The Open Society and its Enemies*, 1962, 1945, Routledge and Kegan Paul.
14 See the petition 'Build Tesco in Torrington!' by Andre Pusey, started on 24 August 2006, at www.gopetition.co.uk/online/9456.html.
15 David Roberts, 'Council "had no idea" about consultants' link to Tesco', 23 November 2006, *Northern Echo*.
16 'Tesco Scheme Rejected – Now Council Looks To The Future', press release, 2006; see www.darlington.gov.uk/Democracy/Consultations/Town+Centre+Development/Town+Centre+Development.htm.

Index

NB: page numbers in italic indicate figures and illustrations